Clyde E. Palmer

Arkansas Newspaper Publisher

Lawrence J. Bracken

ISBN 978-1-4696-6596-2 (cloth: alk. paper)
ISBN 978-1-4696-6597-9 (paperback)
ISBN 978-1-4696-6598-6 (ebook)

This book is a revised version of a dissertation originally
published in 1987 as part of Lawrence Bracken's graduate work at the
University of Arkansas at Little Rock.

Published by the UNC Hussman School of Journalism and Media

Distributed by the University of North Carolina Press
www.uncpress.org

CONTENTS

FOREWORD

By Walter Hussman Jr.

I WAS ONLY TEN YEARS old when my grandfather died, so I later learned more about him only from the stories — and there are many, as you will read in the pages that follow. His name was Clyde Eber Palmer, and he began a commitment to local journalism in the public interest that now spans four generations of our family.

I was two years old when my parents bought the *Camden News* in Arkansas from my grandfather and moved my two older sisters and me from Texarkana to Camden. My sister Marilyn was eight, and Gale was eleven. They had grown up in Texarkana where my grandparents also lived. My father was away in World War II for several of those years, so they spent meaningful time with our grandparents and knew them much better than I.

Marilyn recounts fond memories of our grandfather. For about six weeks when our parents were in New York awaiting word for dad to ship off to World War II, both of my sisters lived with my grandparents. Marilyn remembers playing checkers and other games with our grandfather in the upstairs study, and she attributes her love for games to those experiences with him. She also remembers him teaching her how to water ski on Lake Hamilton outside Hot Springs. She remembers being pulled around the lake on a water board — and that he, in his seventies, also rode the water board.

Gale shares lasting memories of times at the lake with grandfather, when he taught her to swim and ski. And she remembers him sitting at the breakfast table with her drawing Europe and North Africa on a tablecloth to explain the battles being fought in World War II. Gale will tell you that our grandparents were the most important people in her formative life, teaching her the love of books and ideas. She remained close to them the rest of their lives.

There are so many stories that have been passed down to me about C. E. Palmer. Here are a few of my favorites.

After I started working for the company in 1970, the advertising director in Texarkana—also an aviation instructor—told me he had taught the seventy-five-year-old Palmer how to fly. He specifically remembered the day of Palmer's first solo flight. He told Palmer to simply take off, make two left turns, get into the downwind leg, turn on the base leg, and then turn 90 degrees and come down for a landing. As a pilot, I know this is the standard for a first solo flight. The instructor watched Palmer take off, make one left turn—and then just disappear over the horizon. The instructor went into a cold sweat. Palmer might crash. He might be hurt or killed. He himself would lose his job. And worst of all, my grandmother, Palmer's wife Bettie, would learn he was secretly teaching her husband to fly. He waited nervously. A half hour later, he saw a plane headed west coming his way. It approached the Texarkana airport and landed. It was C. E. Palmer. Relieved, he asked Palmer where he had gone. Palmer replied he simply followed the highway and flew up to Hope, Arkansas, and back. Palmer always followed his instincts and rarely fit a mold.

My favorite story is about when Palmer met William Dillard. Dillard was from Nashville, Arkansas, and opened his first store there when he was twenty-four years old. After eight years, he was ready to expand, and he came to Texarkana. One of his first meetings there was with the local publisher, C. E. Palmer. It was 1946; Dillard was now thirty-two years old, and Palmer was seventy. He told Palmer he wanted to open the town's first department store, but he didn't have enough capital to do it. He said if Palmer bought stock in his company, he would become Palmer's largest advertiser and that Palmer's retail advertising would increase 50 percent. Palmer had never done anything like that, but he later agreed. After he had invested and the store was up and running, Palmer called Dillard one Christmas Eve and asked him to lunch. At lunch, Palmer said that Dillard had not been honest with him. This puzzled Dillard, a man of high integrity. Palmer then told Dillard he had indeed become his biggest advertiser, but his business had doubled, not increased by merely 50 percent. Palmer said that if he never got a nickel out of the stock, it would be the best investment he ever made.

I first heard this story from my father, then I heard Dillard tell it himself. It was January 9, 1990, at the annual convention of newspaper advertising executives in Palm Springs, California. I flew out on American Airlines early that morning so I could hear Dillard's keynote speech at noon. (Listen to the speech at arkansasonline.com/wdillard01091990.)

After lunch, major advertisers like Sears, JCPenney, Kmart, Macy's, and of course Dillard's, participated in roundtables where newspaper ad executives could come talk with them. I went to the table with William Dillard and stayed as ad executives from newspaper companies like Tribune, Knight Ridder, McClatchy, and Gannett came by to visit. As the discussion concluded, Dillard looked over to me and asked when I was going home. I told him I had a flight later that afternoon on American Airlines. He invited me to instead fly home with him on his plane. I noticed with some satisfaction that the representative from Gannett, with whom we were in fierce competition in Little Rock, overheard the invitation. On the flight back to Arkansas, I learned a lot about Dillard and his business philosophy. It was quite a day.

Another story featured Ross Perot. Perot grew up in Texarkana and was a paperboy at age fourteen for Palmer's *Texarkana Gazette*, delivering the paper on horseback. He was given a route in a poor part of town where the collections were often difficult, so the carrier got a low wholesale rate to compensate. Perot not only solved the collection problems, but he expanded subscribers and managed to have a very profitable route, given the low rate. The circulation director noticed—and raised his rate. Perot objected. He was told his only appeal would be to the owner. So he went to see Palmer, and Palmer sided with him. When Perot ran for president, he addressed newspaper publishers at their annual meeting at the Waldorf Astoria Hotel in New York. Like William Dillard, he told his C. E. Palmer story, and I was fortunate enough to be in the audience to hear it.

In reading this book by Larry Bracken, I have reflected on how my career has differed from my grandfather's. While I worked on consolidating ownership within our family, he often sought outside investors. While I followed my father's strategy to buy and hold properties to realize a return by operating them, Palmer would often buy a newspaper and sell it within a few years. My grandfather's passion was business—mostly in newspapers and then broadcasting— but he would invest in anything he considered profitable, including real estate, oil, and gas. Palmer once started a newspaper in Fort Smith, and when it proved difficult and unprofitable, he pulled out after a year. In contrast, we bought the struggling *Arkansas Democrat* in 1974—and despite enormous challenges competing with the larger *Arkansas Gazette* (first owned locally for more than a decade of our competition and then owned by the country's largest newspaper company, Gannett, for the next five years), we persisted, and we prevailed.

In this book, you will read about Palmer's crusade against the Arkansas Louisiana Gas Company and its chief executive officer, W. R. "Witt" Stephens. Witt bought control of the gas utility at a bankruptcy auction, and as the story goes, brought enough cash with him to convince the judge he was financially capable of the purchase. He was a self-made man, starting his career selling belt buckles door to door, and later buying Arkansas bonds in default for cents on the dollar that later paid off in full. He was one of the most colorful individuals in Arkansas in the twentieth century, renowned in both business and political circles.

Ironically, when I moved to Little Rock many years after my grandfather died, I became good friends with his one-time rival. Witt often invited me to lunch with interesting and influential guests. And as the newspaper war waged on for more than a decade, Witt more than once offered to loan me the money to buy the *Arkansas Gazette*. I never accepted the offer. But when we eventually did buy the *Gazette*'s assets with a loan from the Bank of New York, Witt told me, "You deserve it. You worked your tail off." I remember later going to visit him about a business challenge I was confronting. As his assistant waved me into his office, he had his head down underlining a book, and he didn't look up for a few moments, even after I arrived. I sat down, and he placed the book, a Bible, on the table. I had never heard him speak of his religion. He was the real deal, and I respected him. Our two families had come full circle.

While I have had a far more varied, challenging, and exciting business career than I would have ever imagined, my real passion has always been journalism more so than business. I realized when I joined the family business many years after my grandfather died, and with my father nearing retirement at age sixty-four, that I was drawn to the allure of carrying on into a third generation the legacy of a family business, a legacy started by a remarkable man and publisher, Clyde E. Palmer.

I am grateful that my own children have chosen to extend the commitment to journalism for yet another generation.

THE CHARACTER AND NATURE of the publishers dominates the history of newspapers in Arkansas, a tradition as rich and varied as the succession of the publishers themselves. Clyde Eber Palmer is an important part of this rich and varied history. For almost fifty years Palmer played a critical role in Arkansas newspaper publishing. He served as the patriarch of a publishing family that continues to lead in Arkansas journalism as publishers of the *Arkansas Democrat* and other state newspapers. Palmer was known both regionally and nationally as an enterprising publisher and a pioneer in modern newspaper technology. During his career, he published almost forty newspapers in Arkansas and Texas. In addition, he owned radio stations, television stations, and one of the nation's earliest cable television companies. As a successful businessman, he held diversified interests in real estate and oil, in addition to his media enterprises. Politically active, he called numerous politicians close friends and engaged in some of the most important political events and controversies of his era. And he was a strong influence on many newspapermen and women who knew and worked with him, many of whom became editors and publishers of newspapers throughout the United States. His influence, especially through the Palmer Circuit, extended beyond the borders of the state and impacted the technological developments in newspaper publishing following World War II.

I aim to present a historical record of Clyde Eber Palmer's career and to highlight those elements of his publishing life that helped shape Arkansas journalism in the first half of the twentieth century. I chronicle Palmer's publishing, radio, television, and political career and provide a historical overview of his various enterprises, with special emphasis on the Palmer Circuit, which was an important technological influence on newspapers and wire services throughout the nation in the late 1940s and early 1950s. Here, I present evidence to prove that importance. I carried out research in secondary sources in order to place the chronology in a proper sequence. I conducted primary research (interviews and correspondence with associates and family members) in order to ascertain additional details of events and to attempt to answer questions raised by the research. The primary question centered around what motivated Palmer to attempt to put together a conglomerate of newspapers, radio, and television stations in southwest Arkansas and northeast Texas during the economic depression of the 1930s. Finally, I present an overview of the Palmer legacy, still significant in Arkansas journalism. Other questions concerned his political motivations and his humanitarian motivations, especially with regard to the Palmer Foundation and the Golden Rule Readers. A primary consideration was also to detail the development of the Palmer Circuit, the multinewspaper teletypesetting circuit, for which he was best known.

Palmer's role and impact have long been ignored in studies of Arkansas journalism and should be acknowledged as important to any study of the news media in the state. Palmer deserves to be ranked in importance with William E. Woodruff and J. N. Heiskell, both of the *Arkansas Gazette*. The scope of this book spans the career of Clyde E. Palmer and his various enterprises related to the Palmer Group, as his holdings were known, established in 1933. His publishing career began in 1909 and ended with his death in 1957. Some attention is given to the continued growth of the Palmer holdings after his death. While I consider some of his Texas activities, the scope primarily focuses on his Arkansas enterprises. The legacy of Clyde Palmer today lives in a network of newspaper, television, radio, and cable television operations known as WEHCO Media Inc. WEHCO Media represents the third generation of the family publishing business through which Palmer's importance and his influence are still felt in Arkansas journalism. Indeed, it is hard to discuss the history of Arkansas newspaper publishing and not mention Clyde Palmer's name.

Palmer's career can be divided into three parts. The first chapter reviews his early career, during which he was the publisher of the *Four States Press* in Texarkana, Texas, a daily newspaper that served both northeast Texas, especially Bowie County, and southwest Arkansas, primarily Miller County. The newspaper also had some circulation in both Oklahoma and Louisiana. In 1926 he sold his newspaper and retired. However, he soon began a new newspaper career in Fort Smith, Arkansas, and, in two years, he faced bankruptcy, at the very beginning of the Depression.

Chapter 2 covers the second part of Palmer's career, beginning in 1933, which was markedly different than his early years; by this date, Palmer had purchased both daily and weekly newspapers throughout southwest Arkansas. Some he purchased outright and others involved complex corporate purchases. Often he purchased newspapers and combined the circulation with existing Palmer Group newspapers, simply eliminating competition. The year 1933 marks the beginning of the Palmer Group, the official name of his various holdings. He began to purchase radio stations in similar fashion, eventually moving into television. He became politically active during this period, serving as chairman of the controversial Farm Tenancy Commission and the Arkansas Centennial Commission. He developed long-standing relationships with several Arkansas governors and the congressional delegations of both Texas and Arkansas. While only a member of the Arkansas Press Association during his early career, he became the prominent member of the APA during the second half of his life. He also dominated the state's Associated Press group during the second half of his publishing career.

During this time he implemented the Palmer Circuit to solve manpower shortage problems and break the unions in his daily newspapers. Chapter 3 reviews the development, implementation, and impact of the Palmer Circuit and outlines Palmer's anti-union feelings, cemented by his chairmanship of the Farm Tenancy Commission.

In the last decade of his life, Palmer became a philanthropist, establishing a private nonprofit foundation to help elementary school children improve their reading and moral capabilities. He assisted several colleges in their development, with gifts and grants. And he waged a battle with the Arkansas Louisiana Gas Company that is still remembered today. Chapter 4 reviews these aspects of Palmer's career.

Ultimately, Clyde Palmer was far more than just the publisher of a chain of daily newspapers in southwest Arkansas. He became one of the prominent citizens of the state, involved in a variety of business, political, and social activities. Palmer was not popular or well liked by those involved in Arkansas journalism. He developed a reputation for ruthlessness in his business activities, deserved or not, and had numerous critics. However, other than the fact that he operated his newspapers as an omnipotent and tight-fisted publisher, visiting each one almost every week, the specifics of discontent with him are difficult to pinpoint. He hired and fired employees at will and created a legion of disgruntled "Palmer Alumni." Many of those very individuals, however, have reconstructed his image in light of the passage of time and their own development. Clyde Palmer was a unique and interesting character, but more than that, he was a pioneer of publishing technology and developed the largest newspaper group in Arkansas. At his death, he was, along with J. N. Heiskell, a dominant force in Arkansas journalism.

The methodology of this book is of a historical nature. I conducted a search of pertinent literature on Clyde Palmer, both in Arkansas and, to some degree, in Texas. I performed research at the University of Arkansas at Little Rock; at Southern Methodist University, in Dallas, Texas; and at the University of West Florida, in Pensacola, Florida. The staff of the Arkansas Press Association proved very helpful in researching information and providing access to historical records and to the archived issues of the APA's monthly publication, *The Arkansas Publisher*. Dennis Schick and several APA staff members provided valuable assistance. Assistance was also given by Lyndell Williams, executive director of the Texas Press Association, who provided several copies of Palmer's correspondence from the files of that organization, and by Thomas A. Prentice, director of services for the Texas Daily Newspaper Association. I conducted some research in the Arkansas State Archives of the Arkansas Historical Commission in Little Rock, Arkansas. I also gathered information from newspapers, journalistic magazines, and trade publications.

I utilized several historical accounts of Arkansas journalism. Fred W. Allsopp's *History of the Arkansas Press Association for a Hundred Years or More*, published in 1922, proved useful in examining Palmer's early career in Texarkana. Clio Harper's 1930 publication, *History of the Arkansas Press Association*, provided additional details on the first half of Palmer's publishing career. Robert W. Meriwether's *A Chronicle of Arkansas Newspapers Published since 1922*, published in 1974, provided details about Palmer's later newspapers. *Arkansas Airways* by Arkansas radio veteran Ray Poindexter supplied a great deal of information concerning Palmer's radio and television business.

I conducted a series of personal interviews with a number of Palmer's associates and family members, between 1982 and 1986, as part of an interview project for the Department of Journalism at the University of Arkansas at Little Rock. I interviewed close Palmer friend and retired editor of the *Texarkana Gazette* John Q. Mahaffey in Texarkana, Texas, in 1984. I interviewed DeQueen, Arkansas, editor Ray Kimball, who worked closely with Palmer on the development of the Palmer Circuit and co-owned several newspapers with Palmer, in the offices of the *DeQueen Daily Citizen* in 1983. I interviewed retired Hot Springs reporter Edna Howe at her home in late 1982. Howe worked for Palmer from the late 1930s until she retired in the late 1970s. The purpose of these interviews was to gather additional information on Clyde Palmer and his publishing practices and personality. I attempted to interview Palmer business associate Alex Washburn, of Hope, Arkansas. Washburn was in poor health during the last few years of his life, and he died in 1983, before I could conduct an interview. I conducted additional interviews with Betty Palmer Hussman and Walter E. Hussman, in Little Rock, Arkansas, in December 1984. Both were in poor health at the time of the interview. I interviewed Palmer's grandson David Palmer Mooney, of Gilmer, Texas, in Hot Springs, Arkansas, in October 1986. I interviewed business associate Sam Papert Jr., of Dallas, Texas, president of the Papert Company, in September 1986. Papert's father was a close business associate during the early years of Palmer's career, and Papert himself was both a family friend and a business partner. Finally, I conducted an interview with John F. Wells, of Little Rock, Arkansas, in October 1986. Wells knew and worked with Palmer for a number of years and was especially knowledgeable in the area of Palmer's political activity and his battle with the Arkansas Louisiana Gas Company. In addition to the interviews conducted with these Palmer associates and relatives, I corresponded with all of them as a follow-up to the interviews.

I also utilized correspondence with a large group of Palmer associates in the research for this book. Following up on suggestions made by Mahaffey, Kimball, Howe, Papert, and others, I attempted to contact a number of former Palmer reporters, editors, and business associates, as well as additional family members. I contacted Palmer grandchildren Gale Hussman Arnold and Walter Hussman Jr. I contacted both former reporters George Brewer, of Little Rock, Arkansas, and Roy Bosson, of Hot Springs, Arkansas, several times. Brewer furnished several photographs of Palmer in Europe in addition to his letters. Other former Palmer employees contacted included Louis Graves, of Nashville, Arkansas, and W. R. Whitehead, of Fordyce, Arkansas, both now well-known editors of their own newspapers. Retired Associated Press executive Clement Brossier, of Orlando, Florida, knew Palmer and provided information regarding the relationship between the publisher and the wire service. Ernie Dean, of the *Arkansas Gazette*, now retired in Fayetteville, Arkansas, provided some insight into Palmer's newspaper purchasing habits. *Kansas City Star* publisher James H. Hale provided details on the Texarkana strikes by the International Typographers Union against Palmer. Former US Senator J. W. Fulbright, of Washington, DC, a one-time co-owner of the Russellville newspaper with Palmer, offered a portrait of Palmer. W. R.

"Witt" Stephens, founder of Arkansas Louisiana Gas Company, provided details of the dispute between Palmer and the corporation.

I corresponded with a number of individuals in the Harte-Hanks newspaper organization concerning the Palmer Circuit, which was implemented in their newspaper group after Palmer successfully developed the circuit. Edward H. Harte, of Corpus Christi, Texas, provided information regarding this, as did Jenny Sakellariou, of San Angelo, Texas. Sakellariou also contacted several other Harte-Hanks employees for additional information. Proceedings of the annual conventions of the Associated Press Managing Editors Association, located in the University of West Florida's Library, also provided details on the implementation of the Harte-Hanks circuit and further development of teletypesetting circuits, based on the Palmer Circuit model, within the Associated Press.

Although several searches have been made for Palmer's business and private papers, very few have been found. His personal business records appear to have been lost or destroyed over the years. A complete search of the WEHCO Media Inc. files might turn up more Palmer papers, but this task was not accomplished. I have found a few items of Palmer's correspondence, and I have also utilized several interviews from a variety of publications. Correspondents sent clippings, photos, booklets, and numerous suggestions of other sources, which were helpful.

Because Palmer died thirty years ago, memories of details concerning many items have dimmed and many questions remain unanswered. For example, Palmer's advertising company, Arkansas Dailies Inc., simply disappeared. There is a good chance that it was sold to Sam Papert Sr., but I found no evidence of this. Other unanswered questions concern Palmer's relationship with Arkansas governors Carl E. Bailey, J. M. Futrell, and Orval Faubus. Research in the state archives and the private papers of these governors might turn up interesting aspects of Palmer's political involvement. There is certainly room for additional examination of Palmer and the Farm Tenancy Commission, especially in the commission's later land use decisions. The scope of Midwest Video Inc. and the connection with Senator Lyndon B. Johnson (Johnson's antagonistic relationship with the FCC over Midwest Video Inc. is noted by several of his biographers) might also reveal items of interest. Palmer's activities in the state of Texas are also well worth examination. He was active in the press associations in that state and may have owned other newspapers

besides those noted in this study. His relationship with the Texas congressional delegation might also provide insight into his activities.

Palmer's ownership of Arkansas newspapers, radio stations, and television
stations eventually made him the most important and influential publisher
in Arkansas for almost six decades. His innovative technological advances
that led to the cost-efficient and labor-efficient multinewspaper teletypesetting circuit, known as the Palmer Circuit, had a far-reaching impact both
in and beyond Arkansas. And his political and business activities made him
one of the most prominent citizens in Arkansas for several decades. He was
at the forefront of several of the most important social and political issues of
his time, such as the farm tenancy issue. His political connections with such
prominent politicians as Senator Lyndon Johnson, Senator J. W. Fulbright,
Senator John McClellan, Congressman Oren Harris, presidential family
member Elliott Roosevelt, Congressman Wright Patman, and a succession
of governors in both Arkansas and Texas, put him in a position of political
influence for several decades.

Palmer is an important element in any comprehensive study of Arkansas
journalism. The first truly modern publisher in Arkansas journalism judged
by today's media conglomerate standards, he operated his publishing operation as a true business before any other Arkansas publisher. Today Palmer
might not be able to assemble the publishing empire that he built in the early
years of the twentieth century, but his vision, drive, and energy, as well as
character, would fit perfectly into today's world of Murdochs, Gannetts, and
Knight-Ridders. Palmer's legacy still plays an important part in the study of
Arkansas journalism, and the newspaper and electronic media chain that he
assembled still survives.

The career of Clyde Palmer focuses attention on several more general questions concerning newspaper consolidations. Are such consolidations valuable
to the democratic idea of a free press and a free exchange of ideas? What manner of press philosophy develops from such chain journalism in the 1930s or
the 1980s? Did Clyde Palmer care about journalism and printing the news, or
was his concern profits from his publishing business, or both? Did his power
improve the quality of Arkansas journalism, or was it simply an end in itself?
And, finally, does any Palmer philosophy carry over into today's WEHCO
Media Inc. operations? I hope that I answer some of these questions in this
book.

CHAPTER I

The Early Years, 1876–1933

The Early Years

Clyde Palmer entered the newspaper business in 1909. In 1926 he sold his newspaper properties and retired. Later that same year he began a second newspaper career, and within two years, just at the beginning of the Depression, was facing total failure as a publisher. By 1933 he had put together a chain of successful newspapers in southwest Arkansas and northeast Texas that became known as the Palmer Group. From 1933 until Palmer's death in 1957, the Palmer Group served as the major media chain in Arkansas, and Clyde Palmer was one of the most influential men in Arkansas.

Clyde Eber Palmer was born on August 24, 1876, in Spirit Lake, Iowa, and died on July 4, 1957, at his home in Texarkana, Texas. Spirit Lake sits in the northwestern corner of the state, a few miles from the South Dakota border. The Little Sioux River runs a few miles west of the town, and Spirit Lake, one of the largest lakes in Iowa, lies about ten miles north of the town. Today Spirit Lake has a population of fewer than three thousand people, and in the 1870s it probably consisted of only a few scattered farmhouses. It was here where Eber and Lydia Denny Palmer settled in 1863 and where Clyde Eber Palmer was born. A Palmer family story claims that the young Palmers moved to Spirit Lake not long after an Indian massacre had taken place in the area, reinforcing the frontier status of the community.[1] Eber Palmer served as postmaster of Spirit Lake for many years, and young Clyde attended the common school in the community and then moved to Fremont, Nebraska.[2] Fremont is located about twenty-five miles northwest of Omaha and was home to Fremont Business College, which Palmer attended.[3] The Palmers probably had relatives in Fremont because Clyde had a sister, Mrs. Waldo Wintersteen, living there at the time of his death.[4] Palmer's first association with newspapers occurred while he was still a student in Fremont, when he worked as a newsboy for a local newspaper.[5] His first job after graduating from Fremont Business College, however, was as a cashier for the Security Mutual Life Insurance Company.[6] He also worked, he often said, as a stenographer for a law firm during his early career.[7]

In 1898 Palmer moved to Chicago, but when the Spanish-American War began that same year, Palmer, then twenty-two, enlisted in Company "H" of the Second Nebraska Regiment.[8] He served the duration of the war as a private.[9] There is no record indicating that he was in any military action during the conflict. At the end of the war, Palmer moved to Chicago and worked for the Chicago, Burlington and Quincy Railroad, and he served briefly as a ticket agent for the Burlington Railroad in Omaha.[10]

On October 14, 1899, Palmer married Helen Maude Locke, of Missouri Valley, Iowa. Missouri Valley is located about forty miles from Fremont, Nebraska, and about twenty-five miles from Omaha. Palmer probably met Miss Locke while in the Fremont area. However, the marriage took place in Greenville, Texas.[11] It is possible that Miss Locke had moved to Texas and that was why the marriage took place in Greenville; that may also be the reason that Palmer left Nebraska for Texas.

In 1902 the Palmers moved to Fort Worth, Texas. Palmer worked a short time for the St. Louis Southern Railroad, which later became the Cotton Belt Railroad.[12] The exact date and circumstances remain unknown, but Palmer's next position was as the credit manager for Washer Brothers Department Store in Fort Worth, which sold men's clothing.[13]

Entry into the Texarkana Newspaper Business

On August 4, 1909, at the age of thirty-three, Palmer joined the staff of the *Texarkana Courier* as the business manager.[14] Texarkana is a unique city, located half in Arkansas and half in Texas. In addition, it lies only thirty miles from the borders of both Oklahoma and Louisiana. Consequently, then as now, it serves as the economic center for small towns in four states. It was in Texarkana, Texas, that Clyde Eber Palmer began his newspaper career in 1909.

In 1930, Palmer told *Editor & Publisher* interviewer Ray Reid that *Texarkana Courier* owner John B. King offered him the position of manager of the newspaper. Palmer said he arrived in Texarkana one day and King left on vacation the next day, leaving Palmer fully in charge. Palmer recalled his surprise:

> That was the most reckless thing I have ever heard charged against Mr. King. His departure the day after my arrival was not in the contract, as far as I knew, and if I had known, Fort Worth probably would have continued to be my place of residence and Texarkana would have probably been passed up. However, I was there and Mr. King was gone, and there was nothing to do except to get down to business and learn about my duties.[15]

Palmer's Texarkana associate John Q. Mahaffey has said that Palmer entered the newspaper publishing arena because of his "business tendencies . . . he didn't know anything about writing. He was a terrible writer as far as any editorials or news stories . . . he was strictly business." How Palmer and King originally became involved remains unknown, but evidence suggests Palmer's Washer Brothers duties possibly brought him into contact with many businessmen in northwest Texas, northwest Louisiana, and southwest Arkansas.[16]

There is another family version of how and why Palmer settled in Texarkana. Palmer's daughter, Betty Palmer Hussman, said that her father returned from his honeymoon in Havana, Cuba, and "got off the train in Texarkana and found out he could buy some stock in the *Four States Press* and, using his honeymoon money, he bought the stock and stayed there."[17]

Palmer's granddaughter Gale Arnold tells a similar story, probably an extension of family lore. "My grandfather was passing through town [Texarkana] with either $3,000 or $6,000 in his pocket for a honeymoon to Cuba with my grandmother," she recalled. "The paper was for sale. With her agreement, they bought it."[18]

Mahaffey tells a different story of Palmer's arrival in Texarkana. "I think he came over here [Texarkana] as a ticket agent for the Cotton Belt or the Texas Pacific Railroad," Mahaffey recalls; "then he became the business manager for the old *Texarkana Courier*." Mahaffey did not recall ever hearing the family story of the Cuban honeymoon from Palmer, but he did remember that Palmer "did draw a pension from the Army, a Spanish-American War Pension."[19]

Family stories are often based on a germ of truth; however, there are historical problems with the family version of Palmer's arrival in Texarkana. For instance, the *Four States Press* did not exist until Palmer established it in 1910 after buying the *Texarkana Courier*.[20] And there is evidence, from both Palmer himself and others, that he indeed served as business manager of the *Courier* prior to purchasing the newspaper. Fred W. Allsopp states that Palmer was in the "mercantile business" in Texarkana prior to his newspaper venture.[21] However, this probably relates to Palmer's previous employment with Washer Brothers. But the most obvious reason why the family story cannot be accurate is that in 1909, the year Palmer moved to Texarkana, he had divorced Helen Locke but had not yet married Betty Maines, his second wife. Consequently, there could not have been a "honeymoon" trip in that time period. How Palmer happened to come to Texarkana is not as important, however, as his association with the Texarkana newspaper, which began his newspaper publishing career.[22]

Most historical accounts agree that Palmer did indeed join the *Texarkana Courier* staff in 1909.[23] Some accounts place him in Texarkana as early as 1894, working as *Courier* stenographer, bookkeeper, and, finally, office manager in 1909.[24] Arkansas newspaper historians Robert W. Meriwether and Allsopp confirm the 1909 date, and Clio Harper and Mahaffey state that Palmer joined the staff of the Texarkana paper as business manager, not owner, in 1909.[25] Mahaffey has written that Palmer's "newspaper career began on August 4, 1909, when he left the passenger department of the Cotton Belt Railroad to become manager of the *Texarkana Daily Courier*. . . . He later bought the *Courier*."[26] Harper, in his history of the Arkansas Press Association, writes that Palmer "entered the newspaper business August 4, 1909, as business manager. . . ."[27] Another source states that Palmer "started work as a secretary for the *Texarkana Gazette* in 1909."[28] Since Meriwether used Allsopp as a primary source, it is not surprising that they should agree on a date. In addition, Meriwether also used the Union List of Arkansas Newspapers 1819–1942 and the Arkansas listings in the *Ayer Directory of Publications*, as well as *The Arkansas Publisher*, a publication of the Arkansas Press Association, as sources. Meriwether seems to have the best evidence of a correct date.[29] Palmer became a partner with King in ownership of the *Courier* in 1909. The two remained in partnership until 1925, when Palmer bought the remainder of King's stock.

J. W. Stuart founded the *Texarkana Courier*, in which Palmer bought controlling interest, in 1898. The *Courier* was the Texas-side Texarkana paper in 1909, while the *Texarkana Democrat* served the Arkansas side of the state line. Stuart sold the *Texarkana Courier* to John B. King in 1908, the year before

Palmer joined the newspaper staff. Within a year of acquiring the *Texarkana Courier*, Palmer changed the name to the *Four States Press*, which he published as a Texas-side morning daily.[30] This reflected his intention to serve a wider area, and, more importantly, it reflected his intention to broaden both his advertising and circulation base beyond the city limits of Texarkana. Mahaffey commented on Palmer's name change of the newspaper: "He just wanted to start all over with a new paper and he wanted it to be a regional paper."[31]

Other newspapers served Texarkana and Miller County in 1910. G. H. Wootten and F. G. Wootten established the older *Texarkana Democrat* on the Arkansas side in 1875, and they later sold the paper to Dayton B. Hayes and Ed A. Church in 1882. The paper began as a weekly, but the publishers added a daily afternoon edition in 1883. In 1884, E. A. Warren and C. E. Mitchell purchased the weekly and daily papers and changed the name to the *Independent*, but they changed it back to the *Democrat* in 1890. In 1892, J. W. Gardner bought the papers, and about a year later, he also acquired the *Daily Texarkanian*, which began publication in 1891. He combined all three to create the *Texarkanian*. In the early years of the twentieth century, George S. Valliant bought the papers, and he sold them to James L. Wadley in 1913. They were published by Wadley's sons, Archer F. and James L. Wadley Jr., until 1926. The *Texarkanian* provided the main competition for Palmer in 1910.[32]

The price paid by Palmer for the *Courier* stock is also part of Palmer family lore. While granddaughter Arnold recalls that Palmer had "$3,000 or $6,000" to purchase the paper, others put the purchase price at $900.[33] Palmer's daughter has stated that she was not sure of the exact price.[34] Nevertheless, as Allsopp noted, Palmer "saw a newspaper opportunity in that city [Texarkana] and in 1909 purchased the old *Texarkana Courier*."[35] The generally accepted purchase price for the newspaper, never disputed by Palmer, was $900.

Palmer's marriage to Helen Locke ended in divorce on October 10, 1908, the year before Palmer joined the Texarkana newspaper.[36] However, they did have two children, a daughter, Alden, born in 1904, and a son, Wellington Denny, born in 1907. Both would become part of the Palmer family newspaper business.

Alden Palmer's first marriage was to a man named Davis, but that marriage ended with divorce.[37] On October 16, 1937, she married David A. Mooney in a wedding held at Palmer's home on Lake Hamilton, near Hot Springs, Arkansas.[38] A native of New Orleans, Mooney had come to Hot Springs as an employee of Postal Telegraph and later worked for the Rock Island Railroad.[39] Alden Mooney joined the staff of Palmer's *Hot Springs Sentinel-Record* and the *New Era*, as part of the advertising department, in 1929 with a starting salary of $7 per week.[40] She later became managing editor of the Hot Springs papers. She retired in 1971 and died on May 29, 1980.

Wellington Denny Palmer, son of Clyde and Helen Palmer, also became a part of Palmer newspaper operations in later years. Known as "Duke" Palmer, he worked a number of jobs on Palmer papers. In 1932 Wellington, with the help of his father, leased the *South Arkansas Progress* and the *Norphlet Enterprise. The Arkansas Publisher* stated that Wellington Palmer planned to combine the two papers and publish them as a combination newspaper, making it the largest newspaper in Union County. The article also noted that Wellington Palmer was previously associated with both the *Fordyce Advocate* and the *El Dorado News-Times.*[41] An *Editor & Publisher* article in 1930 stated that Wellington Palmer was on the staff of the *Camden News.*[42]

Wellington Denny Palmer died of a heart ailment on March 11, 1934. According to *The Arkansas Publisher*, young Palmer, who was then twenty-six, died after a month's illness. The obituary noted that he was "associated with several papers in Arkansas."[43] Several children of both Alden Palmer and Wellington Palmer remained involved with the Palmer Group papers in later years. Their roles in the Palmer Group will be detailed in a later chapter of this study.

Details of Palmer's first marriage are sketchy. Family stories and recollections reveal some information. Alden Palmer Mooney's son David recalled only that his grandmother was a Christian Scientist.[44] Helen Locke Palmer died in California in the late 1970s. Betty Palmer Hussman said that Helen Locke Palmer left Clyde Palmer. According to her recollection, her father had been away on a business trip "and came home and found out that she had divorced him." She also thought that the divorce took place while Palmer was still with Washer Brothers in Fort Worth.[45]

In February 1910, Palmer married Betty Maines of Shreveport, Louisiana. This marriage produced one child, a daughter, Betty Maines Palmer. Betty Maines Palmer married Walter E. Hussman in 1931, and they had three children, Gale Ann, Marilyn Clyde, and Walter E. Hussman Jr.[46] Their role in WEHCO Media Inc. is discussed later.

Palmer embarked upon his newspaper publishing career with unique abilities. He possessed a business background rather than traditional newspaper experience. This made him somewhat of a rarity in those days when reporters became editors and editors usually became publishers. Like any good and prudent businessman, he set out to expand his market and increase his sales. This was especially necessary since the newspaper Palmer purchased from King had problems. Palmer told a writer for the Texas Press Association that when he joined the staff of the *Texarkana Courier*, the newspaper had a press run of only seven hundred and was in serious financial trouble, with several judgments against it.[47] Consequently, Palmer faced formidable problems, not only as manager, but also as publisher.

Arkansas, like the rest of the United States, experienced what most historians call the Progressive Era during the first two decades of the twentieth century. Attorney General Jeff Davis, called the "Karl Marx of the hillbillies," ran for the first of his three terms as governor on a progressive, anti-big business platform.[48] Attempts were made toward public school reform during the period, and the state even began to examine the massive literacy problem, which declined from 20.4 percent in 1900 to 9.4 percent by 1920 for white people, and from 43 percent to 21.8 percent by 1920 for black people.[49] As literacy rates increased and urbanization grew, it was a good time to be in the newspaper business.[50]

For the next fifteen years, Palmer seems to have been content with being a newspaper publisher in a small but growing city. He managed his newspaper, became a father, and was active in local Texarkana civic affairs. He was elected president of the Texarkana Chamber of Commerce in 1921.[51] He served as Miller County chairman of the Victory Liberty Loan campaign in 1918, the last of the war fund drives of World War I.[52] He helped establish several city parks, serving as chairman of the Texarkana Park Commission, which raised $100,000 to purchase land for parks. He joined the Masons and the Woodmen fraternal organizations, and he took up golf.[53] He joined both the Arkansas and Texas Press Associations, and he became an active member of the Texas Daily Newspaper Association.

In 1922 Palmer and Sam W. Papert established the Texas Daily Press League (TDPL) with the goal of assisting members in getting national advertising from corporations and agencies.[54] Sam Papert Jr. recalled that his father was the advertising manager for Palmer's Texarkana paper and that the idea for the TDPL was "formed and discussed and planned" in Palmer's offices.[55]

Papert went to work for Palmer in 1916, then served in World War I, and returned to work for the *Texarkana Gazette*, until the TDPL was formed in 1922. Papert then moved to Dallas to manage the affairs of the association.[56] Palmer served as president of the TDPL for two years and was granted honorary life membership after he retired from the presidency. Papert and Palmer began the TDPL with five members; by 1930 that number had grown to thirty-four newspapers.[57] The idea was so successful that in 1928 Palmer established Arkansas Dailies Inc., with himself as president and W. V. Witmer as manager, with offices in Little Rock's Boyle Building.[58]

Palmer and Papert remained close family friends. Mrs. Papert, a native of Texarkana, was a close friend of Mrs. Palmer's and was introduced to Sam Papert by the Palmers. The TDPL eventually became the Papert Companies, today one of the biggest newspaper advertising groups in the nation. Following the death of Sam Papert in 1951, his son, Sam Papert Jr., took over the company and remained close to Palmer, whom he knew well through both family and business connections. In fact, Palmer and Papert supported each other and their respective associations frequently, by urging and encouraging other newspapers to join either the Arkansas or Texas association.[59]

In 1923 Palmer purchased the *Northwest Arkansas Times* in Rogers, Arkansas, from Guy Stafford and W. E. Runway. John W. Nance and Ernest W. Vinson established the paper on January 1, 1910, and it had several owners before Palmer bought it. This was Palmer's first newspaper purchase outside of Texarkana. He renamed the newspaper the *Daily Post*, and Palmer kept the paper until 1927, when he sold it to James P. Shofner.[60]

In 1925 Palmer began his second Texarkana newspaper, the *Texarkana Journal*, an afternoon daily with Texas and Arkansas datelines.[61] This indicates that Texarkana was growing and that Palmer determined the community could support another newspaper. In addition to the *Four States Press*, the Wadleys were still publishing the daily and the weekly *Texarkanian*, which gave the city two afternoon dailies and one morning daily. According to Allsopp, Palmer had invested in a new printing plant, and, writing in 1922, he commented that Palmer had, "by applying business principles to the business[,] . . . built up a good newspaper property."[62] By 1926 Palmer had established a good regional morning daily, the *Four States Press*, and a good city afternoon daily, the *Texarkana Journal*.

As previously noted, in 1926, Palmer bought the remainder of John King's stock in the *Four States Press* and then sold his newspapers to D. W. Stevick.

At the same time, Stevick bought the Wadleys' *Texarkanian* and consolidated all three daily newspapers, plus the Wadleys' weekly, into a new paper, the *Texarkana Gazette*.[63] A native of Illinois, Stevick "came down and bought all of the papers," recalled Betty Hussman.[64] Stevick was the publisher of the Champaign, Illinois, *News Gazette* until March 1926 when he made his Texarkana purchases.

Mahaffey said Stevick put all of the papers together "into a good morning paper. It was a good one, it covered the whole territory."[65] Stevick, according to one source, was a successful publisher in Illinois and had met and married a Texarkana girl, Helen Taylor, who wanted her husband to buy the Texarkana papers to enhance her local prestige.[66] This may not have been the true reason, but local gossip is hard to refute. Many agreed with Betty Hussman's opinion that Stevick was "crazy to begin with."[67] More than likely, however, he was just an "outsider" in the small community.

According to Mahaffey, the purchase of Palmer's papers was owner financed with Stevick giving Palmer "notes on the Papers."[68] Stevick owned all of the Texarkana papers, and Clyde Palmer made a large profit, it was said. At the age of fifty, Palmer was almost out of the newspaper publishing business.

Why Palmer, obviously successful, would sell his Texarkana papers to Stevick is a question that must be considered. The most obvious reason, and the most probable, is that Stevick simply made an offer that was impossible for Palmer to turn down. If, as it appears, Stevick was determined to buy all of the papers in Texarkana, he must have been willing to make serious offers. In addition, as media historians Edwin Emery and Michael Emery point out, there were growing problems in the newspaper publishing business during this period. Emery and Emery contend that World War I was the high-water mark in newspaper publishing and that by the mid-1920s newspaper ownership was becoming more concentrated, the cost of production was increasing, inflation was becoming a serious problem for newspapers, and the general business depressions of the 1920s were taking their toll.[69] Palmer decided that the time was right to sell.

Failure in Fort Smith and Palmer's Expansion

Palmer, however, decided to start over, and he moved his family seventy-five miles north to Fort Smith and started a new paper, the *Fort Smith Journal*. When Palmer decided to start his second newspaper career in Fort Smith, it was already a growing border city with well-established newspapers. A daily newspaper had served the city since 1882 when the *Fort Smith Journal* began publication. On July 1, 1909, the *Fort Smith Times* merged with the *Fort Smith News Record* to create the *Fort Smith Times Record*, an afternoon daily. The *Southwest American*, a morning daily, was established in 1907. This paper merged with the *Times Record* in September 1923, under J. S. Parkes and George D. Carney, who then produced a morning and afternoon paper, with a combined Sunday edition. (It is worth noting that these papers were sold in 1940 to Donald W. Reynolds and what is now the Donrey Media Group, which is the only historical rival of the Palmer Group in Arkansas journalism.) In addition to the combined dailies, the city was served by a weekly, the *Saturday City Item*, which began in 1901 under R. C. Hite.[70] These papers all provided competition for Palmer's *Fort Smith Journal*.

Consequently, Palmer faced a difficult struggle in 1926 when he moved into the western Arkansas–eastern Oklahoma market against a strong and well-managed daily group and a strong weekly paper. Palmer business associate Ray Kimball has pointed out "there was a good established paper there at the time," referring to the *Fort Smith Times Record* and the *Southwest American*. Kimball felt that the combination of being a new paper in the market and going up against a strong, established publishing enterprise doomed Palmer's paper from the beginning.[71] In Texarkana, Palmer had purchased an already established newspaper, thereby having ready-made advertising bases and established name recognition. Palmer's *Fort Smith Journal* had none of these advantages.

Palmer's failure in Fort Smith, after fifteen years of successful newspaper publishing in Texarkana, must have been a shock as well as a major business disappointment. However, it was Palmer's only real newspaper publishing failure.

"He really took a beating up there," Mahaffey said. "The merchants wanted him to come in and they urged him to start a paper there. So he set up his paper and operated it for a year under contract with the merchants to buy so much advertising and they bought the necessary ads for the first years. When he tried to renew the contracts, the merchants were reluctant. So he pulled out." Failure was not something that businessman Palmer took well. "As soon as he saw something was losing," Mahaffey added, "he cut if off. He operated all his papers on a tight budget."[72]

Ray Kimball concurred. "The operation went broke. He had bought a bunch of intertype [typesetting] machines and he let them have them back and they raised hell about it." Kimball added that Fort Smith was an established newspaper market prior to Palmer's entry. "The paper Palmer had was a very new paper and an inferior paper."[73]

Betty Palmer Hussman recalled the family moving to Fort Smith. "Daddy started a paper up there, which was a big flop! He couldn't sell any advertising. He retired [after the Stevick sale], but he didn't like that and that is why he started the Fort Smith paper." She felt that the problem was the difference between the Texarkana and Fort Smith business communities and the Fort Smith business community's reaction to Palmer's new newspaper. "My father just couldn't sell advertising in Fort Smith."[74]

In an effort to support his falling Fort Smith newspaper, Palmer sold his small *Northwest Arkansas Times* in 1927 to James P. Shofner.[75] That did not help. Palmer called it quits in 1928. His paper had entered the Fort Smith market as a weekly, become a daily, and, in 1928, ceased publication.

Failure was something new for Palmer, who had been a successful Texarkana newspaper publisher for more than twenty years. At the age of fifty-two, with money still coming in from the Stevick sale, but with a dismal failure in Fort Smith, he might have abandoned the newspaper publishing business. But in 1928, as he was closing his Fort Smith operation, Palmer purchased five south Arkansas newspapers. By 1930 he owned all or part of twelve Arkansas newspapers, and, by 1933, "the Palmer Group" was well established.

Palmer learned some difficult lessons in newspaper publishing with his Fort Smith failure. He sold his two Texarkana papers to Stevick and watched as Stevick bought the other Texarkana papers, giving the Illinois publisher a dominant position in Miller County—in fact, a monopoly on newspaper advertising. In addition, Palmer saw the combined Fort Smith papers do very much the same thing to him in Sebastian County. He learned firsthand how difficult it was for an outsider to come into a community and compete against a dominant, established newspaper. He learned that it was to his advantage to have the established newspaper, to drive out or buy out the competition, and to monopolize and control the newspaper market in a community. This was a lesson he learned well and would use himself in the future.

In January 1928, Palmer, C. M. Conway, and Louis Heilbron bought the News-Times Publishing Company in El Dorado.[76] Conway and Heilbron were two of Palmer's Texarkana business associates. Palmer was publisher, and the purchase gave him control of the morning *El Dorado News* and the evening *El Dorado Times*. In addition, he established the weekly *South Arkansas*

Progress.[77] He controlled both daily newspapers in El Dorado and a regional weekly, giving him a monopoly on the El Dorado area market.

The *El Dorado Times* began in 1897 as a weekly, published by Neill C. Marsh and Lee Giles. In 1904 the paper was sold to George W. Mason, who served as publisher until 1921, when he leased the paper to J. S. Goodman. In 1922 the *Times* was sold to the Haynie-Avant Company, which in turn sold the paper to the El Dorado Publishing Company. The new publishers suspended the *Times* in 1926. The *El Dorado News* was established as a morning paper in 1921 by J. S. Goodman. In May of that year, the paper was sold to C. A. Berry's El Dorado News Publishing Company. Berry began in 1907. Huttig was a smaller town near El Dorado. By the time Palmer purchased the company, Berry had changed the name of his holding company to the El Dorado News-Times Publishing Company, but it was publishing only the morning *El Dorado News.*[78]

Palmer immediately reactivated the afternoon *El Dorado News-Times,* with Alex Washburn as editor and himself as publisher. This was the beginning of a long business association between Palmer and Washburn. Palmer's new weekly, the *South Arkansas Progress,* began as a rural weekly, with offices in both El Dorado and Smackover, a small community twenty miles north of El Dorado. The weekly was printed in the *News-Times* plant. At the time, Smackover had its own weekly, the *Smackover Journal,* which began publication on November 18, 1922, with B. W. and Floyd Barnes as publishers.[79] The paper coexisted with Palmer's paper until 1935, when Palmer acquired it.

Palmer's El Dorado editor Alex Henry Washburn was born in Toronto, Canada, on August 12, 1899. He received his education in the public schools of Wilkes-Barre, Pennsylvania, and attended the Wyoming Seminary preparatory school in Kingston, Pennsylvania, prior to attending the University of Missouri, where he received his degree in journalism in 1923. Washburn joined the staff of the *El Dorado News-Times* as news editor on April 26, 1923. By 1926 he had become the editor and a minority stockholder in the publishing company. He was Palmer's editor until late 1929, when he sold his minority interest to Palmer and bought the Hope, Arkansas, newspaper in equal partnership with Palmer, a relationship that continued until Palmer's death.[80]

Washburn, who died in the early 1980s, was still writing a daily column in the *Hope Star* at the time of his death. He eventually became the president and editor of the *Hope Star.* After Palmer's death in 1957, Mrs. Palmer sold her interests in the Hope newspaper to Washburn, giving him controlling interest in the paper. He was an Arkansas newspaperman for more than sixty-two years and was given the Golden Fifty Service Award by the Arkansas Press Association on February 20, 1981.[81]

Palmer's acquisition of the El Dorado newspapers not only gave him a monopoly on the market, but it also put him in the middle of the south Arkansas oil boom, a position that allowed him to benefit from the tremendous economic impact that the discovery of oil had on that part of the state. Oil was discovered in Ouachita County in 1920, and discoveries in Union County, where El Dorado served as the county seat, soon followed. Oil was found first near Stephens, then near Hampton, and finally in the vicinity of El Dorado. On January 10, 1921, the great Busey Well Number One gushed oil out of the ground near El Dorado. By the end of that year, more than fifty thousand oil prospectors had moved into the El Dorado area. The population of El Dorado mushroomed during the next few years, increasing from about four thousand to almost fifty thousand by the mid-1920s, with as many as twenty-two trains a day arriving in El Dorado, bringing wildcatters, roughnecks, and drilling supplies.[82] In 1922 more than nine hundred wells were sunk in south Arkansas, and by 1925 the output of oil in the El Dorado area was 77,500,000 barrels.[83] This was the boom community that Palmer moved into in 1928.

Not only did Palmer purchase good newspaper properties in a booming town, but he came into contact with such people as Colonel T. H. Barton, president of Lion Oil, Democratic National Committeeman, and 1944 candidate for the position of US senator.[84] Palmer later got into the oil business himself and had oil investments. Betty Hussman said there was not "too much oil" where her father bought leases.[85] Mahaffey also recalled Palmer's oil investments, which were purchased after the oil was already found, thereby having little risk, but also little return. "He bought oil royalties," the former Texarkana editor said. "I know because I bought some with him. We bought interests in wells after they were drilled."[86] The value of his oil holdings in the area remains unknown, but later in life he would brag about his success in the oil business.

Veteran Arkansas newspaperman Ernie Deane first encountered Palmer in El Dorado in the fall of 1938. Deane had moved to El Dorado from Tulsa, Oklahoma, and was manager of the El Dorado Chamber of Commerce. "Palmer was in town regularly each week," Deane remembered, "and took a lively interest in civic affairs, especially those that might result in better business for his two El Dorado papers, and I had conversations with him from time to time on matters of Chamber of Commerce concern, [which were often] his, as well."[87]

Palmer purchased two other papers in 1928. His News-Times Publishing Company bought the *Jonesboro Daily Tribune* from Harry Lee Williams and J. R. Williams. The *Daily Tribune* began in 1906 as a weekly and became a daily in 1909. After purchasing the paper in 1928, Palmer sold it in 1930 to Bruce M. Phelps.[88] Palmer also purchased the *Craighead County Journal* in 1928. This weekly was established in 1926 by Jared E. Trevathan, although Eli W. Collins took it over not long before Palmer purchased it. The paper was sold to Phelps in 1930, along with the Jonesboro paper.[89]

In 1928 Palmer, as previously noted, established Arkansas Dailies Inc., patterned on the business he and Sam Papert began in Texas in 1922. The group began with five newspapers, by 1930 it included sixteen participating Arkansas newspapers, and by 1931 it had twenty-one members. By working together, members of Arkansas Dailies Inc. sought to bring national advertising to their pages.

Sam Papert outlined the purpose of Arkansas Dailies Inc. when he spoke to Palmer's group at the Kingsway Hotel in Hot Springs on January 11, 1931. Very few newspapers with a circulation of less than fifty thousand are of such importance that they cannot easily be omitted from a national advertising campaign. A small daily cannot hope to receive the consideration it merits if its solicitations are made as a single unit. To get the attention of space buyers and those in charge of advertising expenditures, a small daily must work with other newspapers of comparable size serving neighboring territories and, through concerted effort, sell the market as a whole.[90]

A full-page advertisement in *The Arkansas Publisher* said: "by Co-operative action, the Arkansas Dailies group secures the consideration of national advertisers which an individual publisher could not receive." The ad carried photos of Arkansas Dailies Inc. representatives in New York, Chicago, Kansas City, Detroit, and St. Louis. The same copy noted that "fourteen active salesmen, operating out of seven advertising centers," were "selling every day for Arkansas daily newspapers that are members of the Arkansas Dailies group."[91]

The Arkansas Dailies group did not just wait for the ads to come in, but it also actively promoted itself. In February 1931, the group printed and distributed a booklet titled "The Truth about Arkansas." The booklet presented a bright picture of Arkansas and outlined improvements in the state's economic, commercial, and industrial status. Noting that "it's easy to get a distorted picture of Arkansas," the booklet added that "business in Arkansas key cities is good and rolling right along."[92] On October 25, 1931, the members of the Arkansas Dailies group met in Little Rock and formed a committee to arrange an advertising budget to publicize both Arkansas and the group itself. Members were to contribute to the ad budget and share the costs equally.[93]

In addition to papers that Palmer owned, daily newspapers in Arkadelphia, Batesville, Conway, Eureka Springs, Fayetteville, Harrison, Helena, Newport, Pine Bluff, Rogers, Siloam Springs, and Wynne were all members of Arkansas Dailies Inc.[94] The members of the group met twice a year to hear speakers and discuss topics of mutual interests, such as "inroads on their national revenue being made by metropolitan newspapers, billboards, movies and radio."[95] The consequences of Palmer's involvement with Arkansas Dailies Inc. were obvious. It gave him a better position for his own newspapers in obtaining national advertising; it widened Palmer's influence considerably and gave him a more prominent role in Arkansas newspaper publishing; and it brought in additional revenue for his newspapers.

In 1929 Palmer purchased all or part of eight newspapers and in each case attempted to follow his El Dorado pattern of controlling the advertising and circulation market and removing the competition. This became his pattern for the rest of his publishing career.

Palmer bought the *Camden Evening News* in January 1929. The paper was established by Curtis B. Hurley in 1920, and he ran the paper until it was sold to Palmer. In March 1929, Palmer, M. F. Freison, and J. H. Vogel incorporated the Camden News Publishing Company with capital stock of $60,000.[96]

Palmer then announced, in July 1929, the creation of the *Camden Morning Gazette*, intended to compete with the *Camden Morning Times*, which had been moved from Stephens, a smaller town about twenty miles southwest of Camden. The *Morning Times* was owned by Charles J. Parker, along with his sons Charles E. and Carlton J. Parker. In January 1930, Palmer bought the *Camden Morning Times* from the Parkers. He then discontinued the newspaper later that same month.[97] He discontinued the *Camden Morning Gazette* not long afterward. Palmer countered the Parkers' move into the Camden territory by starting the weekly *Stephens News Herald* in 1929, but he sold it to A. E. Carter in 1930 and the paper went out of business not long afterward. Palmer also soon acquired the Parkers' weekly *Camden Times*, which they started in 1929, and in 1930 he combined it as a weekly version of his own evening paper.[98]

Camden later became the home of Palmer's daughter Betty and her husband, Walter E. Hussman. After Palmer's death, Hussman moved the corporate offices of the Palmer Group to Camden. Camden eventually became the home address of WEHCO Media Inc.

Palmer's next newspaper purchase was in Hot Springs, where, in September 1929, he purchased the *Hot Springs New Era* and in December purchased the *Hot Springs Sentinel-Record.*[99]

Hot Springs became Palmer's second home, and he purchased a lake home at Lookout Point, on Lake Hamilton, just outside of the city. The home remains part of the Palmer family holdings.

The Spa City of Arkansas, Hot Springs had a daily newspaper from 1877, when J. L. Bowers and Kit Ousley started the *Hot Springs Sentinel*. John G. Higgins started the *Hot Springs Record* in 1899 and in 1900 purchased the *Sentinel* and created the *Hot Springs Sentinel-Record*. Higgins sold the paper to Palmer in 1929. The *Hot Springs New Era* began publication in 1906, established by Robert O. Schaefer, who published it under various names and schedules until selling it to John A. Riggs in 1911, who retained the name *New Era*.[100]

Hot Springs was a hotbed of newspaper publishing, and Riggs bought a series of newspapers, which he combined with the *New Era*, including the *Weekly Horseshoe*, the *Daily Horseshoe*, the *Hornet*, the *People's Hornet Horseshoe*, the *Daily News*, and others. It was also the home of the nationally known *Arkansas Thomas Cat*, published by humorist Jefferson Davis Orear. E. Marion Riggs, John's son, acquired controlling interest in the *New Era* in 1928 and sold it to Palmer the following year.[101]

Palmer continued to publish the *Sentinel-Record* as a morning paper and the *New Era* as an afternoon paper. In 1930 he added the *Ouachita Observer* as an area weekly.[102] His papers quickly dominated the local market and became the only major newspapers in Garland County. In early 1930, Palmer upgraded the printing plant of his Hot Springs newspapers, installing a new twenty-four-page Hope Rotary Press, which could run eighteen thousand papers an hour. He also remodeled the offices of the Central Avenue Plant.[103]

While El Dorado had oil, Hot Springs had a combination of thermal baths, horse racing, and wide-open, if illegal, gambling. The city was a tourist mecca during the 1930s and 1940s and presented Palmer with a growing advertising market, a solid circulation base, and minimum competition.

In 1929, Alex Washburn left El Dorado and moved to Hope, Arkansas, where he and Palmer jointly purchased the *Star of Hope*, established on October 14, 1899, by Logan C. McCorkle. The paper became a daily in 1920 and continued as one after Palmer and Washburn bought it. They also bought the *Hope Daily Press* that same year. The paper began as the *Hempstead County Review* in 1926, started by Curtis Cannon. In 1927 D. A. Gean bought the paper and changed the name shortly before selling it to Palmer and Washburn. They combined it with the *Star of Hope* to create the *Hope Star* and the Star Publishing Company, which circulated the paper as an evening daily. This paper had very little competition, although in 1951 they also purchased the *Hope Journal*, a twice-weekly paper, begun in 1940 by Arkansas politician Kelly Bryant.[104]

By the early 1930s, the Palmer Group, as his growing chain of newspapers was becoming known, owned all or part of the papers in El Dorado, Hot Springs, Hope, and Camden. These papers had very little competition and monopolized their respective markets. Palmer's Arkansas Dailies Inc. was attracting national advertising for his newspapers. Palmer had become a major newspaper publishing force in southwest Arkansas at the very beginning of the Depression.

"He expanded at a time when it was easy to get financing," Ray Kimball noted, "then came the Depression and he couldn't make his payments." Kimball said that Palmer told the bankers holding his notes, "If you think you can run these newspapers better than I can, you come and get them," and Kimball added that nobody wanted the papers except Palmer.[105] Mahaffey also recalled Palmer's financial concerns in the Depression. Palmer told Mahaffey, "I owe every bank in Arkansas that will give me credit. I'll never live to see the day that I'll be out of debt."[106] Mahaffey has written that he would "never forget a tag hanging on a Linotype machine in the composing room. It said 'this machine belongs to the Texarkana National Bank.'"[107] Daughter Betty Hussman recalled "there was a banker from Little Rock, from Union National Bank, who sat in the El Dorado paper's offices from 8 a.m. in the morning until the paper closed every day on account of a loan they had with that bank."[108] Apparently the bank felt that it needed to monitor the affairs of the newspaper in order to protect its investment, if the story has any truth to it.

Following Palmer's rapid newspaper acquisitions, the economic depression hit him hard. To make Palmer even more vulnerable, his Texarkana deal with Stevick fell apart in 1933. The same economic problems that befell Palmer during the Depression hit other publishers as well, including Stevick, who could not maintain both his Illinois concerns and his Texarkana operation and was about to default. In March 1933, Palmer, along with business associates Charles M. Conway, J. A. McDermott, and Henry Humphrey, bought back the two Texarkana papers from Stevick.[109] Stevick was seriously injured in a car wreck in Chicago Heights, Illinois, in November 1928, and his lengthy recuperation might have had some impact on his problems.[110] According to Kimball, Stevick "went broke and Palmer bought them [the Texarkana papers] for $50,000." Even though the original Stevick deal turned sour, Palmer had nine years of revenue from the Texarkana sale, which helped him finance his other purchases, and he then got the Texarkana properties back for a small sum. Kimball marveled at the money that Palmer made on the deal. "How many million dollars do you think it [the Texarkana papers] would be worth now? And Palmer got it for $50,000 on a turn-back basis." Kimball also noted that Stevick, like Palmer, was having credit problems. "I assume that other creditors were after the Stevicks and so Palmer finally took it back."[111]

Mahaffey also recalled the return of the Texarkana properties to Palmer. "He [Stevick] couldn't meet his notes to Palmer, so Palmer repossessed the papers."[112] Daughter Betty Hussman put it in simple terms: "Mr. Stevick came down and bought all the papers, but he couldn't pay for them, so my daddy got them back."[113] For the second time in his publishing career, Palmer owned the Texarkana newspapers, both the evening *Texarkana Daily News* and the morning *Texarkana Gazette*.

Following his pattern, Palmer immediately set about consolidating his Texarkana holdings and eliminating competition. During Stevick's ownership of the Texarkana papers, a competing afternoon daily was started in May 1931 by E. S. Fentress and Charles H. Newell. Their paper had a circulation of about eight thousand, with a Sunday edition. In June 1934 Palmer bought the Fentress and Newell properties.[114] The only other competition that Palmer ever faced in Texarkana was from a weekly, the *Two States Press*, which began in 1935, but it was never a major paper in the market.

On June 6, 1933, Charles M. Conway died in Nashville, Tennessee. Conway had interests in Palmer operations in Texarkana, Hot Springs, El Dorado,

Camden, and Hope.[115] In addition, Conway was involved with Palmer in several radio station purchases, as will be detailed in a later chapter.

Palmer reporter Louis "Swampy" Graves recalled the Texarkana newspaper market under Palmer's domination. Graves resigned from the *Texarkana Gazette* in 1948 to begin his own printing business, with the idea of eventually starting his own weekly or daily newspaper. The business did well but never really had the capital to get into the newspaper market. He sold his stock in the business, Southwest Printers, in 1950 and bought the *Nashville News*. He recalled, however, that his printing business "attempted to get a contract printing a Red River arsenal weekly which the *Gazette* printed. We were never able to get a bid on that job, and certain moves were made to discourage the establishment of another newspaper in Texarkana, but I could never prove anything. My merchant friends did feel some pressure."[116] Although Graves offered no hard evidence, it is likely that Palmer attempted to maintain his printing contract with the arsenal, through a variety of means. In addition, it is also likely that he put pressure on merchants not to place advertisements with an upstart newspaper, by offering them better rates in his paper or by threatening that they would lose placement position in his newspaper. Most businessmen can't afford to lose access to their area's daily newspaper, and Palmer knew that fact well.

By 1933, Palmer monopolized the newspaper publishing business in five major south Arkansas cities. He was not only the major publisher in south Arkansas, but he was also a growing force in newspaper publishing statewide. But Palmer, like all other newspaper publishers, had to face the economic depression of the decade. Many Arkansas newspapers could not survive the period, and many publishers faced bankruptcy. Arkansas newspapers, however, were no different from those in the rest of the nation and faced the same problems that other newspapers encountered in the 1930s.

The economic depression of the 1930s forced a large decline in the number of newspapers published in the United States. In addition, as Emery and Emery pointed out, it aided the growing trend of ownership concentration. Despite a decrease in payroll and production costs during the period, and even a dramatic drop in the cost of newsprint, the number of daily and weekly papers declined sharply. While there was a period of economic recovery between 1934 and 1936, the business recession of 1937 caused even more newspapers to cease publication or be sold to bigger groups, and, most often, consolidate with bigger papers. In writing about the newspaper publishing business in the 1970s, Emery and Emery have pointed out that "these were in many respects the blackest years in the history of American newspapers, with one third of salaried employees in the newspaper industry losing their jobs," and, as he also points out, "daily newspaper suspensions and mergers accelerated."[117]

Arkansas newspaper publishing mirrored the national trends during the 1930s, as did Palmer's growing group of newspapers. An examination of Arkansas newspapers listed by the Arkansas Press Association indicates that between 1921 and 1930 a total of eighty-eight newspapers suspended publication or combined with other newspapers. This followed a trend of concentrated ownership and population changes. Another eighty-four newspapers went out of business between 1931 and 1940.[118] The two trends of concentrated ownership, which Palmer used to his advantage, and the economic depression cut deep into Arkansas newspaper publishing. And, reflecting national changes, the new technology of radio was beginning to cut into the advertising revenue available. While advertising revenue for the nation's newspapers dropped 45 percent between 1929 and 1933, the revenue of radio almost doubled during the same period.[119] Palmer, like other newspaper publishers, took careful note of this fact.

Evidence that the economic depression of the 1930s hit Arkansas newspapers hard is also shown in the curtailment of traditional activities of the Arkansas Press Association. In 1931 the APA membership voted to cancel their annual excursions, which had previously been made to Mexico and Chicago, "due to the depression." In 1932 the APA reported "that district meetings of the APA had not held during the year because of the country's depression." And the 1934 annual meeting of the APA devoted "a major portion of the meeting" to the "Graphic Arts Code, a New Deal program sponsored nationally by the National Editorial Association and in Arkansas by the APA." In fact, the following year the APA even suspended publication of the convention proceedings, as a cost-cutting measure.[120]

Arkansas newspapers not only suffered the obvious economic difficulties that befell newspapers throughout the nation, but also emerged from the Depression fewer in number and with more concentrated ownership. To compound these problems, Arkansas followed another national trend. Media critic George N. Gordon has pointed out that "newspapers came into the depression era as the main, if not the only, mass medium that reached the bulk of American people . . . but by the time the decade was over, this was no longer true."[121] Arkansas emerged from the Depression with a huge growth in the number of radio stations, movie theaters, and outdoor advertising, which competed with newspapers for both advertising revenue and attention. These changes did not escape the notice of Clyde E. Palmer.

By 1933 Palmer owned the newspapers in almost all the major cities in southwest Arkansas. His publishing business had grown from a $900 newspaper that had a marginal market into a multicity chain of newspapers that monopolized news in the major cities of southwest Arkansas. His chain of newspapers became known as the Palmer Group and, from 1933 on, the Palmer Group would continue to grow and diversify into other markets as well as radio and television. The year 1933 marks the true beginning of the Palmer Group and, eventually, today's WEHCO Media Inc.

CHAPTER 2

The Palmer Group, 1933–1957

The Growth of the Palmer Newspaper Group

The Palmer Group began in 1933, and from that year until his death in 1957, Clyde E. Palmer consolidated his growing media organization. His newspapers in Hot Springs, Hope, Camden, El Dorado, Magnolia, and Texarkana gave him daily newspaper circulation to about one-fourth of the geographical area of the state and an almost equal portion of the state's population. His various regional weeklies added to the reader count of Palmer's papers. His numerous newspaper holdings gave him considerable influence with the Associated Press, both in and beyond Arkansas. By the end of the 1930s, Palmer was involved in radio, as well as newspapers. He expanded the scope of his interests to include politics, education, and technology during the 1930s and 1940s. At the same time, his influence grew and his family publishing business increased in size. Additionally, Palmer became very active in several press organizations, and he established a philanthropic foundation to promote peace and the Golden Rule.

"Our newspapers are keenly interested in development of the communities which they serve," Palmer told an *Editor & Publisher* interviewer in the early 1930s, "and the editorial and news policies are shaped with this in mind." Palmer claimed that he had no political interests beyond the issues that confronted the communities in which he operated. "I have less interest in politics than any other newspaper publisher in the world," he said. "Only in matters of utmost public interest do we deal with political issues and then it is for the defense or establishment of principles and not the advancement of individuals," he added.[1] Palmer was operating during a depression, and it was no easy task for him to hold his group of newspapers together. With local business in a slump and his papers in debt, Palmer had to try creative means of bringing in revenue. In 1934 he was sending advertising agencies a letter of "good news concerning Texarkana and the four states area."[2] Palmer's letter encouraged them to place advertising in his Texarkana papers. *The Arkansas Publisher*, the official monthly publication of the Arkansas Press Association, encouraged other publishers to follow Palmer's example. At about the same time, Palmer's Arkansas Dailies group published the promotional pamphlet entitled "The Truth about Arkansas" to advertising agencies throughout the nation.[3]

Another means that Palmer used for raising money for his operations during the Depression era involved the selling of stock in his newspapers. Mahaffey vividly recalled Palmer's financial difficulties in the early 1930s, after he regained the Texarkana papers.

> After he got them back, he was still in trouble in El Dorado. I don't know if he owned the Magnolia paper then, but he owned Hot Springs. But he was in deep financial trouble in all of them. Well, everyone was at that time. I know he was in trouble because he insisted that I buy stock in the Texarkana papers. I took the statement in the Texarkana papers. I took the statement up to my father, who was a lawyer here and he said, "Why son, this outfit is broke!" And I said that I knew it, but that I didn't think it could stay broke under Palmer. I could already see that he was a good businessman. He insisted that I buy stock and I bought it at $50 a share. There were only 1,000 shares in the whole thing. I bought quite a few shares and I later sold them to Hussman at quite a profit.[4]

Mahaffey's recollection of Palmer selling stock illustrates this aspect of Palmer's publishing enterprise. It was not only a means of raising cash, but it also tended to tie his employees to his papers. It was a long-term investment, during a period when salaries were not good. Mahaffey also recalled the low wages of the day:

> I'm pretty sure that his employees were paid less than some other papers' employees. All I could hire in the early days were girls because they were the only ones that would work at those salaries. But Palmer is responsible for my being fairly well off, because he required me to buy his stock he compelled me to do it, but it paid off. And I still get $18 a

month from a pension fund he set up. He also set up a profit sharing plan in his later years.[5]

Edna Howe, one of Palmer's employees at the Hot Springs papers, also recalled Palmer's stock-selling activity.

I was the first employee he hired after he bought the *New Era*. So he asked me if I would write some letters. He was going to sell stock because he was buying the *Sentinel-Record* and he wanted to sell stock in it. So, I told him sure, I would. He said he would pay me $50, if I could do it on my own time. So I took the $50 and bought me a portable typewriter and I'm still using that . . . a 1929 typewriter! I wrote the letters at night, at home. Oh, it took me . . . I don't know how long, days and nights to write those things. Back then they didn't have fancy copiers like they do now, so each one had to be an original and I had to address all the envelopes and everything![6]

Another reporter recalled working for Palmer during this difficult period of the early 1930s. Roy Bosson, who was a Palmer reporter in Hot Springs, said that in the middle of thef Depression "my salary was $7 a week, seven days a week, up to 12 hours a day, on call any times, no overtime, and my first Christmas bonus was a silver dollar. . . . And sometimes you got your salary in script which you could trade for groceries at stores which advertised in the newspaper and had difficulties paying their bills. There was simply not much money around, but Mr. Palmer kept the newspapers alive and kept people at work."[7]

By utilizing the issuance of stock, by forming corporations and holding companies, by borrowing wherever he could, by taking advantage of virtual monopolies in several south Arkansas cities, and by employing good newspapermen, Palmer managed to survive the early Depression years, when many newspapers did not, instead being sold to other newspapers or, in many cases, simply quitting. Palmer got his financing wherever he could find it. He borrowed from banks, friends, and local financiers. Louis Heilbron, of Texarkana, loaned Palmer money on several occasions and was a co-investor in several newspapers.[8] Heilbron was a Texarkana businessman who was associated with Palmer in many business deals. According to Mahaffey, Heilbron and Palmer also developed an area of Texarkana called Beverly Heights, a suburb of the city.[9]

Palmer kept his newspapers alive during the most difficult period of the Depression in the 1930s. Many newspapers in Arkansas were not so fortunate, as has already been pointed out, but Palmer seems to have been able to balance his various enterprises and keep his plants operating, his employees working, and his creditors satisfied.

In 1930 Palmer's daughter Betty was a student at Lindenwood College in St. Louis, and in 1932 she entered the University of Missouri, working on a degree in journalism.[10] On December 24, 1931, Betty Palmer married Walter E. Hussman in a wedding held at the Palmer Texarkana home.[11] Walter Hussman became an important element in Palmer's publishing business.

Walter Hussman was born in Bland, Missouri, the son of W. J. and Anna Vaughn Hussman. His family later moved to St. Louis. He attended the University of Missouri, where he studied journalism. He was a fraternity brother and roommate of Donald W. Reynolds, who later launched his own newspaper career and company. Betty Palmer also attended the journalism school and earned her degree there. Prior to his marriage to Palmer's daughter, Hussman worked briefly in the advertising department of the Palmer papers in Hot Springs.[12] After his marriage to Betty Palmer, Hussman attempted to find a position in the St. Louis area. "You couldn't get a job in St. Louis then," recalled Betty Hussman, "so we went to El Dorado where my husband became business manager." Hussman worked in the advertising department of the El Dorado newspaper during his early years with the Palmer Group and eventually became its business manager.[13]

When Palmer got the Texarkana papers back from Stevick in 1933, he formed Texarkana Newspapers Inc., a corporation owning the properties. Partners in the corporation included Charles Conway, a local real estate man, who also owned the building that housed Palmer's newspaper offices; J. A. McDermott, who had been Stevick's business manager; and Henry Humphrey, who was editor of the *Texarkana Gazette* under Stevick's ownership and under Palmer.[14] In 1936, after his stint in El Dorado, young Hussman became the business manager for the Texarkana papers and vice president of Texarkana Newspapers Inc.[15] Hussman's rise with the Texarkana group may have been due, in part, to the death of Charles M. Conway, who died in Nashville, Tennessee, on June 6, 1933. Conway was a co-investor with Palmer in newspapers in Hot Springs, Camden, El Dorado, and Hope, as well as being associate publisher of the Texarkana papers.[16]

Hussman remained associated with the Texarkana properties during the early 1940s. He became active in the business affairs of the Texarkana area, and on April 26, 1940, he was elected president of the Arkansas Junior Chamber of Commerce.[17] On June 22, 1942, Hussman was commissioned as a first lieutenant in the US Army and was named public relations officer of Camp Robinson, just outside Little Rock, by order of President Roosevelt.[18] In December 1943, Hussman was transferred from Camp Robinson to New York City and assigned to the staff of the Army newspaper *Yank*.[19] According to Betty Hussman, Donald Reynolds requested his friend be transferred to Europe where they became copublishers of *Yank*. In December 1944, Hussman was discharged from the Army with the rank of major. He had served for thirty-one months, parts of which were spent in European and Caribbean theaters. Hussman helped establish the European edition of *Stars and Stripes*, which succeeded *Yank* at the end of World War II.[20] He returned to Texarkana as business manager for the *Texarkana Gazette*.[21]

From 1945 until 1948, Hussman continued to serve Palmer as the assistant publisher of the Palmer Texarkana newspapers. By December 1945 he was listed as president of Camden Radio Inc. and had received a Federal Communications Commission license to begin a radio station in Camden set to go on the air in the spring of that year. The 250-watt station was to operate at 1,450 kilocycles.[22] More details on both Palmer and Hussman and their radio involvement are outlined below, but the purchase of the Camden station indicates Hussman's involvement in expanding the Palmer Group.

Mahaffey recalled the young Hussman: "They lived at Hope for a while and then came over here [Texarkana]. This was during the Depression and nobody had a job, so Hussman began selling ads for the *Hope Star*. Then Palmer brought him over here and he became advertising manager and business manager for the *Gazette*."[23] Mahaffey does not mention a Hussman tour in El Dorado, but Hussman did work in several of Palmer's locations before moving to Texarkana.

Walter Hussman Jr. remembers his father explaining that he moved to Hot Springs after the newspapers went into receivership during the Depression. While there, Hussman launched a Mail-It-Away edition for subscribers to buy extra copies of the paper, which they could mail to friends out of town. The special section promoted all the benefits of Hot Springs as a resort community, and it included lots of advertising. Hussman explained that it got the newspaper back to profitability again, allowing it to exit receivership.

But the newspaper had a cumulative preferred stock outstanding, and with dividends unpaid for a number of years, it took until 1950 for the company to pay all the dividends in arrears before they could resume paying a common stock dividend.

Mahaffey also recalled Hussman's active role in the political side of Palmer's business. He remembered Hussman being close to Arkansas Congressman Oren Harris, of El Dorado. "Harris was chairman of the Interstate and Foreign Commerce Committee," Mahaffey said, "and he handed out television and radio rights." In addition, Mahaffey and others recall Hussman arranging social events for the Arkansas and Texas congressional delegations in Washington, DC.[24]

In the late 1940s, Palmer began to tell people that he was going to ease out of the business and turn "the main operation over to Huss." As Palmer reporter George Brewer recalled, "that turned out to be sort of a joke because the old man couldn't let go of the reins and he and Huss had sort of a discussion, I heard that Walter threatened to leave the organization and CEP [Palmer] gave him full charge of the *Camden News*. Walter moved his family to Camden and ran the works until CEP died. . . ."[25] Brewer added that the temporary disagreement had more to do with "a strong difference of opinion over who would run the Palmer chain rather than money." He also recalled talking to Palmer in France, in 1945, and asking him about the newspaper situation after the war. Palmer told Brewer, "You'll have to discuss that with Huss, I'm going to let him handle the situation after the war." Brewer himself added, "Huss never handled the situation, as I heard it. CEP . . . second-guessed him [Hussman] all over the place. Thus, the move to Camden was to keep Huss at least in the fold, and Hussman did have full control in making all decisions for the *Camden News*."[26]

Hussman did move to Camden. In July 1946, when he was elected president of the Texas Newspaper Publishers Association, he was still listed as business manager of the Texarkana newspapers.[27] And a 1947 listing of Arkansas newspapers in *The Arkansas Publisher* gives Palmer's name as publisher.[28] But by June 1948, Hussman was listed as publisher of the *Camden News*.[29]

Walter Hussman Jr. remembers his father telling him that when he returned from the war, he loved the newspaper business but wanted to own his own newspaper. He found a newspaper for sale in Midland, Texas, got an option to purchase it, then secured enough investors. He went in to tell Palmer he planned to buy the newspaper in Midland, some five hundred

miles west of Texarkana. Palmer did not like the idea of his daughter Betty
and three grandchildren moving such a long distance away. He told Hussman
that he would sell him and his wife Betty the *Camden News*, only eighty miles
to the east. He reasoned that they could together own 100 percent of the
Camden News and not need other investors. In 1949, at age forty-three, Hussman
moved his family to Camden.

Hussman's efforts for the Palmer Group were considerable, even while he
was determined to set his own course. He helped move the Palmer Group
into new fields, especially radio and television, and later he helped diversify
the Palmer Group holdings. With his academic training in journalism and
his growing experience in Arkansas newspaper publishing, Hussman became
increasingly important to the Palmer Group. It was Hussman, for instance,
who arranged for funds to finance the implementation of the Palmer Circuit, and he helped form Palmer's Southwest School Printing Company.[30]
After Palmer's death, Hussman expanded the business even further, forming
WEHCO Media Inc., the successor to the Palmer Group and the owners of
today's *Arkansas Democrat* (after 1991 the *Arkansas Democrat Gazette*) and
other Arkansas daily newspapers, along with radio, television, and cable operations. Surely Hussman and Palmer had their disagreements, especially given
Palmer's gregarious nature, but Hussman remained, even after moving to
Camden, an important element of the Palmer Group. A later chapter details
Hussman's role in the Palmer Group. When Palmer again became publisher
of the Texarkana newspapers, he inherited Arkansas newspaperman John Q.
Mahaffey as well. Henry Humphrey was the editor of the *Texarkana Gazette*
when Palmer regained the newspaper, and Humphrey had a young reporter
on his staff who would one day succeed him. John Quincy Mahaffey was not
only a reporter and editor, but he also later became Palmer's business associate
and known as the "man who knew Palmer the best." It is impossible to talk
to newspapermen or women from Palmer's era and not be told, "You should
talk to J. Q.—he knew Palmer better than anybody."

Mahaffey acknowledges that role. "I made a kind of career out of talking
and writing about Palmer," he said. "I used to make speeches to journalistic
groups and I always used Palmer for the light side of my talk, tell all the really funny things he did."[31] Mahaffey, now retired in Texarkana, continues to
write a column for the *Texarkana Gazette*, and his favorite topic is still Clyde
Palmer.

Mahaffey attended Furman University and graduated with a degree in English in May 1929. He returned to Texarkana, his home, and went to work for the *Texarkana Gazette* on July 5, 1929, when Stevick still owned the paper. He was trying to break into the journalism profession at the beginning of the Depression. Mahaffey recalled his beginnings in journalism:

> I worked for peanuts, but nobody made any money in those days . . . but I had to begin for nothing. The managing editor Henry Humphrey told me, "I'll give you a job, but I can't pay you anything until you are worth something to me. I can't pay to train you." I worked for three months and didn't draw a dime. I finally wrote a story about some black people out on my father's farm and it was such a good story that the Associated Press picked it up and sent it all over the country. The *Denver Post* used it as a feature. I told Humphrey that if I was good enough for the *Denver Post*, I was good enough for the *Texarkana Gazette*. So I began to get paid. From 1929 until 1968 I held practically every job in the news department except sports editor and proofreader. Outside of that I was city editor, telegraph editor, night editor, managing editor and, finally, executive editor.[32]

Mahaffey became very active in the Associated Press Managing Editors (APME) Association and became the voice of the Palmer Group. On November 10, 1948, Mahaffey attended the APME meeting in Chicago for the Palmer Group and chastised the Associated Press for not involving the average man in political campaign coverage. Mahaffey said, "Our night watchman at the paper said during the early part of election night, 'The trouble with you newspapermen is that you talk to the wrong people, the Chamber of Commerce, the country club, NOT [sic] the barbers, the Negroes, the bus drivers and the poor white trash.'"[33] Mahaffey encouraged the AP to improve the political pulse coverage in pre-election stories.

In 1949 he took the floor of the APME meeting in Fort Worth to complain about competition and the careless use of adjectives in AP reports, and he received the proceeds of the "J. Q. Mahaffey Benefit Fund" after complaining on behalf of the Palmer Group about special AP charges.[34] (See Palmer's Professional Activities, the next section in this chapter.) He served on the 1950 Subcommittee on State Services of the Committee on State Studies, which examined the physical setups of Associated Press circuits and problems of service to and by AP members. The report was issued at the 1950 APME meeting in Atlanta and was the first major step toward allowing AP members to have a far greater say in the types of news they wanted to receive, as well as the beginning of the wire service use of the Teletypesetter circuit, which Palmer pioneered in the 1940s.[35] Mahaffey, of course, has close working knowledge of this development, which was nothing new to Palmer's papers. (See chapter 3 of this study.) In 1956 he was elected to a two-year term on the organization's Board of Directors.[36] In addition, he served on the 1955 APME Newsfeatures Committee, along with representatives from newspapers much larger than the *Texarkana Gazette*, including managing editors from the *Miami Herald*, the *Chicago Sun-Times*, and the *Los Angeles Mirror-News*.[37]

The Newsfeatures Committee concerned itself with competition from television and the need for better features to compete with that growing medium in the mid-1950s. Other concerns included the growing demand for color photos, better drawings, and feature packages such as "Keeping Your Home Up to Date."[38] Mahaffey participated actively in these attempts to improve the Associated Press services.

Mahaffey was a popular speaker at the APME meetings, and some of his speeches were so well received that they were reprinted in the APME proceedings.[39] His topics ranged from the frustrations of being an editor (with Palmer as publisher) to the growing role of women in journalism. Mahaffey delivered his messages with humor and was always in demand at the meetings.

Mahaffey represented Palmer well in the APME meetings and became a respected member on a national level. The concerns he expressed concerned Palmer as well. Palmer usually sent a sizable delegation to represent the Palmer Group at APME meetings, including Mahaffey, editor Robert T. Hayes of El Dorado, and editor Robert S. Dean of Hot Springs.[40]

Both Palmer and Mahaffey, like other editors and publishers during and shortly after the war, were concerned with the great number of women entering journalism, due in part to shortages of men and in part to low wages. In 1951 Mahaffey told the APME meeting in San Francisco that "my experience with women is that you can't ride them . . . and once you find a good woman reporter she is very good. And what's more, you don't have to look for them in beer parlors or pool halls." Mahaffey also told the group that he found women newspaper employees to be more conscientious in their work than men.[41] His remarks reflected a growing concern shared by all newspaper editors about the labor market. Members held a lengthy discussion on labor problems surrounding the role of women in the newspaper business at the 1955 APME meeting.

Mahaffey told the convention that getting women to compete against men was not the right approach, but rather they should get the women to compete against each other. "Until you've seen one green-eyed babe going against another green-eyed babe," he said, "you ain't seen no competition."[42]

Palmer encouraged women in journalism and hired many women to work at his newspapers. He often credited his wife with a great deal of his success. Both of his daughters were involved in newspaper work, Alden Palmer Mooney in Hot Springs and Betty Palmer Hussman in Camden. Palmer was a leader in bringing women into the newsroom, although he might also be criticized for using women as a means to lower wages. Still, the record indicates that Palmer's papers did employee large numbers of women.

Palmer and his papers survived the first half of the economic depression of the 1930s. In 1935 Palmer bought the *Smackover Journal*, his first purchase after the buying spree of 1928–1933. Located about twenty miles northwest of El Dorado, Smackover was part of the El Dorado oil boom. The *Journal* began in 1922, and in 1935 Floyd Barnes sold the paper to Palmer's Smackover Journal Inc., a new corporation jointly owned by Palmer, Margaret Brent, and Clyde E. Byrd. The *Journal* was first printed at the News-Times plant in El Dorado, as a companion paper to Palmer's *South Arkansas Progress*, which he acquired in 1927. Each paper retained its own name, but advertising and circulation figures were combined.[43] In 1963 the *South Arkansas Progress* was discontinued, but the *Journal* continued as a Palmer Group paper.

Arkansas newspaper publisher Ray Kimball became a business associate of Palmer's in 1939 when the two purchased the *Magnolia Banner News* together. They first met at a meeting of the Arkansas Press Association in Hot Springs in 1931.[44] Kimball and Palmer later had numerous joint business ventures, and Kimball played a key role in the development of the Palmer Circuit in the 1940s.

Kimball was born in Beaver, Oklahoma, where his father, A. L. Kimball, published a newspaper. The younger Kimball attended the University of Oklahoma and worked for the university as the manager of student publications following his graduation. But he sought his own newspaper to purchase.

"I noticed in one of the trade papers that a newspaper in Horatio, Arkansas, was for sale by the bank, which indicated to me that it had gone through the wringer," Kimball recalled. "So, I came down and looked at it and that's how I came to Arkansas."[45] In 1931 Kimball and his father bought the *Horatio Messenger*, a Sevier County paper, with a circulation of about one thousand.[46]

In 1932, however, Kimball moved his paper ten miles north to the larger town of DeQueen. DeQueen is located north of Texarkana, almost on the Arkansas and Oklahoma border.

In that same year Kimball purchased half interest in Earl Ramsey's *Sevier County Citizen* and then discontinued his Horatio paper. Within a year Kimball purchased the remaining half interest in the *Citizen* and combined his Horatio printing plant stock with that he had purchased from Ramsey and began to publish the weekly *Citizen* himself. On May 10, 1933, Kimball purchased the *DeQueen Bee*, a paper that began in 1897, and combined it with his *Citizen*. The *Citizen* became the *Daily Citizen*, and the *Bee* became a weekly.[47]

Kimball later owned all or part interest in numerous Arkansas papers, including the *Calhoun County Arkansas Plaindealer*, the *Fordyce News Advocate*, the *Malvern Daily Record*, and, with Palmer, the *Stuttgart Daily Leader* and the *Magnolia Banner News*. A well-known Arkansas publisher, Kimball also served as president of the Arkansas Press Association in 1941.[48]

Kimball's role in the development, implementation, and later use of the Palmer Circuit has been overlooked. His association with Palmer is usually confined to their joint ownership of the *Magnolia Banner News* and the *Stuttgart Daily Leader*, but Kimball, more than anyone else, was crucial in the implementation of the Palmer Circuit.

In 1939 Kimball went to Magnolia, Arkansas, "where they had an oil discovery and it was really the only boom town in the whole southwest," he recalled. "So I thought it would be a good idea to buy a paper there, if I could." The weekly *Banner News* began in 1928 and the daily *Banner News* on March 11, 1938. The Banner News Publishing Company published both. Kimball recalls the circumstances: "It was owned by a number of local people, local merchants. I went down there with a handful of dollar bills and some options and signed up enough of them to get controlling interest in the paper. Then I found out that I couldn't borrow the money from anybody to exercise those options. Mr. Palmer had newspapers in Texarkana, Camden, Hope, El Dorado, and Hot Springs, and I thought he might be interested in this and he was. So he helped finance the purchase of the *Banner News* stock and that is how we became acquainted."[49]

After the Kimball–Palmer purchase in 1939, Kimball became editor and publisher of the *Banner News*. While he served in the US Navy from 1942 until 1945, his wife, Evelyn, took over the management of the paper.

On February 26, 1946, Palmer, Hussman, Kimball, and Edgar Brown purchased the *Stuttgart Daily Leader and Arkansawyer*.[50] Palmer was listed as the publisher of the Stuttgart paper, with Brown as the editor. In 1951 Kimball traded his *Banner News* stock to Palmer for Palmer's interest in the Stuttgart newspaper. "I had the majority stock in the *Banner News*," Kimball recalled, "and we had an equal amount in the Stuttgart paper. So we made the trade and I kept a couple of shares of *Banner News* stock and I just sold it to Mr. Hussman last week" (March 1983).[51]

Kimball also noted that the Stuttgart paper cost them $35,000, with Palmer, Brown, and himself owning one-third each, for an investment of slightly under $12,000 per partner. In writing about the costs of Arkansas newspapers during the 1930s, Kimball said that a paper usually cost an amount equal to the paper's "annual gross revenues."[52]

Not only was Kimball a co-investor with Palmer, but he also often served as an advisor to Palmer on potential newspaper properties. "Palmer," Kimball said, "was interested in expanding, but he wasn't pushing."[53] But as Kimball recalled:

> If someone wanted to sell a newspaper, naturally they would contact Mr. Palmer. Mr. Palmer didn't say, "Hey, let's go over to Monticello and see if we can buy a newspaper!" But, like at Warren, if someone wanted to sell, they would contact Mr. Palmer because he had a number of other papers and probably would be able to pay the money that somebody else would not be able to pay. But it wasn't that he was trying to expand, that wasn't my impression at all. But when we had the opportunity to get Stuttgart, he said, "I'll help you, but I don't want to have anything to do with running it; you are going to have to run it." I said, "I can do that!" It just became available and we bought it.[54]

Kimball also remembered looking at the newspaper at Crossett for Palmer: "Right after the war, the Crossett people, their town was just a company town—the owners, asked Mr. Palmer to come over and operate the *Crossett Observer*. Mr. Palmer asked me to go over there and look over the situation and I did. I told him it wouldn't be profitable, that it was a company town... who would you sell advertising to? So we turned it down."[55]

The Crossett Lumber Company established the *Crossett Observer* in 1906. The company discontinued it in the 1930s, and but the paper reappeared in 1939, owned by the Enterprise Printing Company of Bastrop, Louisiana. It

was discontinued again during World War II and born again in 1946 as the
Crossett Enterprise Observer.[56]

Palmer did, however, continue to take an interest in the Crossett newspaper, according to Ernie Deane, who was invited to publish the Crossett
newspaper in 1948. "While considering the potential there for success, I got
a call from Palmer who suggested that we might enter into a joint venture at
Crossett. I was disinterested in a joint venture with anybody.... Palmer didn't
get into the newspaper business at Crossett, either, but I don't know why."[57]

Kimball also cited the problems of getting personnel to operate papers in
the 1930s and 1940s. "I looked at Warren for him one time, but who would
run it? Yes, newspapers were available, all right, but it was difficult to get personnel and to get publishers who were capable of running a small operation."[58]

Palmer did not always listen to Kimball's advice. In 1951 Palmer was part of
a group that bought the *Russellville Courier Democrat*. In addition to Palmer,
the group consisted of J. William Fulbright and the Fulbright newspaper interests. Fulbright was the former University of Arkansas president and then
US senator. The Russellville paper was the result of a merger of two previous
newspapers with the same name—the *Russellville Democrat*—one established
in 1875 and one in 1898. The Palmer–Fulbright group bought the papers from
Rita Faye Livingston in 1941. The group kept the paper until January 1, 1985,
when they sold it to the owners of the rival *Russellville Weekly Tribune*.[59]

Kimball said that the Palmer–Fulbright connection was a business interest between Palmer and the Fulbright family, which owned the Fayetteville
paper and other media interests. He remembered the Russellville purchase:

> Russellville was for sale and Mr. Palmer asked me to go up there and
> look at it. I did and I told him what I thought about it. At the time,
> the former publisher at Stuttgart was looking for a position and when
> Palmer and Mr. Fulbright bought the Russellville paper, Edgar Brown
> became publisher. I advised him [Palmer] against it. Actually, what hap-
> pened was the weekly paper there became the dominant one in the field
> and eventually took over the daily paper ... that was a mistake that Mr.
> Palmer made. They didn't go broke, but it wasn't any huge success. Ful-
> bright wasn't managing it, but he had his publisher up in Fayetteville,
> Sam Gearhart, overseeing the Russellville operation at one time. I think
> I advised Palmer correctly on that deal. But it could have been a real
> good deal if it had been handled right. The management didn't turn out

well for Palmer and Fulbright, so that the opposition paper, naturally, took over.[60]

Former Senator J. William Fulbright also noted that Sam Gearhart was the monitor of the Russellville paper purchase for the Fulbright family interests. Fulbright recalled Palmer well and said "Mr. Palmer was a very shrewd observer and an excellent businessman."[61]

Kimball contributed to the continued expansion of Palmer's newspaper publishing business as both business partner and advisor on newspaper properties. His role in Palmer's business affairs is overlooked because Kimball consolidated his efforts in the DeQueen papers. Today he is recognized as one of the state's best newspaper publishers.

In addition to Hussman, Kimball, and Mahaffey, others contributed to the success of Palmer's publishing enterprises in the 1930s. W. A. "Bert" served as the bookkeeper at El Dorado, then comptroller of the Palmer Group, and, finally, general manager of the El Dorado papers.[62] Alex Washburn was an important business partner and played a key role in the establishment of the Palmer Circuit and in the anti-Palmer union strikes against the Palmer Group that came later. Bill Whitehead in Magnolia and Paul T. Morgan, the business manager in Texarkana, were also important. The Palmer Group could not have survived the economic depression without the assistance of such Arkansas newspapermen, working with and for Palmer.

During the war years, Palmer busied himself with the development of the Palmer Circuit and the consolidation of his various newspapers. After the Smackover purchase, he made no new acquisitions until 1946, when, as noted above, he bought the *Stuttgart Daily Leader and Arkansawyer*, along with Kimball and Edgar Brown.[63] Palmer, as noted previously, traded Kimball his stock in this paper for Magnolia newspaper stock in 1951.

In 1949 Palmer purchased the *Stephens Star*, forming the Stephens Publishing Company as a part of the Palmer Group. Palmer had previously owned the *Stephens News Herald*, which he purchased in 1929, but he sold it in 1930, shortly before it ceased publication. Stephens is located only a few miles from Camden. The purchase of the *Star* allowed Palmer to operate an area weekly as a companion to his Camden dailies. In the 1960s Walter Hussman combined the Stephens paper with the *Camden Times*.[64]

Several associates have mentioned that Palmer once owned all or part of a Little Rock newspaper. However, none of his close associates have been able to provide any details of a Palmer paper in the Little Rock market. Meriwether does not mention Palmer's involvement in a Little Rock paper, but Palmer may indeed have owned a paper there, or part of one, and it may have escaped attention. Brewer wrote that Palmer "did operate a paper in Little Rock at one time, the *Little Rock Times*, I think, but that didn't work out."[65] *Arkansas Gazette* editor Robert S. McCord, whose family had newspaper interests in the Little Rock area, indicated that he thought Palmer once owned a North Little Rock paper called the *North Little Rock Daily News*, but added that it was only in existence for a few years.[66] There is no record of a Palmer paper in Little Rock, however.

From 1951 until 1955, Palmer was a partner in the *Russellville Courier Democrat* with the Fulbright family interests. This was one of the few papers that Palmer ever owned north of the Arkansas River, since he promoted south Arkansas and knew that territory better. On July 11, 1951, Palmer and Alex Washburn bought the circulation and goodwill of the *Hope Journal* from Arkansas politician Kelly Bryant. This allowed for consolidation with the *Hope Star*, adding 1,730 subscribers to the *Star* circulation. In 1953 Palmer purchased the subscription list of the *Columbia County Journal*, a paper published in Waldo, a small town northwest of Magnolia. The weekly was established in 1938 and ceased publication on February 19, 1953, when it was absorbed by Palmer's *Banner News*. On July 1, 1955, the El Dorado News-Times Publishing Company bought the printing equipment and subscribers list of the weekly *Huttig News*. The subscription list was combined with the *South Arkansas Progress*.[67]

This was the last newspaper Palmer purchased before his death. During his career he owned all or part of at least thirty-one Arkansas newspapers and owned the Texarkana papers twice. His control of major dailies and area weeklies in south Arkansas gave Palmer a strong voice in that part of the state. A later chapter details how Palmer used his papers to promote social and political issues, such as candidates for governor and his battle with the Arkansas Louisiana Gas Company (Arkla). His major papers in Texarkana, El Dorado, Magnolia, Hope, Camden, and Hot Springs covered all of the major population centers in south Arkansas.

Palmer also owned a number of newspapers in Texas and was active in several of that state's press associations. His Texarkana operation sat on the Texas side of the line, giving him a base in that state. Recalling that "I heard he owned some newspaper in Texas," Sam Papert said, "in 1951, he [Palmer] purchased 25 percent of the *Jacksonville (Texas) Daily Progress*, a small daily paper in east Texas."[68] Mahaffey thought Palmer may have owned a paper in New Boston, the *New Boston News* or the *Bowie County News*, at one time and perhaps a newspaper in Mt. Pleasant.[69] Papert, however, said that he "did not think that New Boston and Mount Pleasant might have been part of his [Palmer's] estate at any time."[70] Kimball has stated that he was sure that Palmer owned a Mt. Pleasant paper.[71] And Texarkana reporter Louis "Swampy" Graves also recalled that Palmer "had some working relationships with the papers at New Boston and Mount Pleasant."[72]

In January 1955, Palmer wrote to Vern Sanford, secretary of the Texas Press Association (TPA), concerning some of his Texas holdings and the potential TPA membership of some of his employees. "We happen to own the *Morris County News* at Daingerfield, Texas," Palmer wrote, "but we lease it on a flat rental to Olin Hardy and his wife." He pointed out that if Hardy had not yet joined the TPA, he would "go after him again."[73]

A few months later, Palmer again wrote to Sanford:

> We have three weekly newspapers in Texas. The *Morris County News* at Daingerfield, the *Lone Star Journal* at Lone Star and *Hughes Springs News Era* at Hughes Springs, Texas, which we had leased to Mr. and Mrs. Olin Hardy. Mr. Hardy died in February and Mrs. Hardy has been attempting to carry on the publishing of these papers since; however, we feel that is too much of a task for her and are looking for someone, whom we could lease the *Hughes Springs News Era* to, or possibly lease all three of these papers. If you know of anyone that might be interested, will you please have him or her get in touch with Paul Morgan [business manager of the *Texarkana Gazette*]? I would appreciate it if you would keep this information as confidential as possible, and should you desire to run this in your bulletin, please do not use the names of the papers.[74]

A 1965 atlas lists Daingerfield as having a population of 3,133; Lone Star with 1,513; and Hughes Springs with 1,813. The 1984 *Editor & Publisher Yearbook* does not list any of these papers as still in circulation. Palmer's grandson David Palmer Mooney recalled that R. T. Bentley "handled the sale of the Daingerfield newspapers to a man in Daingerfield in the late 1960s. I believe he was selling them on behalf of Mrs. Palmer and J. Q. Mahaffey."[75]

Lease arrangements, such as Palmer had with the Hardys, sometimes make it difficult to trace both his Texas and his Arkansas holdings. But Palmer was very active in Texas newspaper publishing and played a role in east Texas journalism. Both Palmer and Hussman were involved in the Texas Press Association, the Texas Daily Newspaper Association, and other professional groups within Texas.

It is not difficult to assess the total impact of Palmer's papers; he owned newspapers in all of the major southwest Arkansas cities for almost three decades. The 1947 population of the combined counties in which Palmer owned papers was 242,179 individuals. And, in that same year, Palmer's newspapers printed an average of 60,945 daily newspapers and 3,943 weekly issues.[76] Palmer's papers dominated Union, Ouachita, Garland, Columbia, Hempstead, Arkansas, and Miller counties. While the 1947 *Arkansas Gazette* printed a larger average number of daily papers, 87,709 per day, Palmer's in fluence outside of Little Rock far exceeded this. And Palmer's papers did address and influence local issues in numerous communities, while the *Arkansas Gazette* tended to address Little Rock and state issues. Palmer was willing to play the role that his papers gave him. "The newspaper must be a step ahead of other community agencies and must take the lead in community betterment," he said, "else the community will not be bettered to any great extent."[77]

Palmer, as illustrated in a later chapter, was involved in the communities in which he owned newspapers. He supported local charities, and he got involved in local issues (gambling in Hot Springs, defeating a proposed race track in Texarkana, etc.). He supported local chamber of commerce activities, such as lobbying for an airport in Hot Springs. He did not champion any underdog causes, although he did not forbid his reporters and editors from supporting such local issues. Palmer's real interest was not the editorial side of his newspapers, but the business of publishing. As Mahaffey noted, Palmer was not a writer and he had no background in journalism. While he argued with editors about editorial topics, he did not seem concerned with First Amendment issues. Details of his relationships with reporters and editors follow in chapter 4. Palmer expanded in an era when other newspaper groups were also being formed. It is possible that many of the newspapers he purchased might not have survived the Depression, or, of course, they might have been purchased by others.

Palmer's policy of seeking a monopoly in the cities in which he owned newspapers left the community with only a single voice, a single point of view, and a single outlet for community expression. That is the great weakness of chain journalism, of course, and the weakness was as evident in Palmer's newspaper group as any other chain.

Palmer's Professional Activities

As the publisher of the Texarkana daily newspapers early in his career, Palmer was automatically an influential and prominent citizen in the area. He served as president of the Texarkana Chamber of Commerce in 1921 and proved instrumental in the city's attempts to raise money for the purchase of Spring Lake Park.[78] He also became active in the state Chamber of Commerce, and in February 1940, Palmer presided over a Little Rock meeting of the state Chamber of Commerce to discuss state activities for the upcoming World's Fair.[79] In October 1948, he was granted honorary membership in the Chamber of Commerce of the South, which honored "men who have had a part in the South's development and who, by their own achievements, have added to the South's fame."[80] And he was honored by the Texarkana Junior Chamber of Commerce "for his support of community projects and for the up building of Texarkana."[81] Both Mahaffey and Arnold recalled an award given in Texarkana, begun by Palmer. "He did originate the C. E. Palmer Award," Mahaffey said, "for the person judged to have performed the most meritorious service to the town [Texarkana]. All Palmer did was to buy the original cup. Each year the person who won had his name engraved on it."[82] In January 1947, for example, Palmer attended the Texarkana Chamber of Commerce annual banquet to present the C. E. Palmer Achievement Award to local businessman Homer Wommack, an event that Palmer participated in every year.[83] Palmer took his civic duties seriously, it appears.

Throughout his career, Palmer was active in the Arkansas Press Association, the Texas Press Association, the Texas Daily Newspaper Association, the Arkansas Associated Press group, the Associated Press, and other newspaper organizations. "He was a great supporter of newspaper associations," Mahaffey recalled.[84] It was Palmer who helped arrange the May 1928 joint meeting of the Arkansas Press Association and the Texas Press Association at Texarkana's Hotel Grim.[85] He served on the Board of Directors of the Arkansas Press Association for several terms, but he never served as president of the organization. He was president of the Texas Daily Newspaper Association in 1954.[86] In March 1956, the Texas Daily Newspaper Association honored Palmer at the organization's annual convention for his service to Texas journalism.[87] In May 1930, Palmer joined the National Editorial Association and remained active in that organization for many years.[88] And in 1939 he became a member of the Board of Directors of the Southern Newspaper Publishers Association at their annual meeting in Olde Point Comfort, Virginia.[89]

Palmer also encouraged his employees to take part in newspaper organizations. Just as he encouraged Mahaffey to be active in the Associated Press Managing Editors group, he assisted other staff members of his newspapers to be involved in such associations. In April 1952, Palmer attended the New York City meeting of the American Newspaper Publishers Association. In addition, Walter Hussman of the *Camden News*, Mrs. Alden Palmer Mooney of the *Hot Springs New Era* and *Sentinel-Record*, and Thelma Papert of the *El Dorado News-Times* also attended.[90] He also frequently sent Robert Dean of Hot Springs, Bert Estes of El Dorado, and W. R. Whitehead of Magnolia to press association meetings.

After his death, an *Arkansas Democrat* editorial praised Palmer for being a "generous supporter of the Arkansas Press Association."[91] Edna Howe vividly recalled the fun of going to Arkansas Press Association (APA) meetings at the Hot Springs Arlington Hotel and to press parties at Oaklawn Park race track with Palmer, although she remembered his horrible driving more than anything.[92] Ray Kimball first met Palmer at an APA meeting. Kimball served as president of the APA in 1941. He also remembered that Palmer was active in the Associated Press, especially after the development of the Palmer Circuit.[93]

Palmer remained active in the APA for all of his career, from 1909 until his death in 1957. He was the only Arkansas publisher to have two covers of *The Arkansas Publisher* devoted to him, in September 1930 and July 1957.[94] Not only did he serve multiple terms as a Board of Directors member for the APA (1946 and 1951), but he also spoke frequently at APA meetings. In February 1932, Palmer addressed the APA meeting at the Marion Hotel on the topic of "Needed State Legislation Which Can Probably Be Best Secured by Initiated Acts of Constitutional Amendments."[95] In July 1938, when Palmer was chairman of the state's World's Fair Committee, he addressed the APA meeting in Hot Springs on "Arkansas Exhibits at the World's Fair."[96] And in May 1939, Palmer addressed the APA on needed legislative actions, saying, "We need a more reasonable inheritance tax, abolition of special attorneys for the state, the adoption of a billboard tax, a permanent committee to study legislative problems and a workmen's compensation law," adding that "it behooves the press to organize and protect not only their own interests, but the best interests of the state in a legislative program."[97]

In January 1957, the APA honored C. Hamilton Moses with a lifetime honorary membership in the organization. He was the first non-publisher to receive this honor, presented by Governor Orval Faubus and *Fordyce News-Advocate* publisher Bill Whitehead. Moses was president of Arkansas Power and Light and a state civic leader, and the assembled publishers heaped praise upon him, Palmer among them.[98]

Palmer was "a staunch supporter of the Arkansas Press Association," according to Fordyce publisher W. R. Whitehead, and he "attended all meetings and sessions right along with the predominantly weekly publishers in attendance. Even though he owned numerous newspapers, he did not act as if he was above the weekly publishers. When the APA met in Hot Springs he would host the refreshments hour with the finest hors d'oeuvers [sic] including shrimp. This has not occurred since his death."[99] Palmer frequently hosted the "socials" at the APA meetings. In 1941 he had the entire APA annual meeting to a barbecue at his home on Lake Hamilton, near Hot Springs.[100]

Louis "Swampy" Graves also recalled that Palmer was a frequent host at APA meetings held in Hot Springs: "Palmer supported Arkansas Press Association activities. At least one of the semi-annual meetings would be held in Hot Springs and he and Mrs. Palmer were frequently hosts at some of the events. He also sent employees to the meetings. I felt that he deferred to the more numerous small newspapers, and made no effort to be dominant in the APA."[101]

Mahaffey recalled that Palmer was very active in the Associated Press Managing Editors Association.[102] Palmer is listed as a participant at several APME meetings. He was active in the affairs of the Associated Press and was a member of the auditing committee of the Associated Press Board of Directors.[103]

The Associated Press Managing Editors met in Fort Worth's Texas Hotel on November 2, 1949, with nearly three hundred Associated Press managing editors attending, including Palmer, Mahaffey, and other representatives of the Palmer Group.[104] Mahaffey recalled Palmer missing one of his famous speeches: "The closest he ever came to hearing one of my speeches was at the national convention of the Associated Press Managing Editors Association convention. . . . Thinking I could make some points with him, I launched a denunciation of the rates being charged by the Associated Press. CEP always thought ours were too much. After covering myself with glory, I sat down and looked around for his approval. He was nowhere to be seen, having gone to the restroom just before I started speaking."[105]

In representing the Palmer Group, Mahaffey did indeed complain about the Associated Press rates and "special assessments" of members. "Every time there is something special, we have a special assessment. Of course, I don't want regular assessments increased," Mahaffey told the assembly.[106] In fact, Mahaffey's plea for more moderate charges became an important part of the meeting. James S. Pope, of the *Louisville Courier-Journal*, started the J. Q. Mahaffey Benefit Fund and raised a total of $3.06, which was presented to Mahaffey during the meeting. Pope said that he had been "deeply touched" by Mahaffey's remarks. "Because of this sympathy," Pope told his fellow managing editors, "I undertook to establish the J. Q. Mahaffey Benefit Fund and I now turn over to him $3.06 to reimburse him for the phone charge so unjustly imposed on him."[107] Mahaffey's photo was taken accepting the proceeds of the fund on behalf of the Palmer Group. This "frugality" became a trademark of the Palmer Group papers.

The Fort Worth meeting was typical for the association, and Palmer was in the middle of it, surrounded by his various editors. It was an important meeting hosted by Amon Carter, publisher of the *Fort Worth Star Telegram*. Representatives of the Palmer Group included Mahaffey and Palmer, along with Bob Hayes of El Dorado and Bob Dean of Hot Springs. The only other representative of an Arkansas newspaper was Harry S. Ashmore, of the *Arkansas Gazette*. Carter hosted the assembly with cocktail parties and barbecues and a dinner at his Shady Oak Farm, at which he shot out electric lights with a pistol. Carter also arranged for several Texas oil men from the American Petroleum Institute to address the editors and arranged a dinner for editors and wives at the Fort Worth plant of Consolidated-Vultee Aircraft Corporation, where almost one hundred editors were photographed standing on the wings of a B-26 bomber, which was being built by the company. Another lavish dinner followed, hosted by Carter's friends, at the Northwoods Stock Farm, where the editors wore cowboy outfits and watched square dancing. The ladies were treated to a fashion show at the Fort Worth television station WBAP, where $8.5 million in jewels were displayed. At the closing dinner, Amon Carter and AP Executive Director Kent Cooper sang duets (Cooper played the piano).[108] Palmer, Mahaffey, Hayes, and Dean took it all in, and if any of them had any doubts that the Depression had ended and the severities of the war years were over, the Fort Worth meeting should have served notice to them all.

Mahaffey recalled that Keith Fuller, then president and general manager of the Associated Press, talked about Palmer and the AP at Palmer's funeral in 1957.

> We sat in my office before the funeral and talked about the veteran publisher, "If you could talk to Mr. Palmer today, what would you say?" I asked Fuller.
>
> He thought for a moment. "I would have said: 'Mr. Palmer, the AP was three minutes ahead of UPI on the story of your death. What do you say to that?'"
>
> CEP would have liked that. He would have hit the desk with his fist and yelled, "Good, by golly!"[109]

Palmer was not always happy with the Associated Press. But his newspapers and his radio stations were Associated Press members, and Palmer played a powerful role in the Arkansas AP group. In fact, his papers and radio stations were AP's biggest users. Palmer was often host to the Arkansas Associated Press Group. In 1931, for instance, he hosted the State Association of Associated Press Editors in El Dorado.[110] And, again, Palmer's various editors were deeply involved in the Arkansas Associated Press Group. In June 1941, the group met at the Arlington Hotel, in Hot Springs, hosted by Palmer. Mahaffey was elected chairman of the AP group, while others attending included Robert Hayes of the *El Dorado News-Times*, Henry Humphrey of the *Texarkana Gazette*, Paul Morgan of the *Camden Times*, Charles Goslee and Robert Dean of the *Hot Springs New Era* and the *Hot Springs Sentinel-Record*, along with other representatives from Palmer's papers.[111]

In 1948, Palmer served as chairman of the state Associated Press group and again hosted the group at the Arlington, in Hot Springs, on May 21. The association heard a special radio address from NBC in New York by Frank J. Starzel, the assistant general manager of the Associated Press, on the 100th anniversary of the AP.[112]

Bosson, a Palmer reporter in Hot Springs before joining the Associated Press in Little Rock, recalled a story about Palmer visiting the *Arkansas Gazette* offices one time, which were separated from the Associated Press offices by only a glass partition:

Mr. Palmer walked into our offices, dapper and Continental, as usual . . . wearing a beret, long cigarette holder dangling out of his mouth, grey spats, and looking the part of a Broadway stage performer.

The young guys in the AP office, who had never seen him before, crowded around their windows to laugh at the character who had just entered.

Seeing no one that he knew except me, Mr. Palmer came back to my desk and we visited for 15 to 20 minutes.

As he was leaving, he glanced over at the AP office with that little half-grin he always wore, looked back at me and winked.

After he went out they asked me, "Who was that character?"

That "'character,'" I told them, "was Mr. C. E. Palmer who owns the *Texarkana Gazette*, *Hot Springs Sentinel-Record* and *New Era*, as well as newspapers at El Dorado, Camden, Magnolia, Hope, and Russellville, and also some radio stations who get your radio wire." You should have seen the scramble to catch him![113]

In 1952 Clement P. Brossier became bureau chief and head of the Associated Press office in Little Rock and remembered Palmer's involvement with the Arkansas Associated Press Association, comprised of the publishers of all of the AP papers in the state.

Clyde Palmer was an original, and there are no copies. . . . [In the AAPA,] Mr. Palmer was an original there, too. Each member newspaper was eligible to join and thus all of his papers including Hope, DeQueen, Magnolia, Stuttgart, Hot Springs, El Dorado and Texarkana had representatives. Mr. Palmer, during my tenure, always was there, too. And he usually spoke for all the papers in a single voice.

The AAPA was an advisory group designed to provide a forum for the members to air their gripes and compliments on past service and provide leadership as to what they wanted in their news report in the future, Mr. Palmer always had very firm ideas in all three areas.

I believe he did serve as president maybe more than once but not during my time in Arkansas. Election was by voice vote in the last few minutes of the annual meeting and usually there was only one candidate.[114]

Today Brossier is retired and lives in Orlando, Florida, but still vividly recalls Palmer, whom he calls "one of the legends of southwestern newspaperdom."[115]

Palmer's role with the Associated Press Board of Directors and on the AP auditing committee does not appear to have been major. Still, it brought him into contact with a wide variety of other publishers and with Associated Press management personnel, which could not have hurt his publishing influence.

At the time of his death, Palmer was listed as a member of the National Press Club of Washington, DC, and the Overseas Press Club of New York City.[116] His involvement with press and newspaper associations on both state and national levels gave Palmer an opportunity to have a voice far greater than that of any other newspaper publisher in Arkansas. It increased his influence, and it gave him a platform for his ideas, which became important in the development of the Palmer Circuit.

Palmer's influence with press associations, coupled with his monopoly of newspapers in southwest Arkansas, gave him the possibility of even greater control of the news. This was as great a weakness for journalism as it was a strength for Palmer's organization. It heightened the monopolistic situation. There is no evidence that Palmer used his press association influence to play gatekeeper, but the possibility existed with his publishing monopoly.

The Golden Rule Publishing Enterprise

At the time of Palmer's death, the *New York Times* noted his newspaper publishing career, his development of the Palmer Circuit, and that "Mr. Palmer was also president of the Palmer Foundation, a philanthropic enterprise that financed research for the preparation of the Golden Rule Reader, a modern reader for elementary grades."[117]

The Golden Rule Readers were a pet project of Palmer's late in his life; the books have long since disappeared and are no longer printed, but in the early 1950s they received considerable publicity. The books were the most tangible outgrowth of the Palmer Foundation, established on September 21, 1945.[118]

Palmer funded the Palmer Foundation with an initial endowment of $100,000. The stated purpose was "to contribute to a true peace by promoting among people an attitude of fairness and unselfishness in personal and public affairs." "This is an undertaking which I hope will contribute to the true peace for which we as a nation have been striving," Palmer said. "We have learned by now that peace is not something to be taken for granted but is a condition which can be maintained only by the unselfish devotion of many millions of people. Peace, then, or the maintenance of peace, must begin at home in the relationship of one individual to another," he added. Palmer called for proposals, which received awards of $500 and $1,000, that could answer the question: "How best may we inculcate in young people a consciousness of, and a devotion to the principles of morality that are embodied in the Golden Rule—'Do unto others as you would have others do unto you.'"[119] The Palmer Foundation quickly became known as "The Golden Rule Foundation."

Palmer recognized that some might object to the moral tone of his foundation's purpose. "It is understandable that objection should be raised to the teaching of any religious creed in America's public schools," he said, "but surely no sect or creed can take exception to instruction in the personal satisfaction, and the individual and public benefits, that accrue from gauging one's conduct by the Golden Rule."[120] Palmer invited individuals or groups in any college or university to submit proposals to the foundation, and he set up a panel of judges to review the submissions.

The premise of the Palmer Foundation was naive, at best. But it was probably a sincere attempt to establish some means of promoting the Golden Rule among people. The religious overtones were evident in the entire concept, but it was an attempt to do good, coming at a time when so much of life was filled with war and death. "We have solved the problem of keeping the peace in a city and a country and between communities and states," Palmer said, "but we are far from a solution industrially as well as internationally."[121]

The Palmer Foundation made the first awards in January 1947. A prize of $1,000 was awarded to Frank E. Burkhalter, director of the Department of Journalism at Baylor University. Charles M. Reinoehl, emeritus professor of education at the University of Arkansas, won the second place prize of $500.[122]

The *Texas Press Messenger*, a publication of the Texas Press Association, carried a story about the Palmer Foundation and the Golden Rule Readers. Noting that Mr. and Mrs. Palmer felt that a "vacuum" existed in the elementary schools, the story indicated that the Palmers "established the Palmer Foundation in 1945." The article described the Palmer Foundation: "A philanthropic institution, dedicated to character development in children through books directed at specific age groups, the Palmer Foundation is the harvest from years of successful work in the newspaper field."[123]

The article states that the Golden Rule publishing enterprise began at several colleges where Palmer sponsored a series of workshops, leading to a variety of publications. The first publication was a book entitled *Parents' Responsibility in*

Character Development, which was the result of a workshop in Washington, DC. The General Federation of Women's Clubs published and distributed the book, which was aimed at the parents of preschool children.

The next workshop was held at the University of Michigan and resulted in a book by Dr. William Clark Trow titled *Human Values in the Elementary School*. The topic of this book was character development among students in the fourth, fifth, and sixth grades. The Palmer Foundation printed the book, but the National Education Association in Washington, DC, distributed it.

Dr. Vernon Jones, a professor of educational psychology and the chairman of the Department of Education at Clark University, next prepared a teacher training syllabus with the title "Character and Citizenship Education." The Hugh Burch-Horace Mann Fund of the National Education Association printed this syllabus in collaboration with the Palmer Foundation.

In 1954 the first of the Golden Rule Readers appeared, distributed by the American Book Company in New York City. These books were for use in the first three primary grades. They appear to have been well received, and Palmer said that, by 1956, the sales had totaled "nearly a million dollars." Palmer added, "We are highly pleased and gratified with the success of the readers."[124] Betty Palmer Hussman's recollection of an education professor named Level, from Virginia, who actually wrote the Golden Rule Readers, has not been confirmed. However, the books were successful for a number of years.

Betty Hussman recalled having something to do with their beginnings.

> He asked me one day what he could do that would do a lot of good, something to put his money into, and I suggested that he do something founded on the Golden Rule. He found this professor up in Virginia— Level, I think his name was—and he took some books and rewrote them. They sold real well. But the lawyers wrote us after a while and said the federal government was making it too difficult to have that kind of a foundation, so we gave what money we had left to start a library at Texarkana Junior College. The American Book Company published the books, in New York City.[125]

She added that the books "made $200,000 to $300,000 a year."[126]

Sam Papert remembers that "Palmer was sponsoring a republication of the McGuffey Readers . . . he wanted to be sure that English and reading were well grounded throughout the school system. . . . In other words, he felt a need for more basic 'reading and writing' training way before we were hearing about it on a nationwide basis."[127]

Ray Kimball remembered only that Palmer "seemed interested in promoting" the Golden Rule Readers.[128] Mahaffey recalled that "Palmer had the idea that education needed more character and morality to it and he went back to the old McGuffey Readers. He wanted to publish a series of textbooks that were like the McGuffey books." Mahaffey added that he always thought that Palmer was partially motivated by the possibilities of a charitable tax deduction. He noted that the books "just sort of faded out . . . they were just one of his many projects."[129] As for the books themselves, Mahaffey recalled that in later years he saw them "stacked up and gathering dust in a file room at the [Texarkana] *Gazette*."[130]

George Brewer said that he "was aware of Mr. Palmer's Golden Rule Foundation, but never could figure out exactly what it was supposed to do. Some who didn't cotton to Palmer and his operations averred it was an income tax dodge. I really don't know."[131] Many of Palmer's critics not only felt that this was just another business scheme, but were quick to say so as well.

"I, along with most [Palmer] employees," said Louis Graves, echoing the opinion of many, "thought the Golden Rule Foundation a tax-exempt joke."[132] It was, no doubt, difficult for those who were critical of the Palmer style to understand his interest in promoting language arts among school children.

That the books attracted no small amount of attention was evidenced by the fact that two state newspapers devoted considerable attention to them after Palmer's death. The *Arkansas Democrat* noted that

> In recent years Mr. Palmer took a great interest in preparing young children to be good citizens. The highly successful Golden Rule books reflect his concern.
>
> The second series of those readers to teach children moral values by story example has just been published. An earlier series is in use in the public schools of most states. Extensive research in child psychology and reading habits preceded the writing of these books. The cost was borne by the Palmer Foundation, which Mr. and Mrs. Palmer established in 1945 to further "a true peace by promoting among peoples an attitude of fairness and unselfishness in personal and public affairs."
>
> The foundation has made grants to universities and educational organizations for conferences on citizenship training and for publication of books on the subject.[133]

And the *Pine Bluff Commercial* also editorialized on the Golden Rule Readers.

> The Palmer Foundation, established by the publisher and Mrs. Palmer some years ago, started a research program that resulted in the publication of the "Golden Rule Series" of readers which heavily emphasized character education for school children of tender ages. The first readers—fourth, fifth and sixth grades—sold over $300,000 last year, thus encouraging the Foundation to prepare readers for the first, second and third grades. Seventh and eighth grade readers will be prepared later, Mr. Palmer wrote in a letter to your editor, which arrived on our desk after his death.
>
> The readers teach lessons of cooperation, courage, fairness, friendliness, reverence and unselfishness, yet sustain the pupil's interest at the same time avoiding the attitude of "preachiness." Thus will the younger generations have abundant reason to cherish the name of Palmer.[134]

If, in fact, the books made as much money as Palmer said they did (and as Mrs. Hussman attested they made), it seems unlikely that they would have ceased publication, or that they would have just "faded out," as Mahaffey thought. Mrs. Hussman's recollection of attorneys advising them to quit the Palmer Foundation because of tax law changes could be possible, although charitable foundations have always had a place in modern tax law.

Palmer's Golden Rule Readers were probably a victim of the changes taking place in school systems during the 1950s and early 1960s and of the constant push by publishers to promote new textbooks. The Palmer Foundation was dissolved after his death, and the remaining funds were given to Texarkana Junior College to begin a library building fund. The college named the building in honor of Palmer.

Mahaffey recalled the creation of the library building fund at Texarkana Junior College. "They named it after him because he put up $50,000 to help build it."[135] The Golden Rule Readers and the Palmer Foundation do seem to have been ideas that Palmer really was interested in promoting for the good of school children. While it was easy for critics to say that the entire idea was a tax "dodge," it is probably more true that it was a tax shelter that provided a means for attempting to do good. Palmer could certainly have found other ways of sheltering money, without the cost that apparently went into research, seminars, publishing, and distribution.

The fact remains that many Arkansas school children used Palmer's readers in school each day, while their parents read Palmer's newspapers at home.

Others listened to Palmer's radio stations. And, in the near future, many would watch Palmer's television station.

Radio and Television Enterprises

Unsurprisingly, Clyde Palmer turned his attention to radio in the 1930s and to television in the 1950s. The decline of newspaper revenue and the rapid increase of radio revenue did not escape the attention of the businessman in Palmer. Exactly when Palmer became actively interested in radio cannot be pinpointed, but evidence suggests that he was involved early in the 1930s. Texarkana residents not only picked up early radio signals on their home sets, but the Kansas City Southern passenger line, which ran through Texarkana, also installed radios in its Pullman cars. The railroad gave this innovation a great deal of publicity, and this helped increase interest in the new technology. And Palmer surely noted reports of radio sales, which indicated that, nationwide, $358 million was spent on the purchase of radio receiving sets in 1924. In Arkansas and Texas, radio was coming of age. The first Arkansas Razorback football game was carried on September 27, 1924, and the University of Arkansas began radio courses for credit in the fall of 1925.[136]

The natural connection between newspapers and radio was already made in the state by the time that Palmer became interested. In early 1933 Mrs. Jay Fulbright, publisher of the *Fayetteville Daily Democrat*, purchased station KUOA. And by 1935 the Associated Press, United Press, and International News Service were all broadcasting news, in five-minute segments, containing the tag, "For full details see your daily newspaper," at the end.[137]

If all of this was not enough to cause Palmer to develop an interest in radio, then an important event that took place on June 10, 1936, surely did. President Franklin Roosevelt came to Arkansas to open the state centennial celebration. Palmer served as a member of the state Centennial Commission, which invited the president to visit the state. Roosevelt's speech from Little Rock aired live throughout the state and parts of the nation and attracted national attention.[138]

Palmer was also involved in another 1936 Centennial Commission activity, when five Arkansas cities aired Hot Springs station KTHS for a full day of centennial activity on the radio. Feeds also came from the Biltmore Hotel in New York City and from Washington, DC, where both Senators Hattie

Caraway and Joseph T. Robinson spoke to the state. In addition, Arkansas entertainers Bob Burns and Dick Powell performed from Los Angeles, and Lum and Amber came on from Chicago. The daylong event was sponsored by the Arkansas Centennial Commission, headed by Harvey Couch and of which Palmer was a commission member.[139]

In May 1938, Jesse H. Jones, chairman of the Reconstruction Finance Commission, one of FDR's New Deal agencies, and publisher of the *Houston Chronicle,* and therefore a Texas newspaper colleague of Palmer's, came to Arkansas and dedicated a new radio station at Siloam Springs. The governors of both Arkansas and Oklahoma were in Siloam Springs for the ceremonies, and their speeches, along with the Jones speech, were carried by radio in Arkansas, Tennessee, Oklahoma, Louisiana, and Texas.[140]

Although Palmer did not purchase the Hot Springs newspapers until 1929, the Spa City papers were involved in radio history on August 11, 1926, when the Associated Press results of the Democratic primary from the *Sentinel-Record* were sent by a special phone wire to powerful clear channel radio station KTHS, located in the Arlington Hotel, for broadcast. The radio station had made special arrangements with the Associated Press. The Dempsey–Tunney fight and the 1926 World Series between the St. Louis Cardinals and the New York Yankees were broadcast in the same manner, using the newspaper AP wire and a direct hook-up to KTHS. And Arkansas Senator Joseph T. Robinson accepted the position as Al Smith's vice presidential running mate on August 30, 1928, live from Hot Springs, with KTHS feeding both NBC and CBS.[141] In short, radio was playing an increasingly important role in the daily lives of Arkansas citizens.

Texarkana radio station KCMC went on the air on February 26, 1932, and that evening a celebration attended by both Arkansas Governor Harvey Parnell and Texas Governor E. L. Sterling marked the beginning of Texarkana radio broadcasting. The station's studios were in the Grim Hotel, owned by Palmer business associate Charles M. Conway. By mid-1933, following the death of Conway that same year, the station had been purchased by Palmer's Texarkana Newspapers Inc. In 1936 the studios were moved to the Texarkana Bank, and later, after a 197-foot tower was built on top of the newspaper building, the studios and transmitter were moved to Palmer's *Gazette-News* building. By 1938, Palmer was listed as the president of KCMC Inc.[142]

In 1938 Palmer's station promoted itself with the motto: "serving the four-state area with news of the world, hours ahead."[143] According to Mahaffey, Palmer sold stock in KCMC, just as he had in newspapers, and Mahaffey bought stock in the radio station.[144] In the latter part of 1938, Palmer evidently sold all or part of the station to Henry Humphrey, who was editor of Palmer's Texarkana newspapers and a partner in Texarkana Newspapers Inc., although, according to Ray Poindexter, Palmer was still listed as president of the station in 1941.[145] During this time the station was affiliated with both the Mutual Broadcasting System and the Texas Radio Network, owned by El-liott Roosevelt. Mahaffey recalled that Palmer bought KCMC from Charles M. Conway, another partner in Texarkana Newspapers Inc., and he credits Conway with originally starting the station. "Palmer was interested in anything that made money," Mahaffey recalled in talking about Palmer's radio beginnings.[146]

Poindexter says that Palmer made an attempt to establish a radio station in Hot Springs in 1936, when he made application for a 100-watt station, to be operated at 1,310 kilocycles with the Federal Communications Commission (FCC). He also notes that Clyde. E. Wilson established KWFC radio in Hot Springs on July 26, 1939, with a studio at 819 Central Avenue that went on the air June 21, 1940. He added that Howard Shuman, who had been with KTHS since 1937, left the station in 1939 to "help organize KWFC" as a mutual affiliate.[147] A 1939 biographical sketch of Walter Hussman lists him as being president of KWFC in Hot Springs.[148] It is possible that Palmer arranged the financing for this station, with Hussman eventually acquiring control after Palmer's death.

Palmer's 1936 application was made in the name of Associated Arkansas Newspapers Inc., his corporation that published both the *New Era* and *Sentinel-Record*. At the same time that Palmer submitted the application, however, Col. T. H. Barton's El Dorado group, El Dorado Radio Enterprises, also sought a permit for a station. Barton proposed to buy KTHS, which at that time was owned by the Hot Springs Chamber of Commerce, and move it to Little Rock. The chamber attempted to stop the sale and move by court action. The court did, in fact, approve the sale of the station to Palmer's fellow El Dorado oil investor, Col. Barton. However, the FCC had not approved the sale. The FCC finally reviewed the pending sale of the station to Barton in November 1938. A delegation of Hot Springs Chamber of Commerce members and Arkansas Governor Bailey, along with Congressman-Elect

W. F. Norell (of Monticello) appeared before the FCC. However, on the second day of the hearing and in the face of such opposition, Col. Barton ceased his effort to buy the Hot Springs station, but he was granted an option to purchase the station if the Hot Springs group decided to sell.[149]

At this point, another associate of Palmer's, Elliott Roosevelt, son of the president, appeared on the scene and offered to operate KTHS via a management corporation, if the station increased the power to 50,000 watts. Roosevelt arrived in Hot Springs for a meeting with the Chamber of Commerce Board of Directors on January 3, 1939, to discuss the possibilities of operating KTHS. While in Hot Springs, Roosevelt was the guest of Palmer at his Lake Hamilton home.[150] The plan was not accepted. However, in September of that same year, Harvey Couch (who had been chairman of the Centennial Commission on which Palmer served and an advisor of President Roosevelt) and C. Hamilton Moses (who was a friend and business partner of Palmer's) of Arkansas Power and Light presented a plan to increase the power to 50,000 watts and got NBC to agree to invest $150,000 of the $200,000 needed to increase power. The Hot Springs group would have to come up with the remaining $50,000. This plan was also turned down.[151] What role Palmer played in this series of events is not clear, but it is almost impossible to believe that he was not involved in some way. Barton, Moses, Couch, and Roosevelt were all associates, in one way or another, with Palmer.

Barton and his group, Southland Radio Corporation, had another opportunity to buy the station in 1941, but before the FCC could act, World War II broke out.[152] Radio was having a growing impact in Arkansas, and Palmer became more involved in radio as the decade passed. As Kimball recalled, "Mr. Palmer was interested in the radio station in Magnolia when they organized that. He asked me to go in with him on that, but I didn't want any part of it. I don't know what they did. . . . Mr. Palmer was part owner of that radio station, at that time. At least when they organized it he did have some stock in it."[153]

Radio station KVMA went on the air in April 1948. Palmer was associated with the Magnolia station as a stockholder, although the extent of his interest remains unknown.[154]

Perhaps the most interesting aspect of Palmer's radio involvement concerns the connection with Elliott Roosevelt, son of president Franklin D. Roosevelt. Betty Hussman recalled that Roosevelt "wanted to build up a network of Texas radio stations and he leased stations. They were involved in the Texarkana station."[155] However, she remembers no details of the involvement. Mahaffey also recalled that Elliott Roosevelt "had some dealings with Palmer here [Texarkana] in connection with KCMC radio. I think Roosevelt owned part interest in the station here."[156] Kimball additionally recalled a Palmer–Roosevelt connection, but remembered it as having something to do with a station in Fort Worth, Texas.[157] Graves recalled that "Palmer and associates became owners of KCMC after it was established—my recollection not research—by Roosevelt."[158] There is no evidence that Roosevelt began the Texarkana radio station. In fact, the call letters KCMC stand for Charles M. Conway, one of Palmer's partners in both newspaper and radio ventures. The station went on the air on February 26, 1932, owned by W. A. Blair and John R. Anderson, of Tupelo, Mississippi. Palmer bought the station in mid-1933.[159]

Poindexter notes in his history of Arkansas radio stations that a group including Lt. Col. Elliott Roosevelt and Major Walter Hussman filed an application with the FCC for a station in Camden in December 1944. Betty Hussman does not recall any Roosevelt involvement with her husband in the Camden station.[160] Camden Radio Inc. did receive authorization from the FCC to begin a 250-watt radio station in Camden in December 1945. Walter Hussman, labeled "a Texarkana newspaper executive," was listed as president of the firm.[161] Poindexter notes that the Palmer Group received a permit for KAMD, in Camden, soon after the end of World War II and went on the air on June 19, 1946, using a US Navy surplus transmitter and tower. And Poindexter also notes that the Camden station was managed by Randy McCarroll, of Paris, Texas, with Frank Meyers of Texarkana listed as general manager of the "Palmer radio holdings."[162] Palmer was also listed as a stockholder in the Camden station.[163] In Poindexter's history of Arkansas radio, Meyer's name crops up several times, connected with Palmer sometimes and other times standing alone. The chances are he was fronting for Palmer on radio deals. Poindexter says that Meyers was "associated with Roosevelt."[164]

Poindexter notes that Hot Springs station KWFC let a contract to Elliott Roosevelt and Associates to act as consultants for the station in November 1942. He pointed out that Roosevelt owned a chain of radio stations in Texas as well. A note in this same book, however, indicates that Clyde Wilson of the Wilson Furniture Company was the owner of KWRC.[165] No clear trail of ownership exists at this time. However, on November 3, 1951, Walter Hussman, acting for Camden Radio Inc., purchased controlling interest in KWFC, with one-fourth interest remaining with Clyde Wilson, the station's founder. Hussman was listed as president of Camden Radio Inc. and vice president of the corporation operating KCMC in Texarkana.[166] It is obvious that Palmer was indeed becoming as involved in radio as he had been in newspapers, with interests in stations in Texarkana, Camden, and Hot Springs. By 1953, when KWFC joined the ABC radio network, Walter Hussman was listed as president of the corporation holding KWFC, according to Poindexter.

Elliott Roosevelt's attempt to establish a chain of radio stations in Texas, the Texas State Network Inc., included among its investors John A. Hartford, of the Great Atlantic & Pacific Tea Company, who purchased $200,000 worth of stock in the network. Other investors were a group of New York insurance executives, along with a long list of other stockholders. Elliott himself was a commentator on his network, but was, according to sources, independent of his father's administration.[167]

By 1941 Roosevelt's Texas State Network was in trouble. "The radio station company was insolvent," wrote Roosevelt biographer Ted Morgan; "the entire investment capital of $500,000 had gone down the drain, and not a penny had been paid back to investors." Elliott joined the Army Air Corps, and Jesse Jones, owner of the *Houston Chronicle* and a member of the Roosevelt administration, personally helped cancel out Elliott's outstanding debts.[168] (Jesse Jones, as previously noted, dedicated a Siloam Springs station in 1938, and Roosevelt was also involved in the KTHS Barton/Chamber of Commerce deal that same year.)

Whatever the connection between Palmer and/or Hussman and Elliott Roosevelt, having the son of a sitting president involved with his radio stations was probably a good way to attract both investors and advertisers to Palmer's radio enterprises. Elliott would probably not have been much help in getting FCC licenses, however, since he felt that the FCC unfairly worked against him because of his father.[169]

At the time of Palmer's death, he was listed as president of KCMC Inc., of Texarkana, and president of Midwest Video Inc., of Little Rock. According to David P. Mooney, Midwest Video was another media holding company, and Palmer was an associate of the Lyndon B. Johnson interests through this corporation. "Midwest Video was a holding company for a number of cable television companies," Mooney said, "and it was headquartered in Little Rock."[170] Mooney pointed out that Midwest Video did have connections with Lyndon Johnson interests in Austin and later in Louisiana. Palmer had business and political connections in Texas, and he and Johnson could have been involved. A more detailed discussion is presented in chapter 5. Mooney said that Midwest Video was an early cable company that began in the early 1950s when cable television was just beginning.[171]

It is difficult to say how close any relationship between these stockholders might have been, but it is certain that Johnson would have known the major stockholders who owned 50 percent of his own television operation.

Walter Hussman, in 1957, was listed as president of KAMD, in Camden, and vice president of KCMC, in Texarkana.[172] By this time KCMC-TV in Texarkana had become part of KCMC Inc. At least one associate recalls a Palmer interest in a television station in Louisiana, between Texarkana and Shreveport.[173] Television was the growth area of the company after Palmer's death, when his original radio and television holdings extended into cable television and microwave transmission.

In July 1957, *The Arkansas Publisher* devoted the issue's cover and a large space to the death of Clyde Eber Palmer. The obituary noted that Palmer had pioneered teletypesetting circuits for newspapers. It noted that he had various newspaper holdings, radio and television properties, oil, and real estate. "The value of Palmer's properties could be counted in millions," the writer noted, "although he apparently never made a public estimate himself."[174]

The *Arkansas Gazette* once reported that in 1950, a New York interviewer quoted Palmer as saying that his press, radio, oil, and other interests were worth $150,000,000. His associates said they thought the interviewer was mistaken or Palmer was jesting, although they said his worth was in the millions.[175]

Palmer had, by his death in 1957, improved his $900 investment in the old *Texarkana Courier* considerably. He had become a major business and political force in Arkansas and had gained a national reputation for his tele-typesetting circuit (see chapter 3) and his publishing enterprises. He survived the Depression. He survived the competition of radio and became actively involved in this new medium. And he survived many of his detractors and competing newspapers to build a media group that dominated southwest Arkansas. The Palmer Group was well established and a thriving publishing business. As Mahaffey pointed out once: "It is no exaggeration to say that Mr. Palmer was a business genius. Business was his hobby, his relaxation, and nothing delighted him more than a tough civic or business problem."[176]

Clyde Palmer dominated Arkansas newspaper publishing from 1933 until 1957. He exercised broad influence with the Arkansas Associated Press. He was involved in radio and television as owner of all or part of several stations. He also operated an important, if brief, elementary school textbook operation, of national note. To Palmer's critics, he controlled too much of the Arkansas media. His control did indeed prohibit a variety of views from being spread by the media in the communities he served. Still, there is little evidence that he exercised any policy of censorship in those communities although the possibility obviously existed. Palmer seemed concerned, almost exclusively, with the business affairs of his enterprises.

CHAPTER 3

The Palmer Circuit

History of the Palmer Circuit

Clyde Eber Palmer's reputation is based on his position as an important publisher of Arkansas newspapers and the owner of radio and television stations. However, outside the borders of the state, Palmer's fame and importance rests more on his role in the development of the automatic teletypesetting device that connected his major newspapers. The Palmer Circuit, as the multi-newspaper network was called, was an innovative and important concept that allowed for the centralized typesetting of news for a group of newspapers. The technology involved and the device itself were later used by other newspaper groups and by press associations far larger than Palmer's group of newspapers. In fact, the roots of modern multi-newspaper publishing, such as that utilized by *USA Today*, lie in the technology that Palmer pioneered. Historians of Arkansas journalism have largely overlooked this contribution of Palmer's, for the most part, with the exception of one article in the *Journal of Arkansas Journalism Studies*.[1] As *Fordyce News-Advocate* (and former editor of the *Magnolia Banner News*, one of Palmer's newspapers) W. R. "Bill" Whitehead said, "From a mechanical and production standpoint, C. E. Palmer became known nationally in newspaper circles when he established the first Teletypesetter newspaper circuit in the U.S. or the world."[2] Palmer became nationally known for his development of the Palmer Circuit, and it had a significant impact on the news distribution process in the United States.

The Palmer Circuit became operational in 1942 and was finally phased out in the 1960s, to be replaced by a more modern technology, the company's microwave system. Palmer's "Circuit" essentially comprised a small wire service system that connected his various newspapers, but the system went one step further and allowed for automatic and simultaneous typesetting at each of the newspapers. The circuit was connected by a leased telephone line, which linked the Linotype machines at each of Palmer's daily newspapers with a news copy feed originating at a central point. The Palmer Circuit was the first of its kind in the United States and led to the establishment of such systems at other newspaper groups and press associations. It represented the first use of technology to link newspapers instantly and may be viewed as the beginning of the technological explosion that led to modern newspaper publishing, which today utilizes computers and offset printing techniques.

"The main reason for the establishment of the Palmer Circuit was that it was economical and it was better for the newspapers," one Palmer business associate said.[3] It was economical because it eliminated the need for separate typesetting operations at numerous papers, and it was better for the newspapers because it moved news to more papers in a compressed time period. This technology led to eventual changes in the newspaper publishing industry. The Palmer Circuit appeared at the beginning of a series of problems between the printers unions, who correctly saw the device as a means of displacing them or lessening their power and control of production, and publishers who sought to publish more efficiently. But it was also the beginning of the modernization of newspaper printing. And it was developed at a time when labor shortages caused by the United States' entry into World War II demanded a new technology. Finally, it appeared at a time when the newspaper publishing business faced new competition from radio and cost efficiency became paramount.

More than two hundred thousand people in Arkansas, representing more than 10 percent of the state's population, served in the armed forces in World War II.[4] The per capita income for the state in 1940 was $254, well below the national average of $592.[5] This motivated, in part, young Arkansas men and women to look for work in the growing number of out-of-state defense plants and to seek military service as an opportunity. It began, however, another out-migration of labor from the state, much like the one early in the Depression era. Many Arkansas newspapermen joined this outward migration through both military service and industrial employment.

The pages of *The Arkansas Publisher* reflected this shortage during the early 1940s. Articles with titles such as "*McGehee Times* Suspends Due to Labor Shortage"[6] and "Women Run Shop of the *Chicot Spectator*"[7] were common in the publication during the period. Often the wife of the editor or publisher took over the operation of a small paper during this period, as was the case with Ray and Evelyn Kimball. While Kimball served in the Navy, his wife ran the *Magnolia Banner News*. *The Arkansas Publisher* was filled with like stories during the early and mid-1940s, such as "Mrs. Aydelott Is New Editor of *Monroe County Sun*," which noted that Mrs. John Aydelott was assuming the role of editor while "L. T. Aydelott is with the armed forces overseas."[8] Other newspapers were forced to change their production schedule dramatically during the period. In 1942 the *Carroll Courier* announced that it would appear in "an abbreviated form until such time as it was possible to employ a printer-operator."[9] And *The Arkansas Publisher* also ran numerous advertisements related to the labor shortages with copy such as "If business in your plant is slack because of the war..."[10] and "With key men away on the fighting fronts...."[11]

The critical labor shortages that newspapers faced during the early years of World War II necessitated extraordinary actions on the part of publishers. In July 1942, Enoch Brown, general manager of the *Memphis Commercial Appeal and Press Scimitar*, told the members of the Arkansas Press Association that "every cooperation should be given by the press to the government during the prosecution of the war effort."[12] Telling the assembled editors and publishers that "newspapers, along with other businesses will have to make serious adjustments and sacrifices during the war period," Brown said that the government would try to limit restrictions facing the press.[13]

Palmer, like other newspaper publishers of the time, faced critical shortages of skilled labor, including reporters and pressmen. This labor shortage was one of several reasons that Palmer became interested in utilizing the technology of the automatic Teletypesetter. As Palmer associate Alex Washburn wrote early in the 1940s, "between the demands of the armament plants for skilled workers and of the armed services for fighting men, the newspapers face a perilous shortage in personnel."[14] Palmer sought ways to solve labor shortage problems that he faced in the early 1940s, and the Palmer Circuit, utilizing the automatic Teletypesetter connected to Linotype machines, offered a means of assisting with this problem.

At the same time that publishers faced labor shortages caused by the war effort, organized labor began to put additional pressure on nonunion newspapers. Palmer faced several strikes at his papers over the next decade. The Palmer Circuit was both a cause of and a response to these efforts by the International Typographers Union (ITU), as outlined below.

The creation of the Palmer Circuit depended upon several independent technologies that were evolving in the early 1940s. The Linotype machine was one important element, as it became the standard for typesetting in the industry, due to its ability to automatically set type, replacing the old hand-setting methods. It was, for its day, quick and accurate. The Teletypesetter equipment was evolving at the same time. Finally, the use of telephone lines to transmit information, via a teletype operation, replacing the old telegraph systems, was another important development. The combined use of these three evolving technologies made the Palmer Circuit possible.

Ottmar Mergenthaler developed his Linotype machine in the 1880s, and by 1886 his machines were setting type at the *New York Tribune*. While other typesetting machines appeared on the market, such as the Monotype, the Ludlow, and the Intertype (which Palmer used at his Fort Smith paper), the Linotype became the standard of the publishing industry by the turn of the century.[15] Palmer's papers had, by the 1940s, standardized the use of Linotype machines. In mid-1939 he installed new Model 14 and Model 6 Linotypes in his El Dorado plant and Model 14 Linotypes at the Camden plant.[16] In September of the same year, the Hot Springs papers installed Model 8 Linotypes.[17]

While the Linotypes solved the technological problems of typesetting and printing within newspapers, problems still remained in moving news from one point to another. The telegraph was the first major advance in moving news rapidly from point to point. Ray Kimball recalled that when he was in college, "the *Oklahoma City News* was using a telegraph report, with an old boy listening with a tobacco can at the keys!"[18] In 1913 the Associated Press began to use teletypes, originally called "automatic news printers," and this began to replace the telegraph reports that Kimball recalled.[19] Kimball's description of the stereotypical telegraph office employee, bent over the key, using a tin can to amplify the signal, was quickly replaced by the implementation of the teletype machine. Early in 1928, the Associated Press in Arkansas "replaced Morse operators at 12 state newspapers, including those at Hot Springs, El Dorado and Texarkana" with AP automatic telegraph printers.[20]

In the early 1920s, the use of perforated paper tape as a means of "freezing" telegraph messages for later use came into being. According to Hope publisher Alex Washburn, perforators were being used on the "New York-Boston trunk wire of the Associated Press" when Washburn worked as a rewrite man in the Boston Associated Press offices on Chambers Street in the winter of

1921–22.[21] This was for telegraph purposes only, according to Washburn, who also noted that it took some time before the perforated tape process was standardized.[22] The use of such tapes simply allowed a delay in converting messages from paper encoding to words.

In 1935 the use of perforated (i.e., coded with punched holes) tape as a means of directly setting type was perfected by Walter Morey, of Chicago, who had been working on the process for fifteen years. Morey's device was a mechanical attachment for the Linotype machine keyboard, which would operate the keys of the machine in response to a perforated tape fed into it. The unit received the perforated tape, already encoded with a message (or newspaper story), from a perforator machine. The perforator could receive input from a telephone line and encode a paper tape with the message. This tape, fed into the typesetter, then automatically ran the keyboard, without any need for a Linotype operator.[23] Morey established the Teletypesetter Corporation, as part of American Telephone & Telegraph (AT&T), in Chicago, where he manufactured and sold his units. By 1942 he had sold more than five hundred units.[24]

The first use of Morey's teletypesetting device was in England, where three English newspapers—in London, Scotland, and northern England—were linked by a circuit, as a means of communication between the cities, but not as a means of typesetting news stories. In the United States, *Time* magazine first used the Teletypesetter to send copy between New York, Chicago, and Philadelphia for editorial purposes, not for typesetting. And several newspapers in New York and Illinois installed the devices, again as a means of sending copy back for editing purposes and intercity communications.[25]

Palmer installed a teletypesetting device in the plant of his *Hot Springs New Era* and *Sentinel-Record* in 1941.[26] Palmer's Hot Springs papers used the device for wire service copy, received by telephone line and "frozen" onto perforated tape for feeding into the Linotypes at a later time. After it was fed into the Hot Springs Linotypes, the perforated tape was discarded.[27] According to Washburn, Palmer had an idea: "Since telegraph news and time copy are made available every day in the Hot Springs plant in punched-tape form, why not organize a circuit in Southwest Arkansas, install a transmitter and utilize the tape in other cities besides Hot Springs?"[28] The results led to a unique technological achievement. As *The Arkansas Publisher* reported in October 1942, "To a group of Arkansas newspapers goes credit for establishing the first complete newspaper leased wire system transmitting type in America."[29]

While Palmer's Hot Springs papers utilized the paper tape perforator and a single Teletypesetter device in that plant, he did not have such devices at his other papers. But the idea began to develop, and Palmer started to discuss the idea with DeQueen publisher and Magnolia publishing associate Ray Kimball. Kimball recalled the beginnings of the circuit: "Mr. Palmer and I were talking about this new device that we had noticed [the automatic Teletypesetter] and we were both real interested in it. It sounded like a departure that would be of great service to small newspapers, especially."[30]

Palmer and Kimball decided to contact the Teletypesetter Corporation and ascertain costs of the equipment, installation procedures, and the possibility of utilizing the technology for a multi-newspaper operation. Walter Morey was sure it would work, but there were costs involved. Palmer decided to seek a way to fund the purchase and installation of the equipment. Again, Kimball recalled the early planning of the Palmer Circuit:

> So we got—or rather Mr. Palmer got—the information from the Teletypesetter people about the cost of the equipment and what would be involved. He didn't feel that he had the funds to do it all on his own. He wanted other newspapers to cooperate in the thing. So he got the Texas Daily Newspaper people to make a loan or make a grant—I've forgotten which—to purchase the equipment, or to help purchase the equipment. . . . That's how we got started on the circuit.[31]

Kimball also recalled that Walter E. Hussman, Palmer's son-in-law, helped arrange the loan that Palmer received from the Texas Daily Newspaper Association.[32] Although records of the association have no information concerning this support of Palmer's activity, [33] it is possible, as Kimball suggests, that Palmer did receive some assistance from both the Associated Press and the United Press, as discussed below. The costs were considerable. Transmitting equipment had to be installed in the Hot Springs plant, along with reperforators and Teletypesetters at each receiving point, as outlined below.

The planning for the implementation of the circuit was done in the summer of 1941. Palmer and Kimball brought in Hope publisher Alex H. Washburn as part of the project, and the three of them further discussed the idea. They then established the Southwest Arkansas Teletypesetter Circuit, as the circuit was legally known, but it quickly became known as the "Palmer Circuit," because all of the original newspapers in the group were owned, wholly or partially, by Palmer.[34]

Palmer asked Kimball to go to Chicago and learn more about the possibilities of the Teletypesetter. For Kimball this trip would be the beginning of a long friendship with Walter Morey, the inventor of the Teletypesetter.

> ... my wife and I went up there along with the shop foreman from Hot Springs ... and received instructions from Mr. Morey and one of his engineers by the name of Hudson. ... I received instruction on the installation of the equipment and the operation of it and my wife learned the keyboard, the punching of the tape, so that we were well equipped to teach others.[35]

On Kimball's return trip, he and his wife stopped in Urbana and Champaign, Illinois, where a Teletypesetter was operating between the two newspapers in those towns, as a means of intranewspaper communication, not to set type for actual printing.[36] After returning home, Kimball detailed the Teletypesetter operation to Palmer and Washburn. He also related his observations of the operations at the Illinois papers. According to Kimball, Palmer listened to his report and said, "Well, let's see if we can implement this thing."[37]

Palmer owned the Hot Springs, El Dorado, and Camden papers; Kimball, with Palmer, owned the Magnolia newspaper; Washburn, with Palmer, owned the Hope newspaper. So it was easy to organize a multi-newspaper intercity Teletypesetter circuit. These—the *Hot Springs New Era*, the *Hot Springs Sentinel-Record*, the *Camden News*, the *Hope Star*, the *Magnolia Banner News*, and the *El Dorado Evening Times*—were the original member newspapers in the circuit, although other Palmer newspapers were later added. Non-Palmer newspapers would also eventually join the circuit, as the circuit became more accepted and the advantages became more obvious.

Palmer planned to do far more than communicate among the six newspapers; he also wanted to utilize the circuit to send news from a central receiving point (Hot Springs) and have it typeset directly from the reperforated tapes at the other newspapers in Hope, Camden, El Dorado, and Magnolia. This resulted in editorial responsibility for the Hot Springs editors, but it was not unlike a small news service operation, and later the Palmer Circuit was often called the "Palmer News Service."

Before the circuit could be operational, several steps had to be taken. Equipment had to be purchased, delivered, and installed at all plants. This meant purchasing mechanical Teletypesetter devices for the Linotypes in each paper's plant and the tape perforator machines to receive the wire signal from Hot Springs and punch a reperforated tape at each plant. During the winter and spring of 1942, the Teletypesetter Corporation sent company engineer Paul E. Marsand to Arkansas to observe the installation of the equipment.[38] Kimball supervised the mechanical work in the printing plants, and Washburn taught the techniques of the operation to female filing editors, who monitored the receiving, at each paper.[39] In the beginning, El Dorado had only a teletype printer, instead of the Teletypesetter, but received its signal off of the same wire.[40] Consequently, at the outset, the El Dorado papers still had to set their type by hand on a Linotype. Marsand installed the Hot Springs sending point in early June, then made a tour of the cities that would utilize the circuit to ensure that everything was ready. Palmer then notified the telephone company that they were ready for the leased daily wire that would connect all points within the circuit.[41]

According to Kimball, limited funds caused the system to have some built-in faults. Unable to install a printer at each newspaper, several had to receive the feed on perforated tape only. This meant they could not actually read the copy until it was set on the Linotype or, in most cases, when the page proofs became available. Kimball admitted that this "was not a very good way to do it, but it was done and we operated that way for a long time."[42] Washburn also recalled this problem in an article in *Editor & Publisher*: "We have no Teletype printer pounding out printed copy to corroborate the composing room proofs. The man on the telegraph desk is 'blind' until the proofs come up."[43] But, as Kimball also pointed out, even though the system worked "blind" for a long time, there were some limited means of communicating important news to the person monitoring the tape on the receiving end, which created some humorous problems, as pointed out below.

Since Palmer's Hot Springs newspapers would be the sending point for the circuit, arrangements had to be made with the wire services to receive and retransmit copy on the circuit. The Hot Springs newspapers received both the United Press and the Associated Press service and were already using a Teletypesetter to receive and "save" wire service reports. Palmer, Kimball, and Washburn decided to approach the United Press (UP) first to obtain permission to retransmit their services, on an edited basis. The retransmission of the UP report, state, national, and world news, as well as feature news, even on an edited basis, was seen as a substantial improvement on the UP service that their small newspapers received. Kimball remembered the limited UP service, called a "telephone pony," that he received in Magnolia at the time. The "pony" consisted of short telephone reports, twice a day.[44]

Kimball contacted United Press on behalf of the group. He proposed to UP that they allow them to use, free of charge, the full United Press wire, rather than the shorter UP report already received in Hot Springs, pointing out that it was "an experimental thing" and that the group could not afford the full wire services.[45] The response from United Press was not what Kimball expected.

> I got this letter back from some monkey up in Kansas City, and he said, "Aw, this thing you are talking about will be 10 or 20 years away. It is impractical and can't be implemented for a long time and we wouldn't be interested in going along with it." So then I contacted the Associated Press and I was able to get them to allow us to utilize the AP report, which we received at Hot Springs, and to distribute it to the other smaller papers. But the UP man said "no"![46]

Significantly, the United Press refusal to assist the Palmer Group meant that the Associated Press became involved in the use of Teletypesetters at an earlier date than the UP and, as a consequence of their involvement with Palmer, had a lead in the use of the technology. In fact, as shown later, the Palmer Circuit led directly to the Associated Press beginning its own teletypesetting systems in the 1950s.

Kimball said that several years afterward he told Palmer about the United Press letter; Palmer said that he would like to see it, and Kimball gave it to him. "If somebody could locate that letter," Kimball said, "it would be real interesting for you to say 'here is what the reaction was from UP about this new type of a way to distribute the news!' They said it was so far off that they wouldn't be able to go along with it, that it was just pie-in-the-sky."[47] The willingness of the Associated Press to experiment with Palmer and later with other circuits, such as Harte-Hanks, gave them a lead in the development of the new Teletypesetter technology. The Associated Press implemented nationwide Teletypesetter services much earlier than the United Press, because they took the lead in the experimental use of the equipment and the service. Kimball later recalled that United Press did let them use the UP report at a very low monthly cost of $4 per week at his DeQueen paper, which later became part of the Palmer Circuit, but only after the Palmer Circuit was a big success.[48] The interest of the Associated Press in the Palmer Circuit established a strong link between the Palmer newspapers and the news service, and Palmer became very active in Associated Press affairs, both in Arkansas and on a national level, for the rest of his life. The Associated Press fed the Palmer Circuit and, thus, played a role from the beginning.

On Friday, June 19, 1942, everything was ready. Palmer had permission to retransmit the Associated Press report from Hot Springs to the other newspapers on the circuit. The filing editor in Hot Springs, Mrs. A. D. Christopher, was ready to edit and send the Associated Press report.[49] Alex Washburn was in Hot Springs to assist with the transmission, but he had his mechanical superintendent, George W. Hosmer, standing by his reperforator in the pressroom at Hope, on the receiving end of the circuit.[50] Kimball was ready at his reperforator in Magnolia. Palmer, along with Marsand and Washburn, was ready to watch the originating process in Hot Springs.

Elsewhere on that same day, President Franklin Roosevelt met with Churchill at Hyde Park, where they discussed their joint knowledge of the atomic bomb and the fall of Tobruk to Rommel's forces in North Africa. It was wartime and a time when news was highly valued and awaited eagerly. The Palmer Circuit represented one advance in technology that would bring the events of the world a step closer to newspaper readers in southwest Arkansas.

That Friday morning was supposed to be devoted to simply testing the circuit, Washburn later recalled.[51] Consequently no real Associated Press news transmission had been prepared, and the edited Associated Press report for the Hot Springs papers had already been sent to the composing room of the Hot Springs papers. The transmitter was scheduled to send out a dummy report to the receivers and reperforators in the other cities.

Unexpectedly, however, at 9:15 a.m., Palmer was notified that the telephone company had completed its test of the wire and the leased phone line connecting the newspapers was ready for use.[52] Washburn recalled later that they managed to quickly salvage some edited AP report tape from the composing room for the first transmission.[53] They fed the tape into the machine in Hot Springs, while Palmer, Washburn, and Marsand wondered what was happening in the other newspaper offices. Washburn placed a long distance call to Kimball and others at their respective receiving points. In recalling that moment later, Washburn wrote about his feelings:

Anyone with as much as twenty years in the newspaper business will understand the feeling of suspense when, after a year of planning, the switch is thrown and a little piece of punctured tape starts moving silently through the "Gate" of the transmitter on the complicated business of turning words into type in cities 70 to 120 miles away . . . it was I, calling from Hot Springs to the receiving points that opening day, who heard the gladdest words known to man: "Working? Hell yes—it's pouring in!" [Ray Kimball told him.][54]

In the scramble to pick up some already perforated tape from the composing room of the *Sentinel-Record* and *New Era*, the AP report had been missed, and since it was impossible to tell what was on the tape, which consisted only of a strip of paper punched with holes, the first news sent over the Palmer Circuit was not really usable for local news in Hope, Camden, or other points on the circuit. "There was some kidding at the end of the day," Washburn said, "when the receiving points congratulated us on telegraphing a galley of Hot Springs society news to the state at large."[55] Washburn added that, beginning the next day, the circuit filing editor began sending out the Palmer Circuit feed first, from the edited AP report "before sending it on to the Hot Springs composing room and always knowing what was going out on the wires."[56] This was critical, since the receiving ends could not determine what news copy they were receiving until the galleys came up, because they were receiving it "blind."

On August 19, 1942, as American Commandos stormed the French coast and the wire services reported that a second front might open up in Europe, the news staff of papers on the Palmer Circuit engaged in a new activity, which Alex Washburn described several months later:

In Southwest Arkansas the crowd was not in the editorial office—it was around a Linotype in the newspaper composing room. Elsewhere the news was being received as copy, read and then turned into type. But in Arkansas, already famous for its Ozarks, blue diamonds, Bob Burns and giant watermelons, they have a brand new marvel—the first newspaper leased wire circuit transmitting type, in America. At Hot Springs a girl stenographer copies spot wire news and feature stories onto a perforated tape, which reminds you of the principle of the old-time perforated player piano roll applied to ticker tape; this tape goes into the transmitter, and in the cities, the telegraph machine reproduces the original tape and feeds it into the Linotype, which sets type without an operator. The twentieth-century marvel which makes this possible is the Teletypesetter, which when applied to a keyboard typesetting machine enables it to operate by means of the perforated tape, dispensing with manual work on the keyboard.[57]

The Palmer Circuit was born at 9:15 a.m. on Friday, June 19, 1942, when the *Hot Springs Sentinel-Record* and the *New Era* linked up with the *Hope Star*, the *Camden News*, the *Magnolia Banner News*, and the *El Dorado Evening Times*. Clyde Palmer, Ray Kimball, Alex Washburn, and the others involved saw the new technology as a means of efficiently providing news to a group of newspapers "in the same geographical area, all of them under 5,000 circulation and running four, six and eight pages daily."[58] None of them really foresaw the future large-scale impact of their work. They saw it as a cost- and labor-efficient means of serving small newspapers and did not realize that such circuits would someday link newspapers throughout the nation.

In 1983, more than forty years after the Palmer Circuit began operation, Ray Kimball recalled that the Teletypesetter made it possible for a typist to do the work of a Linotype operator. One monitor could handle three Linotype machines, and the typists could type at least three times the amount of composition that an ordinary Linotype operator could produce, or at least twice the production. This was the primary cost saving involved in the circuit, according to Kimball. The telephone lines were leased for $1 per mile, and the reperforators and Teletypesetters were purchased from AT&T, although Kimball could not recall the exact cost in 1942 dollars. "The real savings, however," Kimball said, "was in the elimination of the Linotype operators and in the speed at which the type could set in this manner, up to 10 lines a minute. It was easier to get Teletypesetter operators than Linotype operators because all they needed to know was the typewriter keyboard and instructions on how to justify the lines."[59]

This was exactly the point that later caused typesetter union problems for several of Palmer's papers and other newspapers throughout the country, but in 1942 it was a boon to his publishing enterprise. In addition to solving a labor shortage problem, it also allowed the Palmer Group to pool their Associated Press costs. The Palmer Circuit, sending re-edited world, national, and state news, became, in effect, the Palmer news bureau, as a sub-bureau of the Associated Press. It was cost efficient, since, as Washburn pointed out, "practically all of the editing-out work usually done on the home-town tele-

graph desk has already been completed by the [Hot Springs] filing editor—
establishing a sort of state wire-bureau-for-small-cities-only, operating within
the state wire network, but owned by, and responsible to, the four newspapers
it served."[60]

It is impossible to detail the actual savings involved in the implementation
of the Palmer Circuit. The real costs were the leased telephone lines and the
Teletypesetter equipment, purchased from AT&T. The savings were in Linotype operator salaries and in the increased speed at which type could be set by
this method. Since the equipment was a one-time purchase and the Linotype
operator salaries were recurring expenses, it probably did not take long for
the actual savings to become substantial. The teletype monitors, as unskilled
labor, were far less expensive than union-scale Linotype operators, and this is
one reason why Palmer was anxious to break the International Typographers
Union's hold on his printing plants.

Technology of the Palmer Circuit

There were still technical problems to solve in the operation of the Palmer
Circuit. Palmer had to establish hours of operation for the circuit that would
allow maximum utilization of his human resources, as well as the Associated
Press flow and the Palmer Group needs. The Palmer Circuit began to operate
between 8 a.m. and 4 p.m. The normal Associated Press wire began transmission at 7 a.m. and closed at 3 p.m. The Palmer Circuit schedule allowed
time for the build-up of early reports and an hour following the close of the
AP wire for catch-up and re-editing, if needed. The Palmer Circuit originally
operated six days each week, ceasing its flow on Sunday.[61]

Since the receiving stations operated blindly, a means for indicating an
important story had to be found, because the machine did not have bells such
as those found on Associated Press teletypes. They soon discovered it was
possible to outline certain letters in holes in the paper tape. They worked out
a system so that a "T," reported several times and followed by several feet of
blank tape, indicated feature material, or time copy, as it was then called. As
Washburn noted, "if any receiving point finds its composing machine lagging
considerably behind the wire, this 'T' or time copy tape is set aside—to be
used after press time—while the typesetter catches up with the live telegraph
news."[62] For a very important story—a "flash," "urgent," or "bulletin"—the
letter "E" was outlined several times, with blank tape before and after. This

called the reperforator monitor's attention to the tape. This was exactly the case for the news of the August 19 Commando attack on the French coast.[63]

In order to have a balance of news, the filing editor in Hot Springs used a combination of about 80 percent "spot" news and 20 percent "time" copy. This ratio of breaking news and features gave a balance to the service, allowed each monitor to back up the feature news for later use, and allowed them to stay on top of hard news in those anxious early days of World War II. If the filing editor ran out of copy, the TTS (as the Teletypesetter quickly became known) wire could idle.[64]

Shortly after going online, problems developed with the paper tape on the receiving ends, becoming too taut and breaking. They developed an "automatic stop," which halted the Linotype operation if too much tension was put on the tape.[65] The receiving reperforator machine was usually set to one side of the Linotypes, with the 3/4-inch paper tape being fed directly into the Teletypesetter, which was mounted on the right side of the Linotype keyboard.[66]

James H. Hale, once the publisher of the *Kansas City Star* and the *Kansas City Times*, was a recent graduate of Baylor University when he went to work for Palmer at the *Texarkana Gazette*, just as the Palmer Circuit was implemented. Hale recalled the technical problems they encountered in those early days of the circuit operation:

> We would receive, in the newsroom, a six level perforated tape simultaneously with copy which moved on a teletype machine. I eventually became the night telegraph editor on the *Gazette*. It was my job as telegraph editor to put the circuit tape together with the teletype copy. This was done by rolling up the tape on a machine that was wound by hand into a roll. Then we took an ordinary clothespin and clipped the two together, so that the person who fed the tape through the Linotype machine and the Fairchild adapter would have something to go by. [The Fairchild adapter was a later version of the AT&T tape feeding device.] The Palmer Circuit was less than ideal. Every time It thundered or there was lightning between Texarkana and Hot Springs there would be a garble and correcting this tape after it was fed through the Linotype was hell on this earth! Often, it was necessary to throw the whole thing away because proofs could not be read or edited. As a matter of fact, editing was not possible unless you were willing to go back to the Linotype and reset paragraphs of type in hot metal.[67]

The leased telephone wire and transmitter were capable of sending sixty words per minute, but the average rate was about fifty-three words per minute. Operators changed the drive pinions on the Linotypes so that the machines could set 8 1/2 lines per minute, rather than the 7 1/3 lines per minute for manual operation. In the first three months of operation, June 19 to mid-August 1942, Washburn estimated that the circuit set an average of four hundred lines of type an hour or nearly eighteen thousand words per eight hours of circuit time.[68]

Ray Kimball noted that this was "the beginning of providing a typesetting operation originating at a central point" and added that the process became standard with press associations and other communication groups. "But this," he said of the Palmer Circuit, "was the first time that they had been able to set type!" Kimball also pointed out that the Palmer Circuit required a certain standardization in the papers on the circuit. Column widths at all papers had to be the same, for instance, although minor alterations were possible.[69] This technology, and the wire service technology that evolved from the Palmer Circuit, was the beginning of standardization of newspaper formats, which would become more evident later as the wire services moved into TTS operations in the 1950s.

Other papers soon joined the original papers on the Palmer Circuit—in Hot Springs, Camden, Hope, Magnolia, and El Dorado. The two Palmer papers in Texarkana joined the circuit in 1949 and the morning *El Dorado News-Times* that same year.[70] The *Russellville Courier Democrat* joined the Palmer Circuit on November 1, 1951.[71] Kimball's *DeQueen Daily Citizen* became part of the circuit in February 1947, when it resumed daily publication, after Kimball came home from the US Navy.[72] The Stuttgart *Leader and Arkansawyer* joined a few years after the circuit became operational, as did the Helena *World*.[73] Several of the papers also added supplementary Teletypesetter units in their shops to receive even more TTS copy. In July 1947, Washburn's *Hope Star* added a second unit.[74]

After a decade of operations, a July 1952 article in *The Arkansas Publisher* noted the success of the Palmer Circuit:

> Ten years ago a small group of Arkansas Newspapers took the first major step in a revolutionary form of newspaper transmission.... Several years after inauguration of the Arkansas wire, similar private circuits were set up by cooperative or chain newspaper groups in other states.

Two years ago the press associations became interested and began establishing state and regional circuits. Ten years after Mr. Palmer pioneered the idea, Teletypesetter circuits throughout the country number more than 50 and serve newspapers in every state in the union. Large circuits are also operating in three Canadian provinces.[75]

There was no doubt of the success of the Palmer Circuit and that it paved the way for newspaper groups in other states. Its impact was far reaching and significant.

Impact of the Palmer Circuit

The Palmer Circuit attracted immediate attention. *Editor & Publisher* ran a full-page story on the Palmer Circuit, complete with photos. *The Arkansas Publisher* printed a story on the development of the circuit. Interest was expressed by newspaper publishers both in the United States and in foreign countries. A Canadian publisher, W. J. Blackburn, of the *London (Canada) Free Press*, wrote a letter to Palmer asking for more information and indicating that he would like "to set up a Teletypesetter circuit in western Ontario."[76] Blackburn also pointed out that labor was "extremely tight at the present time here in Canada, and it may be that a system like yours would ease the situation considerably."[77]

A Pennsylvania newspaper publisher wrote, "It seems to me you have solved out there a problem of great importance to the smaller newspaper, I believe we will come to that eventually."[78] According to Kimball, "there was a lot of interest by newspapers all over the country. We had visitors all the time, coming in here to look at the circuit and see how we were operating it."[79]

Kimball recalled interest by the *New York Times* and from Robert R. McCormick, publisher of the *Chicago Tribune*, as well as other publishers. Several groups, such as Harte-Hanks, also expressed an early interest and eventually brought that interest to fruition. "Most of those who were interested in it were smaller newspaper publishers," Kimball added.[80] He also recalled that neither the Associated Press nor the United Press was interested in adopting such a system in the beginning. Various groups asked representatives from the Palmer Group to come to talk to them about the circuit. "A number of publishers in Oklahoma that were friends of mine," Kimball said, "asked me to come to the Oklahoma Press Association and discuss with them how they could implement a circuit."[81] Kimball and his wife did install several circuits patterned on the Palmer Circuit. "We installed a lot of Teletypesetter equipment out in Oklahoma, in several places, because Mr. Morey couldn't get enough of his people to install the equipment. All of the newspapers were in a big hurry to get this equipment. Mr. Morey would call me up and say, 'Would you go to Clinton, Oklahoma, and install Teletypesetters for Charley Engleman . . . ?'"[82] In July 1947, Kimball finally did help install a Teletypesetter for the *Clinton Daily News* in Clinton, Oklahoma. According to a report, Kimball and his wife assisted publisher Charles E. Engleman in the installation.[83]

Kimball said that both he and Palmer got so many requests for them to come and give presentations on the Palmer Circuit that they just couldn't go to all of them.[84] Kimball did accept some invitations, however, and in February 1949, he addressed the Inland Press Daily Press Association in Chicago.[85] Kimball was instrumental in establishing several other circuits.

During the war, the labor shortage gave publishers an extra interest in the Palmer Circuit, in addition to the obvious cost savings involved. But many publishers who liked the idea of the Palmer Circuit said that they could never implement such a circuit. "They said," Kimball remembered, "that they would never be able to get the unions to agree to it."[86] Union officials opposed the entire concept, he said. "They thought that this labor saving device was going to eliminate the jobs for their union members. They opposed it and held back the development of circuits for quite a while. I know that when I would go to the Inland Press meetings in Chicago, the big newspapers would like it, but say that they didn't believe their unions would go along with it."[87] According to Kimball, the Palmer Circuit was really better for small newspapers than large ones. "The bigger the paper, the smaller the percentage of mechanical expense. Newsprint might be 30 percent of their total expense, composition and composing room maybe 8 percent. While on a small newspaper like we are talking about [the Palmer papers] that [composing] would run 40 or 50 percent. So it was more to the advantage of a small newspaper to utilize this [the Palmer Circuit] than the big ones and the big newspapers just backed off because of the unions."[88]

It is important to understand that the use of the automatic Teletypesetter circuit developed as a wartime labor shortage, and it began to impact newspapers during a period of increased labor union demands. The impact of such circuits closely paralleled the change from hot type to cold type that came about in the 1960s, and publishers faced union resistance to both technologies. In both cases the unions foresaw a loss of jobs and a loss of power. Palmer saw the circuit as a means of solving the labor shortage and breaking the union power in his publishing plants.

In the last years of the nineteenth century, the American Federation of Labor and the International Typographers Union (ITU) made significant progress in collective bargaining with newspaper publishers. Union interest waned during the 1920s, but the severe years of the Depression era brought a return of union activity, especially after the passage of the National Industrial Recovery Act in 1933. The NIRA allowed for collective bargaining in the newspaper industry, and union activity increased in the late 1930s and the years shortly before World War II. In the early 1940s, the ITU began a series of strikes against Arkansas newspapers.

In March 1941, the ITU went on strike against the *Fort Smith Times Record*. The strike against publisher Don Reynolds lasted six weeks, ending on April 18.[89] On May 4, 1941, the ITU walked out on the *Pine Bluff Commercial*. The strike lasted only a few hours, with the typesetters returning to work on the same day. In July 1941, the ITU struck Palmer's two Hot Springs papers.

The ITU was negotiating a new contract with Palmer, when, on July 1, the composing force of sixteen typesetters walked out on the *New Era* and the *Sentinel-Record*. Both newspapers were put out in abbreviated form on July 1, but a new group of typesetters, hired by Palmer, returned the newspapers to normal schedules on July 2. Palmer said that the union sought salary increases of 22 percent and that it "was impossible to meet the demands in view of decreasing revenues from publications."[90] The striking ITU members launched their own rival Hot Springs newspaper on July 11. By July 31 there was still no movement between Palmer and the ITU, and the National Labor Conciliation Service sent representatives to Hot Springs to attempt to settle the strike.[91]

On September 4, 1941, twenty members of the ITU walked off the job at the *Texarkana Gazette* and the *Texarkana Daily News* as a result of a wage disagreement between the members of Local 373 of the ITU and Palmer. Both newspapers were put out in shortened form, with Palmer's Texarkana editor Henry Humphrey, who had learned typesetting in Chicago in 1893, running the Linotypes. According to Palmer, the ITU demanded a 21 cent per hour wage increase, while he offered a 3 cent per hour increase. Commissioner Joseph S. Meyers of the conciliation service of the US Department of Labor arrived in Texarkana and helped settle the strike after three days. The ITU received a 4 cent per hour increase and returned to work on September 7.[92]

These strikes were a major motivating factor for Palmer in establishing the Palmer Circuit. Both the Hot Springs and the Texarkana strikes took place during the year prior to the establishment of the circuit. To Palmer, the use of the TTS system was his insurance against future strikes by the typesetters of the ITU. The potential of the Teletypesetter was the virtual elimination of the need for ITU member typesetters at the Linotypes in Palmer's plants.

The development of the Palmer Circuit in the face of renewed organized labor activity must also be viewed in the context of the times and the particular vision of Clyde Palmer, who was involved in one of the state's most publicized union controversies. Palmer, as a businessman of the time, was strongly anti-union. In addition to traditional management versus labor conflicts, it is important to remember that Palmer had served on the Arkansas Tenancy Commission in 1936. Governor J. Marion Futrell appointed the commission in August of that year to "investigate the tenancy problem."[93] The issue was important in its time, receiving front-page coverage in Arkansas newspapers as well as national attention. Before the issue was settled, it even became a topic of interest in the White House. Palmer was in the middle of the controversy, and it helped him develop a strong philosophical bias against organized labor, to amend his natural management bias against unions. While the tenancy issue did not have a direct impact on the Palmer circuit, it does help put the strong anti-union feelings of the time into perspective. It was a time in which many Americans shared a great fear of organized labor, and the tenancy issue, which spread into several states, increased this fear. The racial overtones of the controversy added to the problem. For many publishers, the Palmer Circuit became a possible means of solving a larger social and economic problem, and such issues as the farm tenancy movement hardened their stand against labor unions. It certainly cemented Palmer's anti-union philosophy.

The "tenancy problem" began in July 1934, during the bleakest period of the Depression, when sharecroppers, both black and white, met at Tyronza, Arkansas, and formed a union, the Southern Tenant Farmers Union (STFU). The leaders were two young socialists, H. Clay East and H. L. Mitchell. Their concern was the fact that most Arkansas farmers—almost two-thirds, according to the statistics for 1935—did not own the land they worked.[94] The STFU organized strikes, calling out cotton pickers in 1935 and cotton choppers in 1936, as their membership grew to over thirty thousand members. In January

1936 they set up a tent colony near Parkin, which began to attract national attention. According to one historian, "across the state most Arkansans looked upon the union with horror."[95] The local business leaders deplored the union and along with planters saw a conspiracy of outside agitators, urged on by socialists and radicals. The biracial element of the SFTU further stirred fear, and many recalled the Elaine Massacre of 1919, in which five white people and twenty-five black people died and troops had to be sent in to restore order.[96]

On August 26, 1936, Arkansas Governor Futrell appointed a thirty-eight-person Farm Tenancy Commission "to study the farm-tenant and sharecropper situation in Arkansas."[97] The governor asked the commission to begin hearings on September 21 in Hot Springs. Clyde Palmer served as the chairman of the commission, and committee members included Palmer's Hot Springs newspaper editor Charles Goslee and Palmer's El Dorado neighbor and south Arkansas businessman Col. T. H. Barton.[98]

On August 28, 1936, the *Arkansas Gazette* carried the response of the SFTU leadership to the appointment of the commission. The farmers union objected to the commission because no members of the union had been appointed as members. The same story reported that a grand jury was appointed to study reports of violence and peonage in Arkansas cotton fields. And the same article noted that Governor Futrell called on other southern governors to participate in such commissions.[99] Various news reports circulated by the SFTU objected to the one-sided aspect of the commission and to the heavy concentration of conservative businessmen on the panel.

On September 21, 1936, the Farm Tenancy Commission held its first hearings in Hot Springs at the Arlington Hotel. Prior to the meeting, Palmer, serving as temporary chairman, "voiced the hope that one result of the sessions may be a plan whereby the conditions of tenants may be improved."[100] The commission then opened the hearings and immediately elected Palmer chairman of the Tenancy Commission. Palmer's Hot Springs editor Goslee was elected secretary of the commission. Palmer did allow one representative of the SFTU to speak for several minutes.[101] That brief presentation focused on the extent of the union's direct involvement in the commission study. The Tenancy Commission existed for several years, eventually turning its attention away from the SFTU problems to state land use recommendations. Palmer served two three-year terms as chairman.

The *Arkansas Gazette* carried a front-page article on the Tenancy Commission's opening day entitled "Roosevelt Asks Plan to Solve Tenancy Issue."[102]

The Arkansas SFTU had inspired the creation of similar organizations in the Midwest and in other southern states. The issue grew beyond the borders of the state, and the Arkansas Tenancy Commission was expected to provide leadership in solving the problem. But the commission did not really solve the tenancy problem. It continued its hearings for several years, issuing reports from time to time. The reports were usually critical of the SFTU and have been described as "harsh" by some.[103] The greatest lasting impact of the commission was in the area of statewide land use recommendations.

During the legislative session of 1939, the Arkansas General Assembly enacted a new "State Land Policy Act." Palmer said that "naturally, I and other members of the Farm Tenancy Commission are greatly gratified by the passage of both houses of the land policy act, as well as by the sympathetic understanding of the purposes of the bill shown by members of the General Assembly."[104] Palmer added that the act "set up procedures for classifying state lands so that each tract may be put to the use for which it is best suited. Cutover lands may be reseeded for forest lands, eroded lands may be reconditioned for production and agriculture lands made available to actual farmers under the present donation statue."[105] By the time that the new land policy act was passed, the Tenancy Commission had turned its attention to the zoning issues of state lands, not the plight of the tenant farmer. The final judgment on that issue was that "tenancy was caused by absentee ownership of land, by mortgage foreclosures and insufficient farm credit."[106] The Tenancy Commission issued a long report, denouncing the SFTU and most of its goals and demands and recommending that state and federal governments assist industrious (non-SFTU) farmers in a plan to purchase land on reasonable terms.[107] The final federal government action was the creation of several tenant farmer communities, where land was financed with federal funds, such as the community of Dyess in Mississippi County.

During the same time period, union activity in the west Arkansas coal fields had turned violent and received a good deal of publicity. And there is no doubt that Palmer, active in national press organizations, heard, like Ray Kimball, many tales concerning the ITU from big newspaper publishers in the North and East. He was determined not to lose control of his papers to the ITU, as other publishers seemed to have done. Palmer's experience with the Tenancy Commission reinforced his intense dislike of organized labor. In December 1939, Palmer was appointed to a second three-year term as chairman of the state Tenancy Commission.[108] When the ITU took on Palmer and his newspapers, they confronted a publisher familiar with union activity and one who would not privately retreat from a public anti-union stand.

Consequently, Palmer's interest in the automatic teletypesetting circuit went beyond simple interest in improved technology. The first series of ITU strikes against his papers, coupled with his experience with organized union activity in the tenant farmer movement, provided him with additional impetus to complete the installation of the circuit. As the United States entered World War II, the circuit provided the additional advantage of solving the labor shortage for his papers, but it also freed him from the ITU. During the war years, the ITU typesetters were replaced with typists, who easily managed the Palmer Circuit transmissions.

As the war ended, the Linotype operators who had been in the armed forces returned home. The defense-oriented industries began to cut back, and American business began to feel the new political power of labor unions. Neither the Linotype operators nor the International Typographers Union liked the changes that had taken place in the newspaper publishing business during World War II. In many cases women were running the Linotypes, and, in some cases, such as the Palmer Group papers, the Linotype operators were simply no longer needed. The Teletypesetter was often seen as a way of breaking ITU strikes or as a threat to forestall both pay increases and strikes. It marked the beginning of a battle between technology and labor that is still taking place. Kimball recalled one incident related to the use of the TTS system in a strike situation:

> One time they were having a strike at the *Chicago Tribune* and Mr. Morey called me one night and said, "I could sell about 50 Teletypesetters to the *Chicago Tribune*, if you would come up here and supervise it." I said, "Mr. Morey, how long would they use those Teletypesetters?" He said, "They just want to use them to break the strike!" I said, "No, I'm not coming." But I was interested in expanding it when the people really wanted to do it, but when they came and said, "We just want to use this as a strike breaker," that was a different story. So, I told him "no." So he didn't sell them any Teletypesetters. They [the *Chicago Tribune*] used typewriters and justi-writers and engraved plates for the press when they had the strike there.[109]

After World War II the returning Linotype operators, who had been employed by Palmer's newspapers, did not like the Palmer Circuit, for all of the obvious reasons. In June 1950 ITU members walked out of the Palmer papers in Texarkana and El Dorado. Both papers continued to publish with non-union printers. The ITU members sought "an increase from $1.80 to $2.27 per hour for day work and from $1.90 to $2.49 per hour for night work."[110] The strike was led by a man named DuVall, who, according to John Q. Mahaffey, had been previously dismissed by the ITU. Mahaffey also said that the ITU tried to raise $250,000 to publish a competing paper to Palmer's *Texarkana Gazette*. It was rumored that the ITU would match the funds with an additional $250,000.[111]

The Texarkana ITU did begin a rival newspaper on July 17, 1951. The *Texarkana Daily News-Digest* was a tabloid, coming out at noon on weekdays. The publisher of the *News-Digest* was J. D. Baynham, and the editor was J. Gladston Emery. Baynham owned a Texarkana advertising agency and had been one of Palmer's advertising salesmen on the staff of the *Gazette*. Emery was a former member of the Oklahoma state senate and a former Oklahoma newsman, who had also worked previously at the *Fort Smith Southwest American*.[112]

The ITU successfully began several newspapers. ITU president Woodruff Randolph called the ITU's publishing enterprises a "success." The ITU had, at that time, union papers publishing in Allentown, Pennsylvania; Meriden, Connecticut; and Monroe, Louisiana. According to Woodruff, the ITU was planning additional papers in Missouri, Ohio, and West Virginia.[113] The *Texarkana Daily News-Digest* lasted for three years, printing its last edition on April 23, 1954.[114]

An interesting aspect of this strike was the fact that the strikers picketed the *Texarkana Gazette* building, and Palmer and his management staff, in turn, picketed the ITU pickets.[115] Palmer walking the picket line was a sight that many of his employees recalled for years. This image strengthened Palmer's reputation as an anti-union publisher.

In 1951, the members of the Hot Springs Local of the International Typographers Union went on strike over the issues of wages, fringe benefits, and the Palmer Circuit.[116] As Hot Springs reporter Roy Bosson recalled, Palmer "could hire girls to punch the tapes and thus eliminate the greater cost of hiring union Linotype operators. In other words, a lot of printers would be out of a job. The printers wanted control of the tape-punching system as well as control in the composing room."[117] The Teletypesetters on the Palmer Circuit had completely replaced the ITU members. Kansas City publisher James Hale noted the conflict over control of the tapepunchers:

> Another argument between Mr. Palmer and the ITU was jurisdiction over the Fairchild teletype machine, otherwise known to us as tape-punchers. Tapepunchers were people who would be classified today as clerk typists and they would punch on a keyboard a six-level tape similar to what the Palmer Circuit generated from Hot Springs[,] only all of this was local. These tapepunchers were located in the newsroom and they did not have to follow the work rules, which were bargained for by the ITU. The local tapepunchers were often times inept and again, the monitor device on the Linotype machine left much to be desired. Thus, it was a madhouse to produce straight matter for the *Texarkana Gazette* in the morning and the *Daily News* in the afternoon.[118]

Those who recall the ITU strikes against Palmer remember the bitterness of it. Hot Springs reporter Roy Bosson recalled the Hot Springs strike:

> The strike was bitter, especially to those of us who had close friends on both sides. The editorial staff, of course, was non-union and in those depression days we had no union to supplement our incomes and we crossed the picket lines. Jobs and money were scarce.... Unfortunately, there were charges of sabotage in Hot Springs... the foreman of the com-posing room killed himself, presumably over grief from the accusations. They still had to use Linotype operators for setting ads but brought in some non-union printers for that. There was great bitterness.[119]

Bosson pointed out that Palmer called in the "Teletypesetter people from up east and they were giving a crew of girl secretaries a crash course in punching tape while they adapted most of the Linotypes to the tape."[120]

The Hot Springs strike did not last long, but while it did, Palmer used other means to publish his Hot Springs papers. The copy was put together and then driven to Hope, where Alex Washburn printed it on his presses. The papers were then hauled back to Hot Springs by truck for distribution. One reporter called it a "haphazard operation" and recalled that "sometimes the papers didn't get there until late in the day, but we made it most of the time."[121] Washburn was described, obviously, as being a "strong anti-union man."[122]

In Texarkana, Palmer faced two strikes. First the pressmen went out, and then the ITU members walked out. Palmer beat both strikes. The pressmen came back, but the ITU members went on strike and never returned, because Palmer refused to settle. He brought in a non-union foreman and introduced him as the new boss of the Linotype operators.[123]

Mahaffey recalled the non-union strikebreakers that Palmer brought in during the ITU strike:

> The strikebreakers were brought in from other cities and were quartered in the Hotel Grim right across the street from the paper. It was my job to escort them from the hotel to the composing room of the paper. A picket line was set up and the printers walked it every day for many weeks, but they never had a chance. CEP [Palmer] was determined to keep the ITU out because they objected to the installation of automatic typesetting equipment.[124]

Kansas City publisher James Hale also recalled the Texarkana strike:

> Since I was sort of the man-in-charge at night, Mr. Palmer informed me that among my duties after the paper was put out about 2 a.m., I was to accompany the group of people commonly known as scabs, back to their quarters at the Grimm Hotel (and it was grim) after the night shift, in the dark of night. I inquired of Mr. Palmer as to my responsibility on that three block journey. (The hotel was across the street, but that was the back side and we had to get over to the front door which, as I recall was on State Line. Thus you had to go down a block south, one block east and one block north to get in the Grimm.) I needed a delineation of my duties during this nocturnal journey. I pointed out to Mr. Palmer that I hoped it would not be necessary for me to defend the honor of the people in the event of a fracas. His reply was that he did not intend for me to have a protective role but simply, if somebody jumped on us, he wanted me to identify the culprits. This was never necessary.[125]

Mahaffey also felt that Palmer may have intended to force the Texarkana strike:

> It was more of a lockout than a strike, because Palmer just brought in some strikebreakers and they marched into the composing room. Palmer brought in a man and said, "Boys, I want you to meet your new foreman," who was a non-union man. So they walked out and we beat that strike. It almost killed me, but we kept bringing in non-union printers and went

through a terrible ordeal. I worked 14 and 15 hour days for . . . I don't know how long. But Palmer was very aggressive in that strike. . . . He wanted the ITU out of there. He wasn't going to let the ITU stand in his way of making mechanical advances on the paper. He just beat them. After they walked out I think many of them wanted to come back, but Palmer wouldn't take them back.[126]

Palmer rubbed salt into the wound. Mahaffey remembered that Palmer hired a young black girl to "parade up and down in front of the office with a sign saying 'ITU is Unfair to Palmer!'"[127] Palmer family friend Sam Papert remembered Palmer out on the picket line with his striking employees:

When the ITU struck the newspaper, Mr. Palmer's position was to hold his line — maintain his convictions and, at the same time, show his concern and his interest in the strikes, who were, after all, employees, in many cases, of long standing. He served them coffee and doughnuts on cold days — he actually "walked the line" with them occasionally — he simply outsmarted them! He killed them with kindness.[128]

James Hale recalled that Palmer wore his beret, which he had acquired in Europe, on the picket line. "He had himself a picket sign painted up and he picketed the ITU pickets. It was a sight to behold!"[129] But Hale also remembered the bitterness of the personal relationships during the Texarkana strikes.

There was a printer by the name of Walter Dykema. He was a makeup man who generally made up the front page of the morning paper. It had been my duty to make a dummy that he could follow and, of course, it was necessary for my presence in the composing room for the purpose of cutting type, etc. I loaned Walter Dykema $5.00 the night before the strike for the purposes of his obtaining certain alcoholic beverages. The strike occurred before the next shift, at which time Walter attempted to spit on me as I attempted to cross the picket line. I never forgave him.

I recall two makeup men who were brought into the composing room. Unfortunately I cannot recall their names, but they were making, what was to us in those days, very big money, working two shifts, one of them at overtime and they lived rather extravagantly. I recall one saying to the other that he had been living in a house of assignation which was on 4th Street not far from the paper and was spending most of his wages there. He hoped to save enough money that week to buy a pair of shoes.[130]

Louis "Swampy" Graves, once publisher of the *Nashville News*, the *Mur-freesboro Diamond*, the *Glenwood Herald*, and the *Montgomery County News*, started working for Palmer at the *Texarkana Gazette* as a proofreader in 1938. He still remembers the low wages, "$17 for a 50-hour work week," but also re-called the higher ITU member salaries. Graves said that his salary "did not com-pare with the $50 for an apprentice in the back shop." Graves was not in Texar-kana during the strike but recalled that "at one point I contacted the Newspaper Guild in Shreveport and discussed organizing the editorial staff at the *Gazette*." However, as Graves pointed out, "fellow employees were totally disinterested.[131]

Kimball has noted that the ITU's opposition failed completely:

> ... the development of the Teletypesetter circuits was hampered by the union's opposition. I noted that when we were working on the instal-lation for the Harte-Hanks people—they were all union shops—the workmen themselves, the journeymen, were interested. They really wanted to do it, there was no opposition. But the union officials were the ones that said, "No, now don't handle this stuff." They struck nearly every paper that put in the Teletypesetter circuits. But they never won a single strike that they went out on to oppose the Teletypesetter circuits. Not a one. They lost every strike.[132]

Palmer persevered, and the strikes at both Hot Springs and Texarkana failed. However, other groups continued to have problems with the union resistance to the change. Even the Associated Press had problems with the ITU when it finally began to implement the Teletypesetter circuit system in the early 1950s. At the 1951 meeting of the Associated Press Managing Editors Associ-ation in San Francisco, members discussed the topic of ITU resistance to the new TTS system.[133]

The Palmer Circuit continued to receive a great deal of attention and in-terest throughout the 1940s and into the early 1950s. Numerous newspaper publishers and groups expressed an interest in setting up similar systems. One newspaper organization, similar to the Palmer Group in scope, had a group of regional newspapers that could utilize the system. The Harte-Hanks group of Texas newspapers expressed a great deal of interest in the Palmer Circuit. Harte-Hanks owned a growing number of newspapers in Texas and was seek-ing the same type of "group" services that Palmer had sought. Working with the Teletypesetter Company and with representatives of the Palmer Group, Harte-Hanks installed their circuit in 1949, and it became operational in January 1950. The original Harte-Hanks system included newspapers in Corpus Christi, Paris, Marshall, Denison, San Angelo, Abilene, Big Springs, and Snyder. Jenny Sakellariou then trained the Teletypesetter operators at Corpus Christi, and Thomas took charge of connecting the circuit with Southwestern Bell lines.[134] The system grew as Harte-Hanks continued to expand in Texas and other states in the region.

Sakellariou and Thomas both remember Ray Kimball's visit to San Angelo, Texas, where he helped start the Harte-Hanks circuit. Kimball installed "the Palmer Circuit on Linotypes . . . that was in 1946 and there were seven Teletypesetters here [San Angelo] for typists to punch the tape that went on the Linotypes," Sakellariou said. She added that Thomas "helped set up the same system in Corpus Christi, Abilene, and Big Springs in 1949" and "in 1950 in Denison and Paris."[135]

In January 1949, the Associated Press Board of Directors met as the guests of Houston Harte in Corpus Christi. Ray Kimball represented the Palmer Circuit and the Teletypesetter Corporation at the meeting and recalled the event:

> After we put the circuit in Texas, the Associated Press Board of Directors were invited to meet in Corpus Christi by Mr. Harte. They met down there and they were entertained out at the King Ranch. All of the AP Directors were touring the *Corpus Christi Caller Times* plant and I was there explaining to them how the circuit worked and the people who were most interested in it were the smaller newspaper publishers.[136]

Kimball said that following the completion of the Harte-Hanks Circuit and the AP Directors meeting, there was increased interest in the Palmer Circuit, "but most of them wanted to get on the existing circuit." He added that the Associated Press and the United Press, at that time, were still not ready to establish a circuit. However, the Associated Press, especially, began to have some interest in the circuits. With the completion of the Harte-Hanks Circuit, there were now two small newspaper groups utilizing the existing technology and several others considering it. These successful circuits, and others being developed around the country, caused the Associated Press to examine the TTS possibilities. Kimball indicated that the Associated Press began to take an interest in the early 1950s, when an Oklahoma group started discussing the possibility of implementing a circuit and contacted Kimball about the possibilities.[137]

Kimball said that most of the smaller newspapers in Oklahoma were United Press clients, not Associated Press members. "I suggested to them that rather than trying to organize a circuit of their own, that they contact the UP and see if they would attempt to set up the circuit. They did that and UP put a circuit in Oklahoma." Kimball said he thought that the United Press Oklahoma Circuit was the second circuit after the Palmer Circuit, followed quickly by the Harte-Hanks Circuit in Texas, which was eventually taken over by the Associated Press. "I believe," Kimball said, "that those were the original beginnings of press associations utilizing the Teletypesetter circuit.[138]

As media historian Edwin Emery and Michael Emery have confirmed, "the Teletypesetter, producing a tape that automatically runs a typesetting machine, arrived in 1951 and both UP and AP set up Teletypesetter circuits for smaller papers, sports and financial services."[139] The Palmer Group led the way for small newspaper groups, and the Palmer Circuit was the first, the pioneer circuit. There is no way today to determine which circuit was the second—the Harte-Hanks circuit or the Oklahoma circuit—and many other groups began to implement the circuits at this time. The Palmer Circuit paved the way for both Harte-Hanks and the Oklahoma Press Association and other newspaper groups. The Harte-Hanks Circuit eventually evolved into the Associated Press Circuit. The Palmer Circuit began the entire change in newspaper publishing toward electronic movement of news by means of a Teletypesetter. Palmer reporter Louis Graves recalled the importance of the development years later: "Palmer and Ray Kimball," he said, "were pioneers in improving communications."[140]

At the 1951 meeting of the Associated Press Managing Editors Association in San Francisco, Victor Hackler, Associated Press General Executive, stated that the coming year would bring "great changes" in the AP wire service due to the planned conversions to Teletypesetter operations.[141] Almost a decade after the Palmer Circuit went into operation, the Associated Press was poised to convert to the same system. At the 1951 APME meeting, the teletypesetting circuits were a major topic. In fact, an entire session of the conference was devoted to the subject, and the Los Angeles distributor of the equipment presented a display of teletypesetting machinery.[142]

Harry T. Montgomery, Associated Press Traffic Executive, addressed the group and told them that AP Teletypesetter circuits were already "established in North and South Carolina and Florida" and that "one will be operating in Oklahoma later this year. By early 1952, circuits likely will be operating in more than 30 states."[143] Lee Hills, of the *Miami Herald*, told the group that his newspaper was setting "around 40,000 lines daily and 50,000–60,000 Sunday" on "six new Comet Linotypes" with Teletypesetters.[144] Mahaffey, who was attending representing the Palmer Group, asked Hills to discuss "the savings in cost through Teletypesetter operations as compared with manual operation."[145] Mahaffey, of course, knew full well the advantages (and the disadvantages) of the system, because he had been using it for a decade.

Roy Bosson recalled the impact of the Palmer Circuit:

> I remember it well! It was innovative. It was the forerunner of the first printing breakout from moveable type. It was a money saver. And it was Clyde Palmer's pride and joy. . . . Palmer took AP, UP and INS, receiving all three via teletype at Hot Springs. This was before the days when services were delivered in TTS [Teletypesetter]. The Hot Springs editor selected their copy, had it punched in TTS tape, used it to set type there and also transmitted the same tape over Palmer's private wire to other papers. It was a 24-hour operation.
>
> Later the wire services began transmitting in TTS. AP imposed an extra charge for use of its tape. No one ever knew what UP charged for and what they gave away to keep business. AP's charge was a basic one for Hot Springs and a lesser one for the other papers since they only received what the Hot Springs editors selected.[146]

Of course, Palmer (along with Mahaffey) objected to the additional charges. "Palmer objected," Bosson said, "saying that the AP was a non-profit organization, which it was and is . . . and that therefore as a member he should have the service free. It was quite a hassle and lasted for some years. Eventually it was resolved. Palmer paid. I think that kind of thing was what made him respect the AP as much as he obviously did."[147]

The first TTS circuits operated by the Associated Press went online on April 23, 1951, in North Carolina and Virginia. Members of the Arkansas Associated Press converted the state news wire to the TTS system in early 1952, after voting to make the change on August 1, 1951.[148] An article in *The Arkansas Publisher* in July 1952 noted that "ten years after Mr. Palmer pioneered the idea, teletypesetter circuits throughout the country number more than 50 and serve newspapers in every state in the union."[149]

By the 1955 APME meeting in Colorado Springs, the Teletypesetter system was well in place and no longer viewed as new technology. Editors lined up to praise the system with such accolades as "content has been improved," "economical and speeded up setting," and as one editor said, the operation has made the "AP more compact. No dead spots during the day. The only problem we have is keeping up with the flow. We have had to shorten our coffee breaks!"[150]

The Teletypesetter Committee report of that year's APME conference noted that "to most newspapers the TTS wire is the Associated Press because TTS is the only kind of service they get from AP."[151] In fact, the AP was promoting a new technical advance, the photofax, and was comparing the development to that of the Teletypesetter circuits. The report of the AP Technical Progress Committee noted:

> Development of the Teletypesetter was somewhat similar. The apparatus, basically the same as it is now, was available in the twenties. In the thirties, the AP assisted several groups of its members in establishing TTS circuits of their own.
>
> More of this was done following the war, but the idea still was not spreading fast. When it became practical, AP applied this development to its own business. Using knowledge gained in earlier efforts, AP established the first wire service TTS circuit, and every one of its TTS circuit, and every one of its TTS developments since has been a first. AP remains exclusive in a number of these.[152]

And the report noted that AP had continued to improve the Teletypesetters, with the development of suitable tables for the reperforators, devices to catch the paper tape, and ways to correct the tapes at the point of transmission. And they were predicting better things to come for the circuits.

> In addition to keeping abreast of current problems, there is the problem of watching developments that might have a useful application. An example of this is AP's work on the so-called 600 word per minute punch and repunch developed by Teletypesetter. In this AP has been working with the Teletypesetter people, Bell Laboratories and the A.T.&T. for over two years. The development could have a practical application in the transmission of stock market tables.[153]

At the 1956 APME meeting in Philadelphia, the Technical Progress Committee Report noted that "AP has available machines that run at speeds greater than 600 words a minute. Faster equipment will require better wires. . . . Actual surveys indicate newspapers are not ready for the high-speed Teletypesetter. Last November the AP offered a faster service on daily stock market tables, utilizing 10 telegraph channels. Of the 90 afternoon newspapers contacted, 63 replied. There were 54 who said they were not interested. Five expressed interest of varying degrees and four indicated future interests."[154]

By this time, the teletypesetting technology had developed to a point that it outstripped the ability of newspapers to keep up with it. Moreover, new developments were on the horizon. Those attending the 1956 Philadelphia meeting heard presentations on "cold type" from J. W. Reid of the Mergenthaler Linotype Company, who said, "We are of the opinion that the entire range of the printing process is undergoing developments and improvements which are calculated to be interrelated and mutually beneficial as time goes on." Companies like Photon, Fotosetter, and Linofilm (the last belonging to Mergenthaler) set up displays, and a new technology was coming into being that would not use the mechanical devices of the Palmer Circuit, but would use electronics and, eventually, computers.[155] Both AP and UP did eventually set up their circuits to serve smaller newspapers, and the system remained the industry standard until the computer/VDT generation of technology and the switch to offset printing and cold type began to bring a new means of mechanical production into being.

By the mid-1950s, the TTS service was fully in place in the wire service's operations, and small newspaper chains, such as the Palmer Group and Harte-Hanks, were also making use of the technology. It took almost fifteen years for the press associations to implement TTS service, which, as pointed out below, is what Palmer originally wanted. In the 1940s, Palmer did not want to establish his own circuit, but instead wanted the press associations to take the lead and provide his newspapers the service. As noted previously, Kimball contacted both the United Press and the Associated Press for assistance during the developing stages of the Palmer Circuit. Palmer also sought financial assistance from the Texas Daily Newspaper Association to implement the circuit, as noted above. It was only when he did not receive help that Palmer decided to proceed on his own. Years later, Roy Bosson recalled the period when "Palmer was pressuring the AP to set up a Teletypesetter system to service its members. When they were hesitant, he set up his own system in Hot Springs, servicing his newspapers and radios." He also recalled that "AP finally relented and installed a similar system."[156] But even after the AP system was in place, Palmer continued his circuit as the Palmer News Service, providing copy to his own news outlets.

The Palmer Circuit was widely recognized as the premier small newspaper TTS system in the United States, and it survived Palmer. Walter Hussman updated the system, and it eventually became an even more modern microwave relay system.[157] Such a system, now state-of-the-art, is used today by numerous groups and chains, most notably by Gannett's *USA Today*, which is simultaneously printed at plants throughout the United States. The technology has changed dramatically, but the roots go back to the Palmer Circuit.

The Palmer Circuit was the one major achievement that separated Palmer from the many other publishers of small newspaper groups that grew up in the 1930s and 1940s. At the time of his death, he was widely recognized for this advancement of the newspaper publishing business. The *New York Times* called him the "pioneer" of newspaper typesetting circuits.[158]

The Teletypesetter Corporation was originally a subsidiary of American Telephone and Telegraph (AT&T), when Walter Morey and Ray Kimball first became friends. Eventually AT&T was forced to divest itself of the operation, selling it to the Fairchild Corporation. Kimball felt that AT&T did not market the devices as aggressively as might have been possible. "They were kind of 'pussy-footing' around," he said. "They didn't want to get into any strike situation, so they weren't pushing it too hard . . . when they [the US government] made them divest it, it was kind of late. Most of the pioneering work had been done.[159]

As for Walter Morey, Kimball fondly recalled the man who perfected the Teletypesetter and who became a close friend and associate. "He knew how to operate it," Kimball said, "but he didn't know how to develop sales and he was not sufficiently compensated for his invention. He was a real fine fellow."[160] He also recalled that Morey was of great help to Mrs. Kimball when she was running the Kimball/Palmer paper in Magnolia while Kimball was in the US Navy during World War II:

> During the war while my wife was running the paper in Magnolia, you couldn't get parts . . . you had to have all kinds of paperwork to get a part, but she would just call him [Morey] up and he would send her down the part. And he came down one time and helped her repair some of the equipment. He was a great fellow! We were the first ones to really help him sell the teletypesetters. If he could have been a salesman along

with his ability to invent this equipment, he could have been a million-aire, no question about it.[161]

Kimball also recalled that Morey once sold an order for Teletypesetter machines to the Soviet Union. Morey sent one of his engineers, a man named Hudson, to Moscow to install one device. Kimball asked Morey if he expected to make a big sale of the devices to the Russian government. "No, they will just steal it and we'll never sell any," Morey replied, "but they got the original equipment."[162]

Walter Morey's invention coupled with Palmer's business acumen and the support of Palmer Group associates Kimball and Washburn did indeed pioneer a new technology in newspaper publishing. The Palmer Circuit was admired by many in the newspaper publishing business, and it led to a major change in the way in which the press associations served their member newspapers and in the way that news and information was communicated throughout the United States and the world. The impact of the Palmer Circuit was significant and lasting. As Alex Washburn wrote:

> The far-reaching value to the newspaper business which C. E. Palmer saw in the Teletypesetter Circuit when we gathered in Hot Springs to plan it in the summer of 1941 is only too obvious today. . . . The Teletypesetter has given us a mechanical right-arm, making bigger and better newspapers in peacetime and in war allowing us to preserve our continuity—which, after all, is the main guarantee that there shall be a free press hereafter.[163]

During Palmer's funeral service in 1957, the Palmer Circuit shut down and observed five minutes of silence in tribute to the publisher.[164] The Palmer Circuit was innovative; it was the pioneer circuit that later became a newspaper and wire service standard. It not only provided a service to his newspapers, but it was labor efficient and broke the ITU hold on Palmer's papers, providing him with independence from the union. And it was the beginning of modern multi-newspaper technology.

CHAPTER 4

Clyde Palmer, the Man

Palmer as a Force in Arkansas Newspaper Publishing

Clyde Palmer was a dominant force in Arkansas journalism for almost half a century. His presence was felt not only in the number of newspapers sold by the Palmer Group or the number of radio or television stations Palmer owned, but also in the character of the man. Chapter 1 of this book chronicled Palmer's entry into Arkansas journalism, and chapter 2 presented the growth of the Palmer Group, as his combined communications endeavors were called. Chapter 3 outlined the development and impact of the Palmer Circuit, his innovative teletypesetting circuit. This chapter explores the character and nature of Clyde Eber Palmer as a personality within Arkansas and presents the side of the man seen by those who knew him, not those who read his newspapers. The circulation of his newspapers was an important factor in his prominence, but circulation figures do not reveal everything about his particular kind of journalism.

While no single newspaper of Clyde Palmer's ever challenged the statewide circulation of the *Arkansas Gazette*, the total combined circulation of Palmer's papers in the late 1940s approached the circulation totals of the *Gazette*. Palmer's newspapers dominated Garland, Union, Miller, Hempstead, Ouachita, Columbia, and Arkansas counties in southwest Arkansas. According to former associates, Palmer disliked Little Rock and its leading newspaper, the *Arkansas Gazette*.[1] John Wells, the city editor of the *Arkansas Gazette* in the early 1930s, first met Palmer through a disagreement between the publisher and Little Rock's leading newspaper. "Palmer came in to complain that the *Gazette* was holding Associated Press stories," Wells said, "which they were supposed to give by carbon to AP. Palmer claimed that the *Gazette* was not releasing stories in a timely fashion."[2] Palmer wanted quicker access to the Associated Press stories for his newspapers.

In the early 1930s, the *Arkansas Gazette* publishers were probably not overly concerned with Palmer's newspapers, since he was only beginning his newspaper chain in that period. By 1947, however, Palmer's growing newspaper chain had a combined daily circulation of 60,945, with an additional 3,943 in weekly newspaper circulation, for a total of 64,888. The *Arkansas Gazette* reported a statewide daily circulation of 87,709. Palmer's papers served a combined county population of 242,179 residents and a combined city population of 92,472. Of the thirty-three daily newspapers published in the state in 1947, Palmer owned all or part of ten, almost one-third. Newspapers belonging to the Palmer Group included the only daily newspapers in Ouachita, Union, Hempstead, Garland, Columbia, Arkansas, and Miller counties. Of the 319,467 daily newspapers distributed in the state in 1947, Palmer's combined sales accounted for almost one-fifth of that total.[3] Palmer's total increased in the early 1950s when he added several other newspapers (the *Russellville Courier Democrat*, the *Hope Journal*, the *Columbia County Journal*, and the *Huttig News*) to his group. Circulation of this magnitude helped give Palmer a place of prominence in Arkansas journalism.

The impact of Clyde Palmer and his family, including Walter Hussman and Walter Hussman Jr., cannot be underestimated. In addition, Palmer's business associations both in and outside of the newspaper business increased his importance in Arkansas newspaper publishing. While the Woodruff-Heiskell-Ashmore continuum at the *Arkansas Gazette* holds a firm place in Arkansas journalism history, Clyde Eber Palmer's primary import and major influence must be considered in Arkansas newspaper publishing and Arkansas journalism. It is hard to find a veteran Arkansas newspaper man or woman who did not work for or against Palmer, and all are quick to detail his importance and characterize him in their own manner. The three major historical accounts of Arkansas journalism provide some insight into Palmer as his newspaper group grew.

In Fred W. Allsopp's 1922 *History of the Arkansas Press Association*, the author gives Palmer a brief six lines of biographical information. In the section that chronicles each Arkansas county, Palmer (in the Miller County section) receives nine lines and a photograph.[4] When Allsopp, who was business manager of the *Arkansas Gazette*, put together his biographical history of

Arkansas newspapermen, Palmer had been publisher of the *Four States Press* for eleven years.[5]

Allsopp wrote of Palmer:

> C. E. Palmer, of the *Four States Press*, Texarkana, came from Nebraska. When he first located at Texarkana, he became a merchant. He saw a newspaper opportunity in that city, and in 1909 purchased the *Texarkana Courier*, which he transformed into the *Four States Press*, installing a good plant. By applying business principles to the business, he has built up a good newspaper property.[6]

In the section of Allsopp's history that examines the newspaper history of each county, more information about Palmer is given:

> The *Texarkana Courier* was founded in 1898 by J. W. Stuart, who remained its editor and publisher until about 1907, when he was succeeded by John B. King, who was superseded in 1909 by C. E. Palmer. Mr. Palmer changed the name of the paper to the *Four States Press* in 1910. This newspaper's office is on the Texas side of Texarkana, in Bowie County. C. E. Palmer, the editor and publisher, came from Nebraska, and was first engaged to the mercantile business in Texarkana. Henry Humphrey is the associate editor.[7]

Obviously Allsopp saw Palmer's business background as an asset to his publishing enterprise. However, he also hints at part of the problem with obtaining an accurate record of Palmer's early career: the Texarkana paper was actually located in Bowie County, Texas. Consequently, early records are scattered throughout the archives of both Texas and Arkansas journalism. The unique nature of the city of Texarkana, located in two states, with most of the business side in Texas, places the city in the Texas realm for most commercial aspects, including newspaper publishing. Allsopp also stated that, in 1922, Texarkana, Arkansas, was "the fourth largest city in the state" and mentions the *Four States Press* on the Texas side and the *Texarkanian* on the Arkansas side.[8]

Eight years later, in May 1930, Arkansas Press Association (APA) historian Clio Harper published his *History of the Arkansas Press Association*. Harper, who had been secretary of the APA since 1919 and was editor of the *Arkansas Democrat*, chronicled the proceedings of the APA by year. In addition, he wrote a brief profile of each member of the APA, which included family information, state commissions on which APA members had served, and other information. His listing on Palmer stated:

> C. E. PALMER—Born Spirit Lake, Iowa, August 24, 1876. Entered newspaper business August 4, 1909 as business manager of the *Texarkana Courier* which was later changed to the *Four States Press*. Sold in 1926 to D. W. Stevick. Now interested as publisher and part owner in *El Dorado News-Times, Camden News, Hope Star, Hot Springs New Era* and *Sentinel-Record*. Founder and president 1928 Arkansas Dailies, Inc. Special representative to 15 Arkansas newspapers.[9]

Palmer had only recently purchased several of the newspapers that Harper listed and had just begun his advertising company. Harper also included a photo of Palmer with his listing.

In 1974 Robert W. Meriwether updated the Arkansas Press Association's activities again in his book *A Chronicle of Arkansas Newspapers Published since 1922 and of the Arkansas Press Association, 1930–1972*. Palmer died sixteen years before its publication, and his son-in-law Walter Hussman was the chief executive of the older Palmer Group, by then called the WEHCO Media Inc. Palmer's name is listed throughout Meriwether's book, which provides a history of Arkansas newspaper publishing by county.[10]

In September 1930, Clyde Palmer's likeness appeared on the cover of *The Arkansas Publisher*, the official organ of the Arkansas Press Association.[11] The press association's monthly publication was only two years old at the time, and the Palmer cover story was reprinted from an August 1930 *Editor & Publisher* feature on the publisher.[12] *The Arkansas Publisher* began publication in the fall of 1928, and from that time until his death, the activities of Clyde Palmer and reports about his newspapers were reported in almost every issue. One of the earliest references noted that Palmer hosted representatives of both the Arkansas Press Association and the Texas Press Association at a "dinner and theater party" on December 10, 1928, in Texarkana.[13] Palmer is, to date, the only individual to have had two entire covers of the publication devoted to him.[14]

To understand Palmer's impact on Arkansas journalism, it is important to have some insight into his character. Certain facets of his character have become a part of his legacy and are reflected in today's operations of WEHCO Media Inc., now run by Palmer's grandson Walter Hussman Jr. While alive, Palmer's nature dominated his newspapers and influenced his employees and associates. After his death, the Palmer Group newspapers continued to reflect the character he had imprinted on them.

Palmer reporter Roy Bosson is typical of those who knew and worked for Palmer. Almost thirty years after Palmer's death, Bosson wrote to John Q. Mahaffey: "I was one of those who worked for him back in the depression days who alternately loved and hated him, but always respected him." Bosson recalled that Palmer was a "tough taskmaster, maybe a little ruthless at times, but you had to be to survive back in those days. However, he was also a very compassionate and understanding man."[15]

Another reporter, George Brewer, who worked for Palmer in El Dorado, recalled the strong and often conflicting contrasts in Clyde Palmer:

> Although reluctant to pay good wages, CEP would go to any lengths to help his employees. He put up money for [El Dorado editor] Bob Hays to buy a house in the country; he would buy him a new suit about twice a year. CEP also has been known to help employees with medical bills and bail them out, etc.
>
> I think it was in this respect that he was able to hang on to good people for years. They were nearly always in hock to him.[16]

John Q. Mahaffey, who knew Palmer well, heard both the praise and the condemnation of Palmer. Mahaffey concluded that, on balance, the good outweighed the bad, and commented, "There is no proof that CEP was an SOB, and he did a lot of good."[17] Bosson also tried to put Palmer into perspective: "There was simply not much money around, but Mr. Palmer kept the newspapers alive and kept people at work."[18]

Palmer's contradictory nature was evident in many things he did. Brewer wrote, "Palmer once raised hell with the New York office of the Associated Press for paying a Little Rock bureau correspondent more than he thought should be the going rate and ruining the labor market."[19] But Palmer also helped an employee obtain a hardship military discharge and then helped set up an insurance program to assist the reporter in meeting medical costs involving an illness with the man's son, even though he knew that the employee was leaving the Palmer Group.[20] Louis Graves, whose own career progressed from reporter at one of Palmer's Texarkana newspapers to publisher of several Arkansas newspapers himself, wrote:

> I confess that during those [early] years I considered him more a businessman than publisher, and one rather niggardly with employee pay.

Since, inasmuch as I've been a newspaper owner with responsibilities on the other side of the fence, I have softened my opinion of him, and acknowledge now that many of his years were spent during the depression times of pre-WWII and that survival could have been uppermost, not the welfare of employees.[21]

Clyde Palmer's impact on the many people who worked for him was lasting and significant. One reason for this was that he constantly visited his newspapers and his employees and was not an absentee publisher. El Dorado reporter Brewer recalled Palmer's typical tour of his newspaper holdings, which began in Texarkana:

He generally started up U.S. 67 to Hope, where he owned half of the *Hope Star.* . . . CEP then went on to Hot Springs where he published the *Sentinel-Record* and the *New Era.* . . . CEP then went to the *Camden News* and onward to the *El Dorado News-Times.* He later bought the Magnolia *Banner News* and stopped off there on his way back to Texarkana. On these trips he carried two bulging brief cases and went over business and news operations with staff members. He used to literally burst into the front door of the paper and everyone came to attention.[22]

Ray Kimball also recalled the visits Palmer made: "He was very attentive to the operation of his newspapers. He came around his newspapers every week or two, made a tour of them. He would drive to Camden, stay all night in El Dorado. *He* operated his newspapers."[23]

Hot Springs society editor Edna Howe recounted that Palmer would "come in in kind of a blustery way and walk all through the building and speak to everybody and then visit the departments . . . once a week or so. You never knew when he was coming, but there he would be!" She added that he would want to know where any absent person was and he would ask about any news stories that were developing. "He made suggestions as to what might work out. It was funny," she said, "how he kept track of what was going on in each place. He *knew* what was going on!" She also remembered his routine in the Hot Springs office: "He would visit with the editorial staff and confer with the bookkeeper in the business office, and talk with the advertising department. He gave instructions as to what he thought were any big stories that ought to be developed, those that he had heard about in making his rounds. He'd mention those to [Hot Springs editor] Bob Dean and we'd get busy."[24] She recalled, however, that Palmer could sometimes be harsh during his visits:

> He read the paper from beginning to end. He wouldn't like the editorials sometimes. . . . Sometimes he was real harsh, but he didn't mean it. It was just the way he came across. And if he liked something, why he'd compliment you! I thought a lot of him and I think everybody did.[25]

Palmer drove an average of six hundred to seven hundred miles a week visiting his newspapers. John Q. Mahaffey, the *Texarkana Gazette* editor, stated, "CEP was constantly on the move. He had that paper at Magnolia and one over at El Dorado and he owned part interest at Hope, and he had a whole bunch of little weeklies all over, too. He was always traveling from one to the other."[26] Mahaffey wrote that "for considerable more than thirty years I tried to keep up with Mr. Palmer and found it was a process that left me exhausted at the end of a day."[27] And he not only traveled to each paper, but when he was home in Texarkana, Mahaffey recalled that he did not slow down a bit:

> CEP, as we called him in the newsroom behind his back, was such a ball of fire, such a consummate bundle of energy that he made me tired trying to keep up with him. He could not understand why everyone did not want to work as hard as he did. Leaning back in an old swivel chair before the most cluttered desk I have ever seen, he was a non-stop dictator from 8 to 5, Monday through Saturday, and from 2 to 6 on Sundays. He not only answered every letter that came to his desk, he answered every circular and turned out a torrent of memos.[28]

Mahaffey also remembered that Palmer:

> fretted about the time he lost in travel and, although he was approaching age eighty, he began to take flying lessons at the airport. Walter Hussman Jr. was told by the *Texarkana Gazette* ad manager that he was a pilot instructor and gave Palmer pilot lessons. He explained that the day he was ready to fly solo, he told Palmer to circle the runway and land the plane. Palmer took off, headed east, and vanished over the horizon. Less than an hour later he reappeared and landed. When asked where he went, he said he followed the highway up to Hope and back. Soon after Mrs. Palmer grounded him.[29]

Palmer's flying also caused problems for Mahaffey, who once wrote:

> Frequently, as soon as he got out of town, another employee and I would
> cut out for the country club to get in 18 holes on the company's time. One
> day we were getting ready to tee off on No. 12 when a light plane began
> circling the golf course.
>
> "I'll bet that's CEP," said my companion, as we watched the plane bank
> sharply to the left and head for our position.
>
> "Watch out!" I yelled. "Make for the woods—he's coming back to strafe
> us!"[30]

"Palmer," Mahaffey said, "took up flying because he wanted a faster way to
make the rounds of his papers . . . which he visited every week."[31]

Hot Springs reporter Roy Bosson remembered that when Palmer was in
town, he tried to get a jump on everyone at the newspaper office. "During the
depression," Bosson remembered, "I was writing sports, covering the horse
races and handling city news, and I developed quite an outside income by writing for out-of-town newspapers and magazines and new services. AP Special
Features, UP, INS, the *Memphis Commercial Appeal, Arkansas Democrat,
Sporting News, Daily Racing Forum,* off-season stores and so on. One of my
jobs was to be down at the office by 7 a.m. to turn on the news service teletypes. In order to handle my outside correspondence, I came down an hour
or two early to have my correspondence cleared before the printers arrived."[32]
Bosson recalled that Palmer "loved to get down to the office just before opening time so he could see who was late. He never beat me to the office. I think
it almost became an obsession to him, and one day he came in about 6:30 a.m.
and found me at my desk and came over to me and asked why I came down
so early since the AP teletype wires didn't open until 7 a.m."

"Roy, why do you come down so early?" Palmer asked. "The wires don't
open until 7 a.m."

"Mr. Palmer," Bosson replied, "I appreciate the fact that you have given me
a steady job and I don't want to jeopardize that, but the salary I make doesn't
quite pay all the bills so I handle some outside correspondence to make some
extra money and didn't want to do it on your time."

He asked Bosson only one question. "Do we get the story first?"

Bosson assured him that he did. Later when some members of the advertising department complained to Palmer that Bosson was working for other
newspapers, Palmer reprimanded them.

"Leave him alone," Palmer said. "He's working overtime for us for nothing!" Bosson also remembered that the following week he got a raise.[33]

El Dorado reporter George Brewer, who worked off and on for Palmer's *El Dorado Daily News* from 1935 until 1942, also recalled Palmer's booming entry into the offices of the newspaper:

> When the front door of the paper banged real loud we all knew that it was CEP, toting a couple of brief cases that would stagger one of Gussie Busch's Clydesdales. He banged the cases on his desk and started hollering for [business manager] Bert Estes, [managing editor] Bob Hays and [circulation manager] John Vogel. They all responded immediately with looks of "what the hell have I done now?" When he stayed overnight at the old Garrett, he would come by the paper after supper to read the AP wire and to visit. The old man had boundless energy and a yen to stir up things.[34]

Palmer had a strong work ethic philosophy, and he believed in two things: hard work and frugality. His personal and professional philosophy was well known among his employees. Mahaffey said: "He was a hard man to work for because he was so full of energy himself and he worked like a dog! All the time, on Saturdays and Sundays and at night. He was a dynamic ball of fire all of the time. He would tell you to do something and if you didn't do it right away, you would get a memo saying, 'What have you done about this?' He reminded me of a feisty dog that was nipping at my heels the whole time I worked for him."[35]

Mahaffey also wrote that Palmer told him: "Do as much as you can do today because tomorrow it might be too late; and after you've done all that you can, don't worry about the things you were not able to do." Mahaffey recalled that age did not slow Palmer down: "The older he became in body, the more agile he became in mind. He never forgot anything, and he was determined that I would never forget anything either as long as he was around to remind me."[36]

Louis Graves noted the energy that Palmer possessed but recalled an oddity about the publisher. "CEP hated all sports," Graves wrote. "He thought all athletes should be chopping cotton, and that no man was worth more than a dollar a day."[37] Palmer, who placed such a high value on the work ethic, obviously saw sports as a waste of time, energy, and effort.

Palmer was frugal, or as his former employees, friends, and associates said, "He hated to pay reasonable salaries."[38] Brewer insisted that "he was a hard man to deal with when it came to money . . . he was noted for his low wages."[39] Mahaffey noted, "my colleagues were always amazed at how tight Palmer was."[40] And several associates echoed Brewer's remark that "Palmer was reluctant to pay good wages . . . he was a tight man with a buck."[41]

W. R. Whitehead, who began to work for Palmer before World War II and became general manager and editor of the Palmer/Kimball-owned *Magnolia Banner News* on November 1, 1947, remembered his publisher's failure to pay higher wages:

Palmer did not pay high salaries, but provided fringe benefits better than most other larger newspapers of his time. Also, he gave security for employees in the event of misfortunes. But he held to the old American idea that every employee should save and have a fraction of weekly or annual earnings [set aside]. Still he would have a Christmas party for employees at a hotel in El Dorado, Texarkana and Hot Springs every year, with employees of the smaller newspapers attending at one of the places.[42]

But Whitehead, who became a Palmer alumnus in July 1955 when he left the Palmer Group to publish the *Fordyce News-Advocate*, credited Palmer with teaching him the business side of newspaper publishing: "At Magnolia C. E. Palmer taught me his method of operating newspapers. I still use much of it and have been successful in pulling out of the red a weekly and a small daily newspaper. . . ."[43]

Publisher Louis Graves also presented a reconstructed opinion of Palmer's management style: "I considered him more a businessman than a publisher, and one rather niggardly with employee pay." But Graves, like Whitehead, admitted that now that he was a publisher himself, he had softened his opinion of Palmer, and "I understand better the role of management of a newspaper and the need to control costs or go down the drain."[44]

Palmer was not unaware of his parsimonious reputation and often used it, along with his sense of humor, to his advantage. He frequently told a story about himself: "I had a note coming due at the State National Bank," Palmer said, "and I told Stuart Wilson, the president of the bank, that I couldn't meet it. He told me that he would give me a little more time on the principal, but

I would have to pay the interest due. I told him that I would be glad to give him my note for the interest. He nearly ran me out of the bank!"[45]

In 1955 Mahaffey addressed the annual meeting of the Associated Press Managing Editors Association in Colorado Springs: "I have been a frustrated newspaperman since 1929. You begin to understand what I mean when you [see] how my publisher opens up our morning conferences. He said, and I quote: 'Well, John Quincy, what expensive brainstorm have you had during the night?'"[46] Mahaffey's audience, which always enjoyed his amusing remarks and knew Palmer and his stingy reputation, roared with laughter at the jibes directed at the publisher.

The creation of Palmer's innovative Teletypesetter circuit was partially rooted in his attempts to save money for his operation and control his means of production. He endeavored to put himself in a position that protected him from union pressure and potential strikes. "Palmer was prepared for the strikes," John Wells recalled, "and he was the only Arkansas publisher who fought the International Typographers Union; the *Gazette* and the *Democrat* just went along with the ITU."[47] Louis Graves also believed that while Palmer's policies were sound, the Palmer Group paid a price. "The Palmer papers were unable to maintain quality staffs because of pay policies," but added that "many competent people began careers there, to move upward and onward."[48]

In the changing economic times between 1909 and 1957, with a depression and two world wars in the middle, employees frequently criticized Palmer's fiscal policies. Brewer recalled "how niggardly he could be at times." He said, "In the middle 1950s he offered me a job as manager of the *Magnolia Daily Banner News* for $1,400 a year less than I was making at an ad agency in Little Rock. He had just run off probably one of the best managers in the chain 'because he was making too damned much money!'"[49] And Palmer did not lavish money on the operational side of his newspapers. "He always operated his papers on a tight budget," Mahaffey said, laughing, adding, "As a matter of fact, he didn't even buy the toilet paper at the *Gazette*! He didn't spend money on luxury items. The typewriters were always old and beat up."[50]

Kansas City Star publisher James Hale remembered an example of Palmer's cost control methods involving the utilities in his Texarkana plant:

> Mr. Palmer was known to me as a frugal man. The newsroom where I worked had a very low ceiling and could be hot and humid in the summertime with lights contributing to the discomfort because of the heat

they generated. Mr. Palmer, when he sometimes worked in his office until 6 or 7 at night, would turn off the air conditioning in the rest of the building when he went home. He hired a security guard by the name of Gans who once had been with the circus. He was a man of considerable girth and he sat in the door making sure that nobody turned on the air conditioning until Mr. Palmer returned the next day.[51]

At the same time, Palmer could be understanding and compassionate. He gave money to Texarkana Junior College. As already noted, he helped Bob Hays, his El Dorado managing editor, purchase a house and purchased news clothes for him several times a year. He helped employees with medical bills and bailed them out of minor scrapes.[52] He gave reporters a bonus after particularly difficult assignments. Hot Springs reporter Edna Howe had to cover a long political court case that involved driving from Hot Springs to Mt. Ida almost every day. During the trial she received numerous threats due to her stories. After it was over Palmer called her in and said, "I'm going to give you a bonus. If you had to put up with all of that, you deserve a bonus." He gave her $25, but as she said, "Back then $25 was a pretty good deal!"[53]

Roy Bosson was one of those that Palmer assisted with family medical problems:

> Mr. Palmer was most helpful in the period in which our youngest son lost his hearing at 18 months. He even set up an insurance program which helped in great measure in meeting the medical bills which we would have had great difficulty in covering.
>
> After the way, when I was about to be shipped overseas, . . . Mr. Palmer pulled some real political strings to help me obtain a hardship discharge because of my son's deafness . . . this although he was aware that I had accepted a job as State Editor of the Twin Falls, Idaho *Times News* in order to see if the higher climate would not help our son. When after a couple of years, it did not help, he brought me back to the Hot Springs newspapers, again knowing that both of the Little Rock papers had offered me jobs at considerably more money than he was paying me. So you can see that I had a genuine affection for the "Old Man," as he was called by the help.
>
> I have met a few people in my nationwide (and quite a bit of foreign) travel who measure up to C. E. Palmer in rank, individualism, and character, along with a compassion that not many people saw.[54]

Mahaffey indicated that he felt Palmer was a "solid citizen in every town in which he operated and that he was very civic minded."[55] At the time of Palmer's death, civic leaders in Palmer paper towns expressed their community loss. "He always had Hot Springs at heart," Mayor Floyd Housley said. He added that Palmer tried to assist the city in improving airport facilities and that Palmer's contributions to local charity drives were considerable sums. The mayor said, "We are going to miss him and his public spiritedness." Hot Springs Chamber of Commerce president Walter Kleinman called Palmer one of the "great individualists in the state of Arkansas" and praised the work he did for Hot Springs. He was also praised for helping start the Boys Club in the city. Louis Goltz, who was Hot Springs' only winner of the C. E. Palmer Award, which the publisher set up for the Junior Chamber of Commerce to present to the state's outstanding citizens, called Palmer "a champion of champions for civic improvements and philanthropic activities." And E. S. Stevenson, founder of the Hot Springs Negro Civic League, said, "I think we have sustained a great loss. He was cooperative in every way. No value can be placed on him. He was wealthy and spent a lot of money for the progress of Hot Springs. He will certainly be missed."[56]

Palmer was a man of extremes. Tight, stingy, compassionate, civic minded, generous, and ruthless all illustrate his character. Those closest to him witnessed all facets of his personality. John Q. Mahaffey, who respected and admired Palmer, was aware of the man's shortcomings and of his warm, humorous, and humane side. Thirty years after Palmer's death, Mahaffey can curse and praise Palmer in a single breath. Many intently disliked Palmer, but he demonstrated little concern for those who opposed him. He expressed his own opinions, started his own crusades, and promoted his individual vision of the region and the state. Sam Papert Jr. praised Palmer's sagacity. "My goodness," the Dallas advertising executive wrote, "he could see further down the road than just about anyone I've ever known."[57]

Not only was Palmer a frequent visitor to all of his newspaper properties, but as president of the Palmer Group, he traveled frequently to New York and Washington. During his travels Palmer frequently called on former employees and friends. Bosson, who left the Palmer organization to work for the US Brewers Association in New York City, recalled that Palmer often called him to see how his career was progressing when the publisher was in New York City.[58]

Aside from his travels in the United States, Palmer made several trips to Europe. His first visit was immediately after the end of World War II serving as a war correspondent. In Paris he met former *El Dorado Daily News* employee George Brewer. In 1942, after working for the El Dorado paper for several years, with short periods at the *Arkansas Gazette* and with the Secretary of State's office, Brewer joined the Army, leaving his position as night editor of the *El Dorado Daily News.*[59]

Brewer was assigned to Paris, where he encountered another Palmer alumnus, Lt. Col. Ed McLaughlin, who had worked for Palmer at the *Camden News.* McLaughlin left the Palmer Group to join the yellow page advertising department of Southwestern Bell in Dallas prior to the war. McLaughlin, like Brewer, was a staff member of the public relations section of the Communications Zone, European Theater of Operations. Brewer first met McLaughlin shortly before VE day, May 8, 1945, and worked for him, but did not know that they were both former Palmer Group employees until later, after Palmer arrived. McLaughlin entertained Palmer royally, including Brewer in the activities.[60]

In the fall of 1945, Palmer arrived in Paris, filling a vacant slot in the foreign correspondent ranks, available after the *Dallas News* recalled a reporter.[61] Brewer was working at the Scribe Hotel, the headquarters for foreign correspondents, which was part of the Communications Zone system, when they received orders "announcing the impending arrival of C. E. Palmer of the Palmer papers, coming as an accredited war correspondent," Brewer wrote. "He made war on the night clubs, fancy restaurants, shows, and in the process plumb wore me out," Brewer reminisced.[62] He added that:

> After a night on the town, he would appear in the office about 10 a.m. bellering, "Well, where are we going tonight?" I would shudder, go out and buy some tickets and brace myself. It was a real fine period, however, and I saw some things I wouldn't have otherwise, such as luncheon at the George V Hotel, hangout for upper field grade and general officers; the officer's mess at various places. He said, "Aw hell, come along. I'll tell them you are my guest." Nobody ever questioned him. Or me.[63]

Brewer recalled the help he received in entertaining Palmer from the Associated Press contingent in Paris: "Naturally the AP field hands paid a lot of attention to him and showed him the town, giving me periodic relief."[64] Ac-

cording to Brewer, the AP people entertained him nearly every night "since
he was a big customer in Arkansas."[65] "Palmer," he said, "was hell bent to try
the escargots and said he liked them pretty well. I never knew whether or
not any of the AP bunch took him to some of the more outstanding sporting
houses, but I'll bet they did."[66]

Palmer arrived in Paris in a full military uniform, which correspondents
were allowed to wear. His uniform attracted a lot of attention, and Brewer
recalled that "the old man looked quite impressive in his army regalia, peaked
cap and three-quarter length overcoat." He remembered one evening when he
and Palmer came out of a Paris night club in the Place Pigalle: "The dressed
up ladies of the evening literally swarmed around the old man, entreating
him to 'come wiz me, Monsieur Generale!' God how he loved it! They could
see who had the dough." Later, when they had both returned to the States,
Palmer took Brewer on the civic club speaking circuit to tell of their adventures in Paris ("to back up some of his adventures," Brewer said), and when
Brewer would tell about the Paris prostitutes swarming the so-called general,
Palmer "would beam," Brewer wrote.[67]

Brewer said that Palmer filed some stories on the effects and impact of the
war in Europe. Palmer made two trips to Belgium, for which Brewer cut his
travel orders. Palmer also traveled to Germany, and he made references to his
Berlin visit later when writing about his 1952 tour of Europe. In the closing
days of the European war, the Arkansas publisher was eager to see everything
Europe had to offer. Brewer wrote:

> CEP liked to take in everything. With him I saw "Arms and the Man,"
> by G. B. Shaw with Laurence Olivier, Sir Ralph Richardson and Dame
> Sybil Thorndike. He damn near ran me to death during those weeks in
> France. He wanted to go somewhere every night and he slept late, took
> a nap in the afternoon and then would walk into my office. . . .[68]

The night before Palmer, a veteran war correspondent by this time, departed
Paris, he threw a big party for Brewer, McLaughlin, and a crowd of Associated
Press correspondents. Brewer said that the party was held at the Bal Tabarin,
one of the leading European night clubs, known for extravagant floor shows.
Brewer recalled the evening:

> The almost naked women, would rise up from the depths of the club
> on a huge revolving stage and the fun would begin. When we were

approaching the club he thrust a wad of 1,000 franc bills in my hand and told me to handle everything and not to spare the horses. . . . Hugh Moore, former AP chief in Little Rock, was with us, along with Col. McLaughlin, and I think Relman Morin and other assorted AP types.[69]

Years later Brewer said, "I spent more of his money that night than he was paying me in a month when I left."[70]

While sightseeing in Paris, Palmer asked Brewer when he was going to return to his position at the *El Dorado Daily News*. Brewer told Palmer that his fate was in the hands of the US Army. Back in Arkansas after the war, Brewer was offered a position with the *New York Sun*, and Palmer encouraged him to go to New York and look over the offer. When he returned to El Dorado, Palmer gave him a $5 a week raise and told him that he would also buy him a country club membership and give him expanded duties. However, much later, in August 1946, Brewer was offered a public relations position in Little Rock that paid $100 more a month than he was making at El Dorado. "The first thing Palmer said after I told him I was leaving was, 'Bert [Estes], cancel that country club membership!'"[71]

Palmer's stay in Europe lasted thirty-five days. On the ensuing civic club speaking circuit, he told his audiences that Europe would face a hard winter due to the lack of food, fuel, and a rebuilt transportation system. He noted that he was pleased with the recovery efforts. However, he was critical of the German people and said they had "no regret or sense of guilt about the war. . . . Their only regret is that they lost. They'll tell you that their soldiers were better than ours, but that it was our supply of equipment that won the war." Palmer called De Gaulle the only "really sound leader France has," and he noted the ruins of Germany and London and the lack of destruction in Paris, along with the black market and the low morality of the German women.[72] Palmer spoke to civic groups in Texarkana, Camden, Ashdown, Pine Bluff, and Hot Springs during the first months after his return.[73]

Palmer demonstrated an avid interest in the war and his many employees and friends who were in the service. Sgt. John E. Murphy sent Palmer a pocket knife with which he had killed five Nazis at Normandy on D-Day, before being wounded. Murphy had worked for Palmer at the Hot Springs papers before he enlisted.[74] W. R. Whitehead, who was in Japan at the end of the war, wrote Palmer about the tremendous destruction in Hiroshima.[75]

And George Brewer wrote a series about his activities in Europe after he returned.[76] All of these received prominent play in the Palmer Group papers.

Palmer's European tour not only equipped him for discourse on the state of Europe, but it also brought out another character trait: Palmer's vanity. His full-dress military uniform and his demands for guided entertainment tours, as well as his self-promoting speaking engagements after his return, are examples of this. The most remembered example, however, of Palmer's vanity was the Palmer beret. Almost every living person who knew Palmer in the 1940s and 1950s still recalls his berets, which caused him to receive attention that he might not have otherwise attracted. Palmer returned from Paris with a supply of French berets in a variety of colors. These berets became a famous trademark of Palmer's and allowed him to combine both his frugality and his vanity.

Hot Springs reporter Edna Howe still laughed about Palmer's red beret thirty years after his death: "He said he got it in Paris. I guess he did. That was so funny! We used to laugh at it back then, because people didn't wear things like that on their heads all of the time, especially not red berets."[77] Mahaffey also recalled Palmer's new headgear: "After his trip to Europe, Palmer wore that red beret all the time. He told me, 'J. Q., these things are handy. You would be amazed at the amount of money I save on hatcheck girls! You just roll this beret up and put it in your pocket!'"[78] Mahaffey experienced some personal embarrassment regarding Palmer's flamboyance:

> I remember that Palmer and I would go for coffee each morning, a kind of editorial conference. But instead of going across the street to the Grim Hotel Coffee Shop, where coffee was a dime, he'd make me walk around the corner to Pete's Place, because coffee there was only five cents. And he'd wear that damned beret! I told him once that I wish he would quit wearing that beret. I told him that in Texarkana some people hated us so much and that beret just added to it. And he would wear a flowered shirt from Honolulu with his beret![79]

Louis Graves also recalled Palmer's "jaunty little black French-style beret he wore in and out of the office, and the cigarette in a holder, which pointed upward somewhat in an FDR style."[80] Publisher John Wells recalled the Palmer beret and Palmer's *café au lait*. "I remember Palmer always smiled and he always ordered a half cup of coffee and filled the other half with cream," Wells said.[81]

These affectations caused Palmer to be noticed, which had to be his object. Miller County, Arkansas, is not a place known for such unique headwear or the FDR-style cigarette holders or café au lait. These became part of the Palmer style.

Palmer made a second trip to Europe in 1952, and the following year he visited South America. In August 1953, along with forty-seven publishers from the United States, Palmer visited Bogotá, Colombia. Guests of the Colombian government, the group toured the capital city and other Colombian towns during a one-week stay. The censorship rules, which had been imposed by the Colombian government, were lifted especially for the visitors; however, Palmer noted that resident foreign correspondents were still covered by the censorship rules.[82] In 1957, shortly before his death, Palmer traveled to Canada on a fishing trip.[83]

Palmer's character and his reputation, for better or worse, grew far beyond that of any other Arkansas newspaper publisher. He was admired, hated, respected, loathed, but he was not ignored. He had become one of the state's leading citizens. His newspapers were his power base, and his force of personality and his unique character became an important part of the history of journalism in Arkansas. He possessed an odd mix of traits that perhaps helped make him, above all, an aggressive individualist, that could not and would not go unnoticed.

Palmer and His Writings

As a newspaper publisher, Palmer was surrounded throughout his career by professional writers and journalists. Palmer did some of his own editorial writing, but in a period in which there were few bylines for any reporter, it is difficult to identify which were his. He associates confirm that he frequently sat at the typewriter and wrote editorials himself, but his editors confess that they usually heavily edited his work.

"He would write editorials," Edna Howe recalled, "and some of them were very harsh and Bob Dean would pace the floor and get mad and Mr. Palmer would kind of calm down after a while. They'd work it out. Bob didn't always agree with him on editorials, but they would work things out."[84] Dean once wrote that Palmer could often be found in his office "dictating an editorial or batting it out on the typewriter himself with an adept hunt-and-peck system."[85] Dean in Hot Springs, Mahaffey in Texarkana, and Bob Hayes in El

Dorado were Palmer's long-time managing editors, and each worked with Palmer for many years. Each had his own way of dealing with the boss and his writing.

Mahaffey said, "Palmer had solid business tendencies, but he didn't know anything about writing. He was a terrible writer as far as editorial or news story. He was strictly business." But, while he did not write many news stories himself, Palmer was always suggesting stories to his editors. "He was constantly suggesting editorial subjects to me," Mahaffey recalled. "If he was in town, he would have me submit any controversial editorials to him and he would make them 'CEP' and check it, if it was o.k. with him."[86]

Palmer filed some stories during his first visit to Europe as a war correspondent, and his reports filed during his second trip, in 1952, were carried by the Palmer Group papers and a few were picked up by the Associated Press. Palmer's stories are more like lectures than newswriting—sources frequently not given, very few direct quotes, and much more opinion than news. Moreover, they are frequently dull, verbose, and filled with various components of Palmer's personal philosophy.

Palmer was eager to return to Europe, and on August 20, 1952, he and Mrs. Palmer boarded the R.M.S. *Queen Elizabeth* in New York and sailed for London. On this trip Palmer returned to France, and also visited England, Germany, Austria, Switzerland, and Italy. He once again was a foreign correspondent, but without his uniform and with Mrs. Palmer along.[87]

Following a seven-day voyage, the Palmers arrived in London, where they toured the city and stayed until September 5. Palmer devoted one of his first stories from England to the topic of British labor unions and took the opportunity to point out the differences between British labor unions and their American counterparts. "British unions," Palmer wrote on September 1, "seem to be much more democratically run than in the U.S. and much more appreciative of what is in the national interest."[88] In another article, filed from London on September 5, he quoted a Mr. Deakin, a British labor union leader, on an incentive offered to workers to produce more. Mr. Deakin was against increased production, and Palmer took the opportunity to disagree with the labor union leaders and their support of low productivity.[89]

On September 6, the Palmers went to Frankfurt, Germany. On September 9, Palmer hitched a ride to Berlin with the US Air Force, which also flew him back to Frankfurt. According to Palmer, "The United States Air Force insisted on flying me to Berlin and back to Frankfurt and extended every courtesy." During his Berlin visit he found the United Press offices in a familiar setting. "I went to the United Press office and was surprised to find it in the apartment where I was billeted in 1945 when I was here with a group of war correspondents," Palmer wrote, adding that "the Press Club is also in its old location, the former home of Nazi official Walter Funk. The means there were outstanding—good old American cooking." Palmer was escorted around Berlin by Claude E. Broom, a former Detroit police chief. They visited all of the various zones of Berlin, except the Soviet zone. Palmer frequently used the term "reds" to refer to anything communist in this story and filled his Germany dispatches with comparisons of the East and West. "The vast majority of West Germans," he wrote on September 10, "are resolute in their stand against communism. They realize there is at present no chance, with the state of the world as it is, for East and West Germany to be reunited although it is universally ardently desired, and catering to this desire is the most powerful factor of Communist propaganda."[90] The last sentence is a good example of Palmer's wordy and convoluted style.

Back in Frankfurt, Palmer's September 10 story notes that he and Mrs. Palmer had just returned from a sightseeing trip and that "the bombing damage here was terrific, although probably not as bad as Berlin." He described a bombed-out cathedral and opera house in Frankfurt, noting that the 1,000-year-old church was no longer usable.[91]

On September 13, the Palmers arrived in Vienna, Austria, going on to Lucerne, Switzerland, on September 19. Palmer's story from Lucerne had an interesting note on farm tenancy, a problem he recalled from his service on the Arkansas Farm Tenancy Commission. "There is no farm tenancy problem," he wrote, "since almost every farmer owns his own land. Consequently, there are few large landowners." And he also gave an overview on the newspaper publishing business in Switzerland. "Switzerland has over 400 newspapers, one to every 500 population," he noted. "Of course, many of these are very small weeklies or semi weeklies, as practically every small town has a newspaper, generally in connection with a commercial printing plant."[92]

On September 20, the Palmers were in Venice, a city that Palmer described as "probably the most fantastic in the world." He wrote about the islands that compose Venice and about the city's churches and paintings. He viewed one painting by Titian and was impressed that Pierpont Morgan had once offered to purchase it for $10 million. "Venice citizens are very proud of having gotten rid of their Communist mayor in an election several months ago," Palmer wrote. On September 26, the Palmers visited Rome. Palmer filed a long article that touched on a variety of topics, from Italian wages to motorcycles.[93]

On October 1 the Palmers returned to Paris, where his first article praised the French for their determination in Indo-China and the Frenchmen for their ability to face what he determined was "an uncertain future with courage and confidence." He also commented on the French press, noting that most papers were in the hands of Nazi sympathizers during the war and were taken over by the government upon liberation. He observed that the government was not leasing the papers to private concerns.[94]

A note in Palmer's story on jet airfields in France, filed on October 2, concerned Palmer's son-in-law Walter Hussman. Palmer lunched with Brig. General C. T. Lanham, chief of public information for SHAPE, and with British General Sir James F. Gault. Palmer recorded that Gault "remembered contacts with Major Walter E. Hussman, now publisher of the *Camden News*, when the latter started the Paris edition of *Stars and Stripes*. He said he was much impressed by Major Hussman's character and ability, and expressed pleasure at hearing of him again."[95] Hussman played a role in the beginnings of the Paris edition of *Stars and Stripes* during his term of service in the US Army.

Palmer's only reference to his previous visit to Paris is also in this dispatch, in which he makes mention of not being able to meet several people, including race car driver Col. Barney Oldfield. Palmer wrote that he had first encountered Oldfield when I was "over here in 1945 and hoped to meet again at Fontainebleau." Oldfield was on assignment in Turkey. However, like his first visit to Paris, the trip also ended on a social note. Palmer wrote" "Our last night in Paris . . . The Follies Bergère with a large and able cast, spectacular stage settings and costumes made the occasion one to be long remembered."[96]

Palmer's last dispatch was filed aboard the *Queen Mary* on October 4, in which he concerned himself with the "communist aggression" in Europe and elsewhere. He noted that the Marshall Plan had provided great assistance to Europe but condemned the "extravagance and incompetence" that went with it. The Palmers arrived back in New York City on October 7.[97]

Palmer wrote one article after his return to the United States, entitled "Frenchman Toils Much Longer Than American for Necessities of Life." The article gave Palmer an opportunity to lecture his readers on the relative merits of the US economic system compared with the French system. He used data from a publication called *French Echoes* as support, and wrote, "The American worker is far better off than his colleagues in other countries. He should do everything he can to protect that advantage by preventing further inflation which, with wasteful government spending, is the greatest threat to our standard of living."[98] This presentation was typical of Palmer's basic contention that people were already well paid, and it served to remind his readers that American workers, including Palmer's employees, were better off than they realized.

A reporter from the Associated Press interviewed Palmer after his return and wrote a story titled "Publisher Says Europeans Do Not Think War Imminent but Realize Reds Call Tune." The article gave Palmer's views on a variety of European topics, including the upcoming US presidential elections. "Everyone," Palmer said in the interview, "seems to have a sincere respect and affection for General Eisenhower and would like to see him have the honor of being president."[99]

The Arkansas Publisher carried one lengthy Palmer article, written after his return. The article rehashed Palmer's opinions on the value of the Marshall Plan ("a good investment"), socialized medicine ("here to stay"), labor unions ("run more democratically than they are in the United States"), farm tenancy ("no farm tenancy problem"), and the Soviet Union ("Russia is still calling the tune and the free world is dancing").[100]

After his return, a collection of his dispatches from Europe, which had been carried in the Palmer Group newspapers, were printed and bound into a volume entitled *Europe Today*, by C. E. Palmer. The cover showed Palmer, arm in arm with Mrs. Palmer, taking what the book described as "a leisurely stroll in the Via Veneto in Rome." Free copies of *Europe Today* were offered in cities where Palmer's papers were published. The Palmer Group papers ran ads inviting people to stop by the local newspaper office for a copy. A Texarkana merchant once told Mahaffey that he was tired of hearing about *Europe Today* and that "Burrus Mill would run out of flour before Palmer ran out of books."[101] Palmer's opinions and observations, set forth in his own writing style, were not in great demand. Copies of the book are rare today.

Primarily, Palmer was content to discuss his ideas with others and let the writers on his staffs carry his thoughts into print. Mahaffey often quoted Palmer in the *Texarkana Gazette*. Mahaffey wrote a column called "A Tale of Two Cities" for years, and Palmer's ideas, such as his thoughts on horse racing in Texarkana, frequently found their way to print in the column. John Wells noted, critically, that Palmer "was too content to work behind the scenes."[102]

But the examples of his newswriting are of a cumbersome style, and it was better that he left the writing to others while he managed the business of his newspapers.

Palmer and Politics

Palmer was a Democrat, but he did not always agree with the policies of the Democratic Party, either at the state level or the national level. "He was convinced that the New Deal and Fair Deal policies of the Roosevelt and Truman administrations tended to destroy individual initiative and pointed the nation toward socialism. His papers supported Eisenhower editorially in both the 1952 and 1956 campaigns," wrote one reporter.[103] Regardless of his political feelings, which were, upon examination, traditionally Democratic and southern conservative, he had associations with many politicians in positions to assist him at both the state and national levels.

US Senator John McClellan was from Camden, where Palmer owned the only daily newspaper and where son-in-law Walter Hussman became publisher. Hussman's association with Elliott Roosevelt and his connections with several major military and political leaders during World War II gave him a power base beyond Ouachita County, Arkansas. In 1938, McClellan lost to Senator Hattie W. Caraway by only eleven thousand votes. Hussman and Palmer were in a position to assist McClellan in his efforts to be elected to the US Senate in 1942. McClellan came in second in the Democratic primary that year and then won the run-off by an almost two-to-one margin, receiving 134,277 votes. He then won the general election as an unopposed Democratic candidate.[104] McClellan served as US senator until his death in 1977. Mahaffey said that "Palmer was close to McClellan."[105]

Palmer also had connections with US Senator J. William Fulbright. The Fulbright family was in the newspaper business in northwest Arkansas, where Palmer himself once owned a newspaper (see chapter 1). His business association with the Fulbright interests in Russellville also gave him a connection with the senator (see chapter 2). Fulbright served as the US representative from District 3 in the 78th Congress from January 1943 until January 1945, and took his seat as US senator on January 3, 1945, and served until January 1975.[106]

In 1986 former Senator Fulbright remembered Palmer warmly, noting that he "knew Mr. Palmer in Washington where he came each year and gave a dinner for the Arkansas Congressional group, including many of their staff members. It was a pleasant evening for all of us. Mr. Palmer was a very shrewd observer and excellent businessman."[107] Although the relationship between the Palmer interests and the Fulbright interests at the Russellville newspaper did not work out well, the two men enjoyed an association that proved useful to both.

If Palmer needed political support, politicians from his newspaper cities were abundant. US Representative Tilman B. Parks of Hope served from 1921 until 1937 and probably enjoyed support of the Washburn/Palmer *Hope Star*. William Kitchens, who entered the US Congress in 1937 and served until 1941, was from Magnolia, where Palmer and Kimball published the *Banner News*. Representative Oren Harris of El Dorado, where Palmer owned the newspapers, entered Congress in 1941 and served until 1967.[108] These members of Congress needed the support and goodwill of Palmer newspapers, which had monopolies on the news in almost all areas in which they campaigned.

Because Palmer operated in two states—Arkansas and Texas—he had political connections and associations in both. Texas Congressman Wright Patman was a friend, and Palmer was acquainted with other Texas state and national politicians. At the time of Palmer's death, then-Governor Price Daniel of Texas said, "C. E. Palmer was one of the outstanding citizens and publishers of Texas and Arkansas. Both our states and the nation will miss him greatly...." And then-Senator Lyndon B. Johnson sent messages of sympathy to the Palmer family. Texas Congressman Wright Patman attended Palmer's funeral, along with Arkansas Congressman Oren Harris.[109]

Ray Kimball noted, "Mr. Palmer's newspapers were very influential in Arkansas politics, because of the coverage of most of south Arkansas. He was very influential in governor races and other activities.... He had good political clout. He was able to help get governmental participation in the development of south Arkansas, to get a highway built or something that was of benefit to the area, because of his newspapers and their influence."[110] And, as Mahaffey said, "there is no doubt that he was a real [political] force. You can't own a local newspaper with 25,000 or 30,000 in circulation and not be a force. And he had all of these papers. He could make his influence felt and he was not above putting pressure on people."[111]

Not only did Palmer have his Texarkana, Texas, paper and his radio and television stations, but his association with the newspapers in northeast Texas and his activities in the Texas Press Association and Texas Daily Newspaper

Association, gave him clout in Texas, as well as Arkansas. Palmer took an active interest in issues before the Texas legislature. In 1954 Palmer took a lead role in attempting to get the Texas State Board of Examiners in Optometry to drop their prohibition against advertising by optometrists. He wrote to Vern Stanford, manager of the Texas Press Association, seeking the organization's support in his effort. "As I understand it," Palmer wrote, "this thing has been pretty full gone into and it has been found that they have no authority to make such regulations or to enforce them. I think about a year ago they put out the same kind of rules and regulations."[112] The regulations were eventually changed in Texas to allow advertising.

Mahaffey noted that Palmer was very close to both Arkansas Congressman Oren Harris and Texas Congressman Wright Patman. However, Palmer had opposed Patman in the Texas representative's tenure:

> For years he tried to beat Patman because Patman was too liberal for Palmer. Patman and Sam Rayburn and that bunch were very liberal. Palmer found out that he couldn't beat them and so I suggested to him . . . I said, "Mr. Palmer, we can't beat Patman. Why don't we join him?" He laughed and said, "That's a good idea!" We became close friends and Patman did many favors for Palmer in Washington. Palmer was also close to Oren Harris. Walter Hussman was closer to Harris because Harris was chairman of the Interstate and Foreign Commerce Committee, and he [had oversight of the federal communications Commission, which] handed out television and radio rights.[113]

Palmer's conservative stance put him at odds with the growing liberal social changes that took place during the 1930s and following World War II. His feelings about the Roosevelt administration were lukewarm, at best. Mahaffey said that Palmer "supported Roosevelt to get us out of the depression, but he also supported Eisenhower."[114] Palmer was, as demonstrated by the Patman story, a pragmatist when it came to politics. Even though the precepts of the New Deal were at odds with his personal work ethic orientation, he became associated with both President Roosevelt and with the president's son Elliott Roosevelt.

During the summer of 1936, Arkansas celebrated its centennial anniversary. The highlight of the celebration was a tour of the state by President and Mrs. Roosevelt. Palmer served as chairman of the state's Centennial Celebration and was involved with Roosevelt's visit. (At some point around the time of Roosevelt's visit, Palmer turned the chairmanship over to Harvey Couch, president of Arkansas Power and Light. Palmer then concentrated on the activities of the State Centennial Publicity Commission, preparing for the 1939 New York World's Fair.) After visiting Little Rock and delivering an address carried live on national radio, Roosevelt visited Hot Springs and stayed at Harvey Couch's home on Lake Catherine, just outside of Hot Springs, near Palmer's own Lake Hamilton retreat. Mrs. Roosevelt was the guest of honor at a breakfast in the Arlington Hotel.[115] Three years later, on January 3, 1939, Elliott Roosevelt stayed at Palmer's home on Lake Hamilton while he visited with Hot Springs Chamber of Commerce officials about radio station KTHS.[116]

President Roosevelt visited Arkansas in June 1936. Shortly before the president's visit, Palmer was appointed chairman of the State Centennial and Publicity Advisory Committee and was charged with preparing the state's World's Fair exhibit. In August of the same year he was appointed chairman of the Farm Tenancy Commission. Consequently, Palmer participated heavily in state activities in the late 1930s.

John Wells recalled Palmer's leadership in the World's Fair exhibit and felt that the state owed him a debt of gratitude for his efforts. "He was in charge of the campaign to raise money for the exhibit," Wells recalled, "including the production of a motion picture."[117] The construction of the exhibition and displaying it at the 1939 New York World's Fair cost $100,000.[118] This was a difficult amount to raise in a state economically crippled by the Depression.

Palmer embarked on a speaking tour to promote the fundraising efforts. His topic at the 1938 Arkansas Press Association convention was "Arkansas Exhibits at the World's Fair."[119] He appeared several times before the state Chamber of Commerce.[120] In November 1938 Palmer went to New York City with Arkansas Governor Carl E. Bailey to meet with officials of the World's Fair. The two then went to Washington, DC, where they met with executives of corporations to seek support for the state's World's Fair project. They also spent some time inspecting the work of various artists bidding on the mural work in the exhibit.[121] In 1939 Palmer was named to represent the state at the opening of the World's Fair on April 30, along with Leo J. Krebs, L. A. Henry, and Mrs. E. W. Frost.[122]

The World's Fair exhibit was a popular idea in the state. According to historian Donald Holley, the centennial celebration "prompted an outpouring of state pride" and helped "people put the troubles of the present in perspective."[123] In May 1939, when Palmer was honored for thirty years as publisher of the *Texarkana Gazette*, Grover Whalen, director of the New York World's

Fair, congratulated Palmer on his work and called the Arkansas presentation "one of the most beautiful exhibits."[124] *The Arkansas Publisher* praised Palmer for his efforts "with the difficult task of raising funds to defray the cost of the exhibit at the World's Fair."[125]

On May 24, 1940, Palmer resigned from the Farm Tenancy Commission, the Centennial Commission, and the State Publicity Commission. In a letter to Governor Bailey, Palmer stated that personal business prompted his resignation.[126] Palmer turned his attention to his family as well as his business. Hussman joined the US Army in 1942 and did not return until the end of the war.

Palmer served on state commissions during the terms of Governors J. M. Futrell and Carl E. Bailey. According to John Wells, who served as Governor Bailey's executive secretary, Palmer and Governor Bailey were close friends.[127] Although Palmer did not serve in any official capacity with the state after his 1940 resignations, he continued to be active in state politics. And his experience with the state Centennial Commission caused him to be named a member of a Hot Springs commission that, in 1941, planned the celebration marking the 400th anniversary of the discovery of the spa area.[128] On May 10, 1941, Palmer presented an award to Governor Homer Adkins for paying off a $137,000,000 bond debt that had faced the state for several years. Governor Adkins praised Palmer for his service on the state commissions and especially for his work with the Farm Tenancy Commission.[129] Palmer still maintained his interest in politics. In a speech to the Arkansas Press Association, Palmer said:

> Newspaper publishers have more civic interest than any other industry in the state. . . . We need a more reasonable inheritance tax, abolition of special attorneys for the state . . . adoption of a billboard tax, a permanent committee to study legislative problems and a workingman's compensation law. . . . it behooves the press to organize and protect not only their own interests, but the best interests of the state in a legislative program.[130]

The eruption of World War II forced Palmer to take more direct interest in his newspapers as many of his associates and employees entered the armed forces. His Hot Springs editor Charles Goslee left in June 1941 to become the state WPA supervisor, and Palmer assumed active management of the *Sentinel-Record* and the *New Era*.[131] In August 1941, the first International

Typographers Union strike against the Palmer papers took place. And in the early 1940s he began to work on the Palmer Circuit. These business concerns took most of Palmer's attention during the early war years.

However, in late 1946, as the war came to close, Palmer offered a novel political idea that did get some attention in the press. He suggested to Arkansas Governor Ben Laney and Hot Springs Mayor Leo McLaughlin that Hot Springs be recommended as the home of the newly created United Nations. Citing the central location of the Spa City within the United States, Palmer noted that ample room was available in the Hot Springs National Park and the Ouachita National Forest. He added that the Hot Springs area had a pleasant climate, adequate air and rail transportation, and cooperative residents, as well as a long list of other features that, in Palmer's opinion, made it an ideal location.[132] It is not known if Governor Laney embraced the idea, but the United Nations found a home in New York City, not Hot Springs.

After the war, Palmer again became interested in politics and supported Eisenhower in the 1952 presidential election. This support of a Republican on a national level caused problems for Palmer on a local level, as Mahaffey recalled:

> He supported Eisenhower. He had this great big headline on the newspaper [the *Texarkana Gazette*] saying "We Like Ike!" After Ike got elected he immediately began closing the war plants in Bowie County [Texas] and Palmer said, "Get on the plane and go up there and see if you can't stop that!" I went with a group to Washington and Lyndon Johnson, Patman and Harris had us all to lunch with Senator John McClellan, too. Johnson leaned over to me and said, "Well, J. Q., how did you get on out at the Pentagon?" [where the delegation had paid a call to protest the closing of the war plants.] I told him that I didn't get on at all because they wouldn't listen to me and showed no inclination to stop closing the plants. Johnson said, "Serves you right! You liked Ike!" and he pulled out one of Palmer's papers that had "We Like Ike!" on it.[133]

Palmer had praised Eisenhower in an article from Paris on October 1, 1952, saying: "There can be no question about Gen. Dwight D. Eisenhower doing a good job over here, considering the great difficulties and the fact that during his last two or three months a great deal of his time was taken up by those who wanted him to run for President." Again, as he returned to the United States on the *Queen Mary*, Palmer wrote, "There is a very great interest all over Europe in the American presidential election. The friendship for, and the admiration of, General Eisenhower is universal. Of course, Europeans know nothing about Governor Stevenson, but they believe he is fully committed to President Truman's policies."[134] There was no doubt about which candidate Palmer supported in the November 1952 election, and his "We Like Ike!" banner was only a confirmation.

In 1942, Palmer began to host annual dinners for the Arkansas congressional delegation, in Washington, DC. Another was Mrs. Brooks (Marion) Hays, wife of Arkansas Congressman Brooks Hays, who served in the US House of Representatives from 1943 until 1959. In her diary for April 15, 1944, Mrs. Hays recorded some details of a Palmer party:

> April 15, 1944. Mr. C. E. Palmer (Hot Springs) has been here and had one of his big dinners for the delegation. I wore my new girdle, because Betty said I was getting bumpy, and it spoiled the evening. We had delicious soup, lovely fish course, and very rich duckling. After all that, the fish and duck seemed to be struggling for possession, but the girdle didn't yield an inch! My breaths became gasps, so I spoke as little as possible, smiled sweetly, and tried to look as if I were enjoying myself.[135]

In 1946 Mr. and Mrs. Palmer hosted a delegation at a dinner party at Washington's Raleigh Hotel. Attending were former US Senator Hattie W. Caraway, Senator and Mrs. John McClellan, Senator and Mrs. J. W. Fulbright, Mrs. Brooks Hays, Representative and Mrs. Oren Harris, and several friends from Little Rock, Camden, and Washington, DC.[136] In April 1949, Palmer hosted not only the delegation and spouses, but Mr. and Mrs. W. L. Beale Jr., who was head of the Washington Associated Press Bureau.[137]

Mahaffey recalled that there had been such parties, but felt that "Walter Hussman did more of that than Palmer did. But it couldn't have been very lavish, because Palmer was so tight with his money!"[138] However, Fulbright seems to have recalled them as being very well presented. John Wells said that "those big dinners for the congressional delegation were just public relations."[139] Mahaffey, who was much more accustomed to seeing Palmer's tight-fisted habits at home in Texarkana, can be excused for not realizing that Palmer could be far more elaborate in his entertaining away from home. The evening at the Bal Tabarin nightclub in Paris and his Washington dinners were examples of Palmer using his wealth to impress people who were important to him, and he seems to have understood the social and political ramifications of scale in his entertaining.

Reporter George Brewer wrote that Palmer may have gotten more credit for the Washington parties than he deserved:

> Many years ago, before the State Chamber [of Commerce] assumed the responsibility for the dinner, CEP and a Magnolia banker, W. C. Blewster, gave such a dinner. According to what I've heard, the affair was such a success the Chamber picked it up, probably at the instigation of Mr. Palmer, who evidently didn't care to keep picking up such a big tab. . . . It used to be a reception *and* dinner, but the tab for both got too high. Usually a delegation of several hundred people would fly to Washington for the blast at the Capital Hilton.[140]

Although Palmer or Walter Hussman possibly attended Chamber of Commerce dinners, Palmer entertained frequently on his own. He obviously wanted to be well known by the powerful and friendly Arkansas delegation.

"I heard a rumor . . . it was generally understood that Palmer wanted to be governor of Arkansas, but knew he couldn't get the support," J. Q. Mahaffey said. "He was not a popular man at all, because he was tight and he was opinionated and didn't hesitate to express himself. He had many opponents in Arkansas."[141] Becoming governor would have been a natural thought for Palmer. His resentment of Little Rock, his obvious political base in south Arkansas, his influence with established politicians, his national and international experience, and his own wealth, power, and political ideology would have all tempted him to give thought to the possibility of running for governor.

Palmer watched as his friend Col. T. H. Barton of El Dorado ran for senator in 1944. Barton spent $127,732 in a losing effort, even though he used his wealth to bring in performers from Nashville's Grand Ole Opry as a draw. And he watched the "G. I. Revolt" led by Hot Springs prosecuting attorney Sidney McMath sweep into the governor's office in 1948 and saw little-known Francis Cherry, with the support of Arkansas Power and Light (Palmer's friend Hamilton Moses was AP&L president), defeat McMath in 1952. Cherry not only had AP&L support, but he utilized live local radio station call-in shows to make himself known.[142] Palmer himself not only owned radio stations, but newspapers as well. The thought of possibly running for the governorship must have crossed Palmer's mind. In the mid-1930s, when he was active on all of the state commissions, he probably could have developed a political base, but his resignation from state commissions reduced his political visibility. Even if he thought of running for governor, he probably saw that it was not possible after the mid-1930s.

Palmer's daughter, Betty Hussman, said that she "never heard any mention" of her father's desire to be governor.[143] And, if he sought advice from friends and associates, Palmer was probably told that, like Col. Barton, he might mount a campaign, but his chances were slim. Palmer was not a popular man. He was an influential man, and he was important in both local and state politics, but he was not the person to run for public office. Perhaps this was on his mind when he told Mahaffey that the root of their power was in the newspapers, not in themselves. "John Quincy, if you were *not* the editor of the newspaper," Palmer once told his Texarkana editor, "you would probably be a ribbon clerk in Ben F. Smith's Dry Goods Co. The paper is the thing that makes us important and don't you forget it!"[144]

Palmer contented himself, it appears, with press association galas at the Arlington Hotel in Hot Springs, press parties at Oaklawn Racetrack in Hot Springs, and other events that involved politics at a state level.[145] And he enjoyed the associations with Senators McClellan, Fulbright, and Johnson, as well as Representatives Wright Patman and Oren Harris. After World War II, or after Franklin Roosevelt, the conservative ideas of an early twentieth-century businessman like Clyde Palmer lessened in popular appeal. Palmer seems to have accepted the fact that his business gave him his importance and that he was secondary to that power.

Part of Palmer's particular political vision involved his steadfast belief that the Arkansas legislature spent too much of the state's tax dollars in central Arkansas, particularly in the Little Rock area, and not enough in other areas, notably in southwest Arkansas. "He felt that every major improvement in the state was always to benefit Little Rock and had no benefit for Hot Springs, Texarkana or El Dorado," Mahaffey recalled. "And I heard him say many times that Little Rock and the papers there [the *Arkansas Democrat* and the *Arkansas Gazette*] felt that Little Rock was the only city in Arkansas and that burned him up! He and the *Arkansas Gazette* never did get along. They were always at odds."[146]

Ray Kimball also said that Palmer's concern for south Arkansas was sincere: "He [Palmer] was always opposed to Little Rock getting anything. He wanted it to come to Hot Springs or El Dorado or someplace else. He was very determined to use his influence to keep and bring any development that he could into these areas, where he had newspapers, as opposed to developments in Little Rock."[147]

It would, of course, be natural for Palmer to attempt to get state expenditures, highway development, and economic development into his area. Not only was he motivated by the fact that it would be good for business, but he had a sense of regional pride and supported the development of communities in which he operated. His attempts to improve airport facilities in Hot Springs, the drive to establish city parks and a junior college in Texarkana, and other civic endeavors offer evidence that he supported the betterment of his communities.

Palmer was a member of the Mississippi Valley Association, which sought to provide flood control and to develop the Mississippi River area. The organization was the beginning of what became the Mississippi River Navigational Project. Mahaffey remembered that "Palmer was a champion of the Corps of Engineers and believed that the Red River could be made navigable from Shreveport to Texarkana."[148] Of course, Little Rock and the Arkansas River eventually got the Arkansas River Navigation Project. South Arkansas and the Red River, as Palmer feared, received nothing.

While it was easy to support highway improvement or to call for increased attention by the Arkansas legislature in south Arkansas, there was one potential and obvious crusade that Palmer did not undertake. Hot Springs was, during the entire time that Palmer operated newspapers there, a unique city. As Hot Springs Palmer reporter Roy Bosson recalled:

> In the '30s and '40s, Hot Springs was a "wide open" town ... elaborate [and illegal] casinos, bookie joints all up and down Central Avenue, gangsters [Alvin Karpis, Lucky Luciano, Pretty Boy Floyd, Frankie Costello, One Madden, et al.]; politicians ... the Pendergast gang from K. C. with Harry Truman, the Ed Crump machine from Memphis, Huey Long and others.... They all gathered here during the period while I was City Editor and Night Editor of the two newspapers.
>
> The Leo McLaughlin Machine ran Hot Springs and Mr. Palmer was constantly pressured by both "reformers" and McLaughlin, but he maintained a firm posture of "let's serve Hot Springs and not the politicians" which never deviated in the years I was with him.... And we did get the pressure.[149]

The illegal gambling was rampant, with casinos such as the Southern Club, the Belvedere, and the Vapors operating much like Las Vegas casinos. Hot Springs offered big name entertainers, floor shows, silver dollars, roulette wheels, and slot machines. His newspapers benefited greatly from the entertainment advertising of the casinos and from the tourist and gambling trade that came to Hot Springs. However, he did cover the news. When Mayor McLaughlin was finally indicted by a grand jury, Palmer's papers covered the entire trial. Edna Howe recalled that it was not easy for her to cover the case: "Every morning when the paper came out, Leo McLaughlin would call Mr. Palmer and complain about what I had written."[150] But Palmer supported her.

Palmer attended parties at Oaklawn Racetrack, and he visited the clubs and casinos. "We used to go to those places," Howe recalled, "to the Southern Club and see the gangsters, they were all there." She said that she thought that Palmer was mostly an "observer. . . . He wasn't a gangster. . . . We just kind of ignored it unless something happened in one of those places; then, as far as the news was concerned, we'd write a story about it. But we didn't editorialize about it or anything like that. A lot of gamblers used to stay at the Arlington Hotel, and we had a lot of prostitution here then."[151]

However, according to John Wells, Palmer did not really ignore the illegal gambling in Hot Springs. Wells recalled that a Baptist preacher from Booneville, who succeeded in obtaining a large amount of evidence about gambling, started a radio crusade against gambling. The minister managed to get the chief justice of the Arkansas Supreme Court to issue warrants for the state police to raid several Hot Springs gambling establishments. Wells said that Palmer was part of a delegation of Hot Springs businessmen who went to Governor Carl Bailey and asked what needed to be done to reopen the gaming clubs. "Governor Bailey told them that the Arkansas State Police could not enter a county without the invitation and approval of the county sheriff," Wells said. "Palmer and the Hot Springs delegation took that message back to Garland County and the gambling resumed."[152]

Another group led by a circuit judge began a second campaign to get Governor Bailey to close the Hot Springs gambling casinos. Again, Palmer was part of a delegation that sought advice from the governor. "Bailey told Palmer to see if they could not get the slot machines and other gambling equipment off the first floor of the Central Avenue casinos and houses," Wells said, "and they moved everything off the first floors and it was all right after that."[153]

But Palmer was not the only person to ignore the illegal gambling. It was fully in view of the Arkansas Press Association, which met in Hot Springs each year. It was thriving during President Roosevelt's 1936 visit to the Spa City. The Arkansas legislature failed to enforce the laws against it. In fact, gambling continued until the mid-1960s, when Winthrop Rockefeller became governor of the state. Palmer simply did what most of his colleagues did: pretended that the gambling was not illegal. His Hot Springs newspapers led no crusade to abolish the casinos. How Palmer personally regarded the Hot Springs gambling is not known, but in 1955, when Texarkana citizens were holding a referendum on allowing pari-mutuel horse racing in the city, Palmer was quoted in the *Texarkana Gazette*: "From what I know about the effects of racing on the business life of a community, I can say without any hesitation that in my opinion it would do Texarkana more harm than good."[154] On July 12, 1955, the Texarkana gambling issue was defeated by a two-to-one margin.

Many of Palmer's critics have charged that the publisher avoided controversial topics that might hurt business. Palmer, however, attacked one of the largest corporations in the state when he started a crusade against the Arkansas Louisiana Gas Company (Arkla). Mahaffey recalled, "Palmer thought that the Arkansas Louisiana Gas Company was making more money on their investments than they should, so he started carrying a series of front page editorials or exposés, on Arkla."[155] W. R. "Witt" Stephens, and associates, bought Arkansas Louisiana Gas Company from Cities Service in 1955. Shortly afterward Palmer began his series of editorials condemning Arkla.

Palmer hired a young reported named Edith Sweezy to do the investigative work on the series. Sweezy had worked for Arkansas publisher John Wells in Little Rock during World War II, but had moved to Washington, DC, with her husband after the war. According to Wells, Palmer was looking for a Washington, DC, correspondent for his newspapers. Wells told Palmer about Sweezy, calling her "one hell of a reporter." Palmer hired Sweezy, and she wrote a column for the Palmer papers called "Capitol Talk," written from Washington. Wells recalled that Sweezy "scooped both the Associated Press and the United Press on the Reynolds Metals plants coming to Arkansas," and that the Palmer papers carried the story two days prior to any other state newspapers. Wells also recalled Palmer giving Sweezy a bonus for the story and inviting Sweezy to visit him at his home on Lake Hamilton in Hot Springs. In 1949, however, Sweezy left the Palmer papers and returned to Little Rock

to work on the *Arkansas Recorder*, published by John Wells. Sweezy is credited by Wells with uncovering a scandal in the Office of State Purchasing and
with exposing the scandal in the state High Department that terminated the
political career of Arkansas Governor Sid McMath. When Palmer began his
attack on Arkla, he asked Wells for the loan of Sweezy. Wells said that he felt
that he owed Palmer for helping him obtain a press seat in the Arkansas legislature in 1943, when he had begun the *Arkansas Legislative Digest*.[156] Since
Sweezy was willing, Wells loaned her to Palmer for the Arkla series.

What exactly provoked Palmer's anger toward Arkla remains a mystery.
More than thirty years afterward, most associates of Palmer's remember only
the unending attacks, not the cause. John Wells said that Palmer was angry
over proposed rate increases. "After Witt Stephens took over Arkla," Wells
said, "he asked his commercial customers to voluntarily agree to a rate increase, with a promise in return that they would then not be cut off. Palmer
was irate."[157] In 1986 Witt Stephens recalled the reasons that he believed initiated Palmer's attacks on Arkla:

> We bought the Arkla Gas Company in '55. Soon after we bought it, we
> laid off 600+ employees and I understand now, two of those people I
> laid off were close friends of Mr. Palmer's and it made him mad and the
> kindest thing I can say is he wrote bad things about me until he died.[158]

To gain access to the corporate records of Arkla, Palmer purchased one hundred shares of Arkla stock in Sweezy's name and sent her to the corporate
offices in Shreveport, Louisiana, to examine the stockholder list. The Arkla
staff refused to let her see the records, and Palmer threatened to sue on her
behalf. The Arkla officers relented, and Sweezy and Palmer published the
list, which contained the names of many prominent Arkansas politicians.
The editorials stated that the politicians gave Arkla special treatment because
they themselves stood to gain. According to Wells, "Witt was so upset that
he called Sam Harris at the *Arkansas Gazette* and asked for help in stopping
Palmer. . . . Witt was hurting, no doubt about it. . . . Sweezy and Palmer had
nailed him to a cross."[159]

Stephens threatened to stop all Arkla advertising in Palmer's newspapers,
but Palmer would not stop the series and told Stephens to go ahead. According to Palmer's grandson David Palmer Mooney, the publisher's main fear
was that Arkla would cut off natural gas supplies to his newspaper plants.
Because of that, Mooney said, "He had butane tanks and pipes installed at

the *Sentinel-Record* and *New Era* plant at 912 Central, just in case that Arkla cut off the gas. The pipes were still there when the newspaper building was moved to Spring Street."[160]

Sweezy continued to examine the corporate records and extract information that appeared in her articles in all of the Palmer papers. According to Wells, Arkla made it as difficult for her as possible, even refusing to let her bring pencils and paper into the office for a while. Sweezy memorized items and then went to the women's restroom to write them down. It soon became apparent that this tactic had failed, so Arkla finally gave Sweezy access to the records, and she continued her articles. Mahaffey recalled that Palmer "carried this on interminably, just one after another . . . people grew tired of it! And I got tired of it! But Palmer raked Stephens over the coals every morning."[161] In the very middle of the anti-Arkla campaign, Stephens paid an unexpected call on Palmer. Mahaffey was a witness to the meeting and wrote:

> During his [Palmer's] career, we waged some terrific editorial campaigns, not the least of which was the one against a rate increase by the Arkansas Louisiana Gas Co. Right in the middle of the campaign, Witt Stephens [W. R. Stephens], the president of Arkla Gas, came to see us. CEP yelled for me to come down to witness the encounter.
>
> "Mr. Palmer," said Stephens, "your newspaper has been writing a lot of mighty bad things about me. I thought I ought to come in and meet you. I'm just an old country boy who never got beyond the eighth grade in school."
>
> CEP hopped up and stuck out his hand.
>
> "I'm an eighth grader too," he said.
>
> After they batted gas and interest rates, profit margins, bonded indebtedness and debentures back and forth across the desk, they told each other goodbye, but not before I had asked them to give me the names of those eighth grade schools. I wanted to enroll.[162]

But the meeting between two of Arkansas's most influential men, who discovered they had much in common, did not cause Palmer to cease his attacks on Arkla. Finally, Stephens went to a mutual friend, C. Hamilton Moses, of Arkansas Power and Light, and asked him to intercede with Palmer. Palmer and Moses were friends and business associates (Ray Kimball recalled that Palmer and Moses were once involved in a cable television business, probably Midwest Video Inc. [see chapter 2][163]). Moses was a law partner of Senator Joe

T. Robinson at one time and became president of the state Chamber of Commerce. He was also the only non-publisher ever made an honorary member of the Arkansas Press Association.[164] Moses and Palmer were neighbors on Lake Hamilton, outside of Hot Springs, as well.

After Stephens asked Moses to assist him in stopping Palmer's attacks, the editorials ceased. Some theorized that Moses was concerned that Palmer's attack on one utility, Arkla, could lead to another newspaper taking on Arkansas Power and Light.[165] Palmer reporter George Brewer recalled that "Moses called upon CEP to stop the investigation and CEP did. It seems that at one time in Mr. Palmer's operation he became strapped for cash and Mr. Moses let him have a considerable sum. It was said that CEP told close associates that he owed Mr. Moses one big favor and he just couldn't turn him down."[166] John Wells said, "Moses loaned Palmer money to keep his papers going in the 1930s."[167]

Witt Stephens said he asked Moses to assist him in getting Palmer to cease the articles:

> It is true that Mr. Ham Moses was a friend of mine and a friend of Palmer's and I asked Mr. Moses to see if he could soften Mr. Palmer on me and Arkla Gas. Mr. Moses passed away some years ago. He was a fine man and president of AP&L....[168]

As George Brewer, who watched the entire conflict between Palmer and Arkla, said, "CEP called off the dogs."[169] Palmer let Sweezy keep the Arkla stock, and, according to Wells, she continued to receive dividend checks on it after she returned to work for him.[170] After the Palmer–Stephens feud ended, a reporter from *Fortune* magazine visited with Sweezy and wanted her to write an Arkla article for them, but she refused.[171] Sweezy continued to work for Wells until her death in February 1984.

Some observers felt that John Wells played a more important role in Palmer's battle with Arkla. Wells has long been a maverick in Arkansas newspaper publishing, but has been called one of the best investigative newsmen in the state by some reporters.[172] Palmer reporter George Brewer recalled, "I don't believe John Wells had any connection with CEP in that business, only the loan of his star reporter and general girl Friday, Edith Sweezy, for the Palmer investigative project. But Wells certainly knew everything that was going on."[173] Wells confirmed that the relationship was limited to his loan of Sweezy.

Wells recalled that Sweezy became furious with Palmer later over the publisher's endorsement of Orval Faubus for governor in 1956. Witt Stephens and Faubus were political allies, and when Palmer came out in support of Faubus, Sweezy was angered, recalling the feelings against Stephens during the Arkla crusade. Wells said, "Mr. Palmer explained to her that his support of Faubus was in appreciation for what one of his friends had asked him to do. Mr. Palmer told her that C. Hamilton Moses had asked him to support Faubus, because Faubus was going to make Moses the chairman of the Arkansas Industrial Development Commission. Mr. Palmer said he had a personal obligation to Moses."[174] In January 1957, C. Hamilton Moses was feted by the Arkansas Press Association with his lifetime honorary membership. Recently re-elected governor Orval Faubus also attended and outlined his plans for the state. Among those making speeches in praise of Moses was C. E. Palmer.[175] Faubus did not, however, name Moses head of the Arkansas Industrial Development Commission, choosing instead Winthrop Rockefeller.

Not long after the end of the Arkla crusade, Witt Stephens announced that Arkla was going to build a new corporate building in the state and that Texarkana might be the site. The Texarkana Chamber of Commerce gave a dinner for Stephens and the Arkla executives. Palmer and Stephens were seated next to each other at the head table. During the dinner, Palmer suddenly slumped over, which frightened everyone. They all stared at Stephens. To everyone's relief, Palmer had simply gotten too hot and fainted.[176]

A final note on the Palmer–Stephens feud came shortly after Palmer's death. Mahaffey remembered that on the day that Palmer died, the Arkla Gas Company was hosting a party at the Texarkana Country Club and Stephens was in attendance. Mahaffey said that Stephens remarked, "I was glad I was out at the Country Club at the time [of Palmer's death] or they would have accused me of doing it!"[177]

On July 4, 1957, Clyde E. Palmer died after suffering a stroke. He was less than a month away from his eighty-first birthday. He had gone fishing in Canada not long before and appeared to be in good health, although he had suffered some minor heart problems in his last few years. He suffered a stroke in his home in Texarkana at about 8 p.m. on the evening of July 4 and was rushed to St. Michael's Hospital, but was pronounced dead shortly after arrival.[178]

Major newspapers throughout the nation noted his passing. Almost all chronicled his pioneering work on the Palmer Circuit, his newspaper group's importance, and his wealth. The *Arkansas Gazette* praised Palmer and quoted his formula for becoming wealthy: "'Making money is a flair,' he once said. 'It's just a matter of being there when it is going by and grabbing it.'"[179] A recent photograph of Palmer ran on the front page of the *Hot Springs Sentinel-Record*, under a banner headline on Palmer's death. Messages of sympathy poured into the Palmer papers from around the nation. Telegrams arrived from business associates, politicians, friends, and fellow publishers all over the country.

In an editorial on July 6, 1957, the *Arkansas Gazette* called Palmer "a self-made man in the most accurate sense of the term" and called the Palmer Group "one of the country's most important chains of small newspapers." The *Gazette* added that "the imprint of his strong personality will continue to be felt in the wide area of South Arkansas where the 'Palmer Papers' operate."[180]

A *Pine Bluff Commercial* editorial writer said that Palmer's death removed "from the Arkansas newspaper picture a colorful and vital personality, and one man who will be sorely missed as both a newspaper man and a big-hearted human being."[181] The *Arkansas Recorder* editorial said that "qualities of genuine greatness sparked the career of Clyde E. Palmer, an Independent if ever there was one." In addition, the editorial called Palmer "an outstanding citizen and crusading publisher, who was not above writing editorials himself when the spirit moved him—which fortunately for us all was often."[182] An *Arkansas Democrat* editorial writer said that Palmer's newspapers "have been noteworthy especially for their close identification with their region. They have contributed to the progress of their communities and they haven't hesitated to take a stand on local, state and national issues."[183] Both the *New York Times* and *Editor & Publisher* called Palmer a pioneer for his development and implementation of the Palmer Circuit.[184]

While editorial writers rushed to praise Palmer following his death and while many newspaper professionals memorialized his importance in Arkansas newspaper publishing, others recounted Palmer's imperfections. One newspaper man praised Palmer for his "widespread" and "beneficial" influence, saying that he "never lost the 'common touch' with either his associates or the public."[185] Another said that he had "a ruthless streak in him."[186] One associate called him "jolly" and, almost in the same breath, called him "harsh."[187] Arkansas publisher and former Palmer reporter Louis Graves recalled the dichotomy: "It was said of him [Palmer], in the depression time, that he could stroll through the city room, pat a reporter on the back for a good story, then cut that reporter's salary."[188] Iconoclast Arkansas publisher John Wells, who was involved in many controversies with Palmer, called him "a pioneer in newspaper technology."[189]

Funeral services were held in Texarkana at 10:30 a.m., on July 6, at the Pine Street Presbyterian Church. Department heads of his Texarkana newspaper, radio, and television operations served as pallbearers. Honorary pallbearers included numerous employees of Palmer's operations throughout the state, as well as friends, including Congressmen Oren Harris and Wright Patman. Longtime Palmer associates Alex Washburn, Bert Estes, and John Q. Holder were also pallbearers. At 10:30 a.m. all of Palmer's newspaper, radio, and television operations halted operation for five minutes. In tribute to Palmer, the Palmer Circuit was closed for five minutes as well.[190]

In August 1956, *The Arkansas Publisher* carried a photograph of Palmer taken at his eightieth birthday party at Walter Hussman's home in Camden. Palmer was surrounded by the women in the Palmer family, including his daughters Mrs. Walter Hussman and Mrs. Alden P. Mooney, granddaughter Marilyn Hussman, Mrs. Palmer, and his sister Mrs. P. D. Vincent. The note with the photo stated that "Mr. Palmer, at eighty, is still active in the Palmer Newspaper chain."[191] In July 1957, the publication carried Palmer's photograph on the cover, bordered in black, with a caption that read "30 – C. E. Palmer."[192] These were the last two notices concerning Palmer in *The Arkansas Publisher*.

Bob Dean wrote, in an editorial in the *Hot Springs Sentinel-Record*: "Palmer had faith in the future of Arkansas and especially in the home cities of his newspapers."[193] That was Palmer's strength, his unending efforts to improve the communities in which he operated. His genuine efforts to improve southwest Arkansas were appreciated by those who worked with him in that cause.

Palmer was a rich, powerful, and well-traveled man. He owned newspapers, radio and television stations, urban and suburban real estate, and oil properties. Yet he also once bought a small peach orchard near DeQueen.[194] He was a friend and associate of the rich and the powerful, of senators, congressmen, and businessmen. But he loved, more than anything, to go to the circus and would go miles out of his way to attend any circus in his area.[195] Palmer was a unique individual, who, for almost five decades, dominated Arkansas journalism with the force of his personality.

CHAPTER 5

The Palmer Legacy

The Palmer Holdings

At the time of Palmer's death in 1957, the Palmer Group constituted a solid-ified chain of daily newspapers in Arkansas and Texas. The Palmer Group newspapers included the *Hot Springs New Era* and *Sentinel-Record*; the *Texarkana Gazette* and the *Texarkana Daily News*; the *El Dorado Evening Times* and the *Daily News*; the *Magnolia Banner News* and the *Weekly Banner News*; and the *Camden News*. Palmer's son-in-law Walter Hussman was an owner and the publisher of the Camden paper, but it was part of the Palmer Group. Palmer and Alex Washburn continued to publish the *Hope Star*. The only weekly of any consequence in the Palmer Group was the *South Arkansas Progress*, which was printed in El Dorado, but with coverage mainly in Smack-over. In addition, the Palmer Group owned KCMC radio and television in Texarkana and radio station KAMD in Camden, with at least some interest in radio station KWFC in Hot Springs. Palmer was president of Midwest Video Inc., in Little Rock, and president of the Palmer Foundation. Palmer also presided over a series of holding corporations: Banner News Publishing Company (in Magnolia); Texarkana Newspaper Inc.; Associated Newspapers Inc. and Southern Newspapers Inc. (in Hot Springs); and the News-Times Publishing Company (in El Dorado).

Palmer's daughter Alden Palmer Mooney served as general manager of the Hot Springs newspapers.[1] Hussman owned the radio station at Camden, while Palmer oversaw the operation of KCMC radio and television in Texarkana, with a manager at each. Palmer had real estate holdings throughout the state. In addition to his home at 902 Olive Street in Texarkana, he owned a home on Point Lookout, on Lake Hamilton, just outside of Hot Springs. He had interests in an area of Texarkana called Beverly Heights. It is not known to what extent he still held oil properties in south Arkansas at the time of his death.

Palmer's ownership of the newspaper outlets in Texarkana, El Dorado, Magnolia, Camden, and Hot Springs, his joint enterprise with Alex Washburn in Hope, and his long-standing business relationship with Ray Kimball in DeQueen, gave him a monopoly on the daily newspaper business in about one-fourth of the geographical area of the state. His radio and television holdings increased that voice. Except for some small weeklies, Palmer had very little competition in southwest Arkansas, and, because of this, he also could provide or withhold political news to this same portion of the state. He had long-standing relationships with numerous Arkansas politicians, and, consequently, he had, through his newspaper chain, considerable political power.

Palmer's influence was not limited to his media holdings or real estate, or even his family, but extended beyond to a group that became known as the Palmer Alumni. Palmer's ownership of the major newspapers in an entire section of the state meant that many young reporters began their journalism careers with papers in the Palmer Group or passed through Palmer's papers as their careers progressed. These alumni remained involved with Palmer, through the activities of the Arkansas Press Association (which his newspapers dominated in terms of numbers), the Arkansas Associated Press (in which he also held a large bloc of votes), and through other professional organizations, such as the Associated Press Managing Editors Association. Add to these the Palmer lieutenants, John Q. Mahaffey, Walter Hussman, Bob Dean, Bert Estes, Alden Palmer Mooney, Bob Hayes, and others who worked for Palmer Group newspapers, and the numbers are substantial.

John Q. Mahaffey, of Texarkana, worked for Palmer for almost his entire newspaper career and has written a great deal about his mentor over the years, much of which is quoted in this book. Roy Bosson was on the staff of the Hot Springs newspapers and wrote that "the training, the work-habit example, and the perseverance example which he set for me ultimately got me all the way up to New York City and Washington, D.C. I shall never forget him."[2] Louis "Swampy" Graves, who later became the publisher of the *Nashville News*, the *Murfreesboro Diamond*, the *Glenwood Herald*, and the *Montgomery County News*, started with Palmer's *Texarkana Gazette* as a proofreader in 1938.[3] George Brewer began his association with Palmer at the *El Dorado*

Daily News in March 1935 and worked for and with Palmer for many years. His recollections are presented in previous chapters.[4] W. R. Whitehead, now publisher emeritus of the *Fordyce News-Advocate*, worked for Palmer in El Dorado and Magnolia. Bert Estes of El Dorado and John Q. Holder of Hot Springs were long-time members of Palmer's newspaper staff. Edna Howe, of Hot Springs, and Francis Cordell, of El Dorado, were two of Palmer's veteran women employees. James H. Hale, now publisher of the *Kansas City Star* and the *Kansas City Times*, began his newspaper career with Palmer's Texarkana newspapers. "I remember Clyde E. Palmer quite well," Hale said, "for it was at the *Texarkana Gazette* that I had my first job in journalism."[5]

One of the best known of the Palmer Alumni group was popular *Arkansas Gazette* columnist Ernie Deane, who began with the Palmer newspapers in Texarkana and later wrote the popular "Arkansas Traveler" in the *Gazette*. Deane wrote, only a few days after Palmer's death, "I had known him since I was a boy. And, in fact, the first dollar I ever made writing for print was on a special assignment for his *Texarkana Gazette*. I complimented him a year or two ago on his business genius and he observed, 'Genius is mostly hard work.'"[6]

Some of the Palmer Alumni stayed with him; others drifted away, came back, and left again. Others learned their writing skills on his papers and left. Some left in anger; others left with regret. They developed names for him. "CEP," they called him when he wasn't around. Or sometimes they called him "the old man." But mostly they called him "Mr. Palmer," and even today many men and women approaching their eighties or more still respectfully refer to him as "Mr. Palmer."

All of them, sooner or later, got the same Palmer lecture that Mahaffey once received about the importance of reporters and editors. Mahaffey recalled the lecture years later:

> "Don't get any delusions of grandeur," he [Palmer] said, "it's the paper and a lot of men are running papers today who haven't got any business running them."
>
> And then he'd give us a lecture on the business of running a paper.
>
> "The trouble with you, John Quincy," he'd say, "is that you want to print the *New York Times* in Texarkana and you just can't do that. You gotta build the town first and the paper will come along!"[7]

Clement P. Brossier, who was head of the Arkansas Associated Press from April 1952 until June 1956, worked with Palmer in the activities of the

Arkansas Associated Press Association. In 1987 Brossier still spoke enthusias-
tically about Palmer. "Clyde Palmer was an original, and there are no copies,"
Brossier wrote.[8] Palmer was the primary personality in Arkansas newspaper
publishing from 1909 until 1957 and greatly influenced journalists in both
Arkansas and Texas for almost half a century.

Palmer, through his newspapers and his business and political associations, changed the history of Arkansas journalism. While he purchased many
newspapers, he eliminated almost as many. Often, he purchased newspapers
to acquire the circulation and eliminate competition. Newspapers that he
eliminated or absorbed included the *South Arkansas Progress*, the *Craighead
County Journal*, the *Camden Morning Gazette*, the *Ouachita Observer*, the
Hope Journal, the *Columbia County News*, and the *Huttig News*. His closely
held business (and family) associations with Alex Washburn, Ray Kimball,
Walter Hussman, John Wells, and the Fulbright family, as well as others,
helped widen his influence. His entry into radio and television extended his
communications control and paved the way for future WEHCO Media advances. His active participation in the state and national Associated Press, his
service on national Associated Press committees, and his membership in the
National Press Club and other professional groups, increased his association
with other publishers on a national level. He was active in the Arkansas Press
Association, the Texas Press Association, the Texas Daily Newspaper Association, and the Associated Press Managing Editors Association. Among his
friends were the rich and powerful of the state, including C. Hamilton Moses,
Col. T. H. Barton, Harvey Couch, and others. His political influence with
Senators John McClellan and J. William Fulbright and Congressmen Oren
Harris and Wright Patman added to his political influence. He was also close
to a series of Arkansas governors, including Bailey, Futrell, and Faubus. He
was influential in gubernatorial races and legislative races, due to the fact
that he controlled the media in so large a section of the state and could en-
dorse, oppose, or withhold coverage of politicians and politics. His banner
"We Like Ike!" headlines and his endorsement of Orval Faubus illustrate his
ability to use his newspapers to influence voters. His service on various state
commissions also extended his influence in state politics.

In conducting research for this book, I contacted more than fifty individuals who knew Palmer. In the course of interviews, correspondence, and
conversations, there were no lukewarm references to Clyde Palmer. While the
names of many important Arkansas publishers, editors, and newsmen arose,

none excited the sources as much as Palmer. Men who had worked for Palmer a half century ago were still enthusiastic about their relationships and their remembrances of the man. Each person seemed to have had a very personal relationship with Palmer, one that persists over the years in memories.

Bob Dean, Palmer's Hot Springs editor, may have understood this relationship between Palmer and his employees when he wrote about his publisher:

> He was intolerant of civic procrastination. . . . A man of action. . . . He possessed great business acumen which was matched by his desire to do what he could for the public good and the courage to take a stand for what he believed to be the right.[9]

And another time Dean had written:

> One of the things we like most about our employer is that he is one of us. He is not just the manager and the coach. He is one of the team. . . . He works alongside us. . . . He sympathizes with us in our troubles . . . ever willing to lend a helping hand, and rejoices in our good fortunes.
>
> He detests bigotry, ostentation and deceit. There is never any doubt as to where he stands on any question. . . .
>
> He shows no partiality to any one department of the newspapers. He is keenly interested in all of them. When he isn't busy in his own office, he is likely to be found somewhere in the plant "talking shop." . . . The subject might be advertising, a news story, an editorial, circulation, mechanical problems or any of the numerous other phases of publishing a newspaper.[10]

In August 1930, as the Palmer Group was beginning, *Editor & Publisher* writer Ray Reid interviewed Palmer. In this article Palmer outlined some of his basic publishing philosophies. "Our newspapers are keenly interested in development of the communities which they serve and editorial and news policies are shaped with this in mind," Palmer said. He claimed to have little interest in politics, saying, "I have less interest in politics than any other newspaper publisher in the world." He added that "only in matter of utmost public interest do we deal with political issues and then it is for the defense or establishment of principles and not the advancement of individuals."[11]

Addressing the business side of his publishing enterprise, Palmer told Reid that he thought that "American newspapers have become too commercialized, and the business office is allowed to dictate too many policies which are not properly in its sphere." Palmer added that "our ideals have become somewhat dim, although the condition is probably no worse than in other professions or lines of business." However, Palmer declared that "a newspaper must be a financial success to continue publication."[12]

Palmer's conviction of the need for less business control and more news may have wavered during the late 1930s as the Depression cut heavily into his newspaper publishing operations. How strongly he felt about the domination of the editorial side over the business side of newspapers may have also changed during those years. And he obviously learned well the lesson of profits supporting news, since his newspapers were eventually successful.

Palmer also told Reid that the "newspaper must be a step ahead of other community agencies and must take the lead in community betterment, else the community will not be bettered to any great extent."[13] Palmer appeared to take this dictum seriously and actively participated editorially, professionally, and personally in the communities in which he published his newspaper. His involvement in the Texarkana Chamber of Commerce and Texarkana Junior College, his support of Hot Springs airport improvements, and his support of the Boys Club and other civic activities attest to his civic endeavors. His newspapers supported local charities and local causes and addressed local issues (horse racing in Texarkana, the Leo McLaughlin trial in Hot Springs, etc.).

Palmer did not receive the permanent rewards that sometimes accompany such civic involvement. The only building that bears his name is the Palmer Library at Texarkana Junior College. In 1941 Palmer was given an honorary degree from Subiaco College, a small Catholic college (now a prep school) in Subiaco, Arkansas. The college conferred an honorary doctorate on Palmer on May 28, 1941, for his support of the college's printing program and for helping the institution meet its printing needs.[14] Civic groups passed numerous resolutions honoring Palmer, such as the resolution of appreciation presented by the Texarkana Jaycees to the publisher "for his support of community projects and for the upbuilding of Texarkana."[15] Resolutions of appreciation were given to him at almost every meeting of the Arkansas Press Association, especially those held in Hot Springs, often because Palmer hosted a reception for the attendees as he did in June 1941, when he invited the entire convention to a barbecue at the Lake Hamilton Lodge.[16] Palmer's permanence was, ultimately, in his newspaper group and his various enterprises, not in monuments.

Overview of Palmer's Importance

Palmer achieved importance, but he also had his shortcomings. Palmer failed to pay his employees well, which caused many of his best reporters and editors to leave the organization. However, some of his harshest critics seem to excuse him for the low wages and note the benefits that he provided. He did monopolize the news in his communities. Palmer faced the same issues that many newspapers today face: most cities are financially able to support only one daily newspaper.[17] Palmer always managed to drive the weaker competing newspaper out of his market, or purchase it, and market monopoly was paramount in the publishing business.

Chain newspaper ownership has its critics. In 1900 there were only eight newspaper groups in the United States; by 1935 a total of sixty-three groups had emerged (among them the Palmer Group); and by 1977 the total number of newspaper groups had increased to 168, controlling 60 percent of all daily newspapers and 71 percent of the daily circulation.[18] Media critic George N. Gordon has written that "for economic reasons alone, chain newspapers prospered, while independents, by and large, had a difficult time." Gordon pointed out that most chains learned that they "were able to cut overhead by, in effect, utilizing feature writers, editorialists, photographers and even compositors economically—somewhat like a small press service."[19] This, of course, is exactly what Palmer did with the Palmer Circuit, and his benefits matched those of other groups that entered the "chain" publishing business. The loss was in the individuality of his newspapers, to some degree. The fact that other newspaper groups (Harte-Hanks, for example) followed Palmer's example demonstrates that the idea was cost effective and, therefore, popular among publishers and wire services. The value of methods and techniques were obvious, and many other publishers and groups emulated Palmer.

John C. Merrill and Ralph L. Lowenstein have written critically of newspaper chains and, because of their concern that the business of publishing dominates the news function, have called such chains "an increasing threat to press freedom."[20] Press critic Ben Bagdikian has written extensively on the topic of newspaper chains, concluding that "never before has so much been under the control of so few."[21] Bagdikian has also decried the "business trend among newspapers" and adds that "newspapers have followed other industries in another form of concentration—the conglomerate."[22] As proof to the dangers of media groups, Bagdikian points to the excesses of William

Randolph Hearst, the DuPont newspapers in Delaware, and the Jesse Jones newspapers in Houston as examples of chain abuse. Bagdikian concludes that "no distinguished newspaper was ever created by a chain."[23] This criticism of the business of publishing is common among the detractors of chain journalism. Peter M. Sandman, David M. Rubin, and David B. Sachsman have written: "When a publisher decides that earning money is more important than advocating a viewpoint, he or she naturally eliminated most of the ideological advocacy from the paper, and care very little about the advocacy that is left."[24]

As the business of newspapers becomes more important than news, the critics note, the editorial values decline. Ralph Thrift Jr. conducted a study of twenty-four newspapers between 1960 and 1975. During that period, sixteen were purchased by media chains. Thrift concluded the editorial pages of those purchased by the chains began to present fewer argumentative and advocacy editorials on matters of controversy. Writing in *Journalism Quarterly*, Thrift said:

> This study demonstrates the chains have had an impact on the editorial quality of the dailies they have purchased on the West Coast. And certainly, the impact is not helpful to readers who seek guidance on local matters when they turn to the editorial pages of their daily newspaper.[25]

Finally, numerous critics have pointed out that the loss of competition between daily newspapers, brought about by the chains' continual purchasing of rivals, is a loss for journalism.

All of these conclusions could easily be aimed at Clyde Palmer and the newspapers of the Palmer Group. Palmer *was* primarily a businessman, a publisher who entered the newspaper profession from the business world. The publishing business was his primary concern, especially during the economically depressed 1930s. His cross-ownership of newspapers and radio stations (and later television), while equally subject to criticism, was also an economic endeavor. Palmer was first and foremost a businessman, in the business of buying, selling, and publishing newspapers. The fact is that many of his former reporters, who agreed with the criticisms above with regard to Palmer, became publishers (James Hal at the *Kansas City Star*, Louis Graves at the *Nashville News*, W. R. Whitehead at the *Fordyce News-Advocate*, and others). Most now condone and support many of Palmer's policies as proof that his business instincts were sound.

It is difficult to judge Palmer by the current standards of criticism that are aimed at today's Gannett, Scripps-Howard, and Knight-Ridder chains. Palmer lived in different times and faced somewhat different circumstances. He did not avoid controversy, the failure to condemn Hot Springs gambling notwithstanding. His newspapers did deal with local issues, such as the Texarkana horse racing vote and the Leo McLaughlin trial. He sought out controversy, as illustrated by the Arkla Gas Company crusade. Palmer's critics during his lifetime were actually far more critical of Palmer the man than of Palmer's newspapers. Finally, critics of chain newspapers often cite absentee ownership as a failure of chain journalism. Palmer, as has been pointed out, was certainly not an absentee owner of the newspapers in the Palmer Group.

Journalism historian Frank Luther Mott, writing during Palmer's lifetime, wrote of newspaper chains:

> The chief values of such organization are supposed to be on the business side, and there is much sharing of techniques and the "know-how" of newspaper management. . . . But the group organization principle itself . . . cannot be said to have been generally injurious to the copious distribution of a good news report. . . . There is nothing reprehensible, or even avoidable, about all this. It is not the result of the machinations of monopolistic publishers, ruthless in their determination to kill off all competition; it is, rather, the effect of a struggle for survival in the face of rising costs.[26]

This view, more than anything, is closer to the record of Clyde Palmer's motivation as he put together the chain of newspapers that became the Palmer Group. In the end, Palmer's impact was that of a publisher of Arkansas newspapers who held power because he controlled access to so many readers. His radio and television enterprises increased that control. Late in his life he invested in cable television, then only beginning, but even then an idea that held promise for additional control of communications profit and communication access to citizens. It is no accident that Palmer and others were interested in this new technology. After his death, his son-in-law Walter Hussman entered this new and highly profitable enterprise.

It is possible that many of the communities that Palmer's newspapers served might have had no newspaper after the Depression era if Palmer had not utilized his particular publishing methods. The Texarkana and Hot Springs newspapers might have survived the Depression, but the likelihood of small communities, such as Camden, Smackover, or Hope supporting newspapers during the heart of the Depression might have been slim. Palmer's methods at least insured that newspapers and information did reach the residents of the small communities that he served. The pages of *The Arkansas Publisher* are full of notices of newspapers going out of business during the mid-1930s and during the early war years of the 1940s.[27]

Politically, Palmer was a force only through his newspapers and his association with politicians, not through any mandate of voters. The issues of the farm tenancy controversy cooled as World War II brought an economic recovery to the area. As the years passed, the direction of the Tenancy Commission turned to planned land uses.[28] The World's Fair helped rekindle state pride, and the Arkansas Centennial did the same, but none of these commissions were political bases of power. His friendships with senators, congressmen, governors, and other politicians were the results of his newspaper influence and power.

Overview of the Palmer–Hussman Legacy

At the time of his death, Palmer was survived by his wife, Bettie Maines Palmer; Mrs. Alden Palmer Mooney, his daughter by his first marriage; and Mrs. Walter E. Hussman, his daughter by his second wife. In addition, he was survived by two sisters, Mrs. P. D. Vincent, of Texarkana, and Mrs. Waldo Wintersteen, of Fremont, Nebraska. He had six surviving grandchildren, including David P. Mooney, Walter E. Hussman Jr., Gale Hussman, Marilyn Clyde Hussman, Denny Palmer, and Virginia Palmer.[29] The Palmer estate passed to his family, mainly to his daughter, Mrs. Walter Hussman. The exact details of the estate are not known, but the Palmer fortune was left in the hands of his immediate heirs.[30]

The details of Palmer's and, after his death, Hussman's involvement and investment in Midwest Video Inc. are not clear. Several of Lyndon B. Johnson's biographers have noted his interest in Midwest and his attempts to ensure Federal Communications Commission approval of a Midwest Video cable operation in Austin, Texas, where Johnson owned KTBC-TV. Johnson and Austin Mayor Tom Miller attempted to merge their dummy corporation, Capital Cable, with Midwest Video. The FCC eventually ruled in favor of Johnson's application.[31] It is always noted that Midwest Video was a Little Rock-based company, which served as a holding company for several cable operations. Midwest Video, at one time, controlled cable companies operating in Greenville, Mississippi; Popular Bluff, Missouri; Dexter, Missouri; Clovis, New Mexico; Victoria, Texas; College Station, Texas; Paris, Texas; and 50 percent of an Austin, Texas, company, with LBJ interests owning the other 50 percent.[32] Stockholders in Midwest Video Inc. included Palmer, Senator John L. McClellan, C. Hamilton Moses, and other prominent Arkansas businessmen. The corporation was eventually sold to McCaw Communications.[33]

Palmer's son-in-law Walter Hussman became the publisher and chief executive officer of the Palmer Group in 1957.[34] The most immediate problem facing the Palmer heirs was the problem of estate taxes. According to several sources, some of the original Palmer holdings were sold to raise cash to pay the estate taxes.[35] This crisis was resolved, and the significant Palmer newspapers and radio stations remained part of the Palmer Group, under Walter Hussman.

Hussman had, during his tenure in Camden as publisher of the *Camden News*, developed several of his own enterprises, including a real estate company, and invested in a local hotel corporation. In 1963 Hussman went to Sapporo, Japan, to examine the microwave transmission systems used by *Asahi Shimbun* and other Japanese newspapers.[36] This type of microwave system was installed in Texas and Arkansas during the early 1960s as part of a "multi-million dollar internal expansion program."[37] According to *Editor & Publisher*, "the Palmer Group . . . was the first in the country to be electronically interconnected by means of microwave transmission." The same article pointed out that the success of this operation, replacing the old Palmer Circuit, connected by telephone line, with a new microwave relay system, provided the base "for a multi-million dollar expansion in broadcast radio and television located in Arkansas, Texas and Louisiana."[38]

Hussman then formed a corporation called Research Associates, which was a partnership of his newspaper corporations. The purpose of Research Associates was to operate the facsimile microwave system that connected the newspapers at Texarkana, Hot Springs, El Dorado, Magnolia, and Camden, and to transmit editorial and advertising copy between newspapers, much as the original Palmer Circuit had done.[39] In the early 1960s the company entered the cable television market in Arkansas, Mississippi, and Texas, and in the mid-1970s constructed a common carrier microwave system to carry cable television signals from Dallas to the cable systems in

Texas, Louisiana, and Arkansas.[40] In 1973, Hussman combined all of the Palmer Group holdings into a single corporate body called WEHCO Media Inc.[41] The first purchase of WEHCO Media was the *Arkansas Democrat* in 1974, which Hussman called "an excellent publication with a tremendous potential."[42]

Named publisher of the *Arkansas Democrat* was Walter Hussman Jr., age twenty-seven, the grandson of Clyde Eber Palmer. The younger Hussman is a graduate of the University of North Carolina, where he majored in journalism, and Columbia University, where he earned a master's in business administration. After graduation he worked for *Forbes* magazine and at the Palmer Group newspapers in Camden and Hot Springs before becoming publisher of the *Arkansas Democrat*.[43] Under Hussman's direction, the *Arkansas Democrat* embarked on a campaign of head-to-head competition with the *Arkansas Gazette*. The battle culminated with a $23 million antitrust suit, which the *Arkansas Gazette* brought against the *Arkansas Democrat*.[44] The suit was resolved when a federal jury dismissed the charges against the *Democrat* in March 1986.[45] In late 1986, the Gannett newspaper group purchased the *Arkansas Gazette*.[46]

Clyde Palmer's reaction to his grandson's battle with the *Arkansas Gazette* would be interesting. Palmer could never stand competition and drove most of his out of the market. The battle for Little Rock (and Arkansas) between Gannett and the Palmer descendants will be worth watching. Gannett is a giant corporation, but WEHCO Media has resources as well. Several years ago, Walter Hussman Jr. said, "The principal interest of the WEHCO company now, as in its beginning, is in the daily newspaper field. Yet the great success experienced in related communications fields has complimented our efforts to produce newspapers."[47] Hussman was speaking of the radio, television, cable television, and microwave transmission systems that WEHCO Media owns and which provide WEHCO with resources. Shortly after the end of the *Arkansas Gazette* suit, Walter Hussman Jr. announced an $11 million expansion of the *Arkansas Democrat*.[48]

WEHCO Media Inc. is a modern, complex, diversified corporation The company is part of a larger company called Camden News Publishing Company. In 1980, when Walter Hussman was 74, and Betty Hussman was 79, WEHCO was 100 percent owned by the Hussman family. Walter and Betty Hussman owned 100 percent of the voting stock and 25 percent of all of the common stock. Their children and grandchildren owned the remaining 75 percent outright or as beneficiaries. Camden News Publishing Company owned 90 percent of WEHCO Media in 1980.[49] Camden News Publishing Company is comprised of four major corporations: WEHCO Media Inc., the Marigayle Realty Company, KCMC Inc., and Camden Radio Inc.

WEHCO Media Inc. has essentially become the new corporate body of the old Palmer Group. The companies within WEHCO Media Inc. are Texarkana Newspapers Inc. (the *Texarkana Gazette*); the Sentinel-Record Inc. (the *Hot Springs Sentinel-Record*); Banner News Publishing Company (the *Magnolia Banner News*); and the New-Times Publishing Company (the *El Dorado News-Times*). The new components are Little Rock Newspapers Inc., which owns the *Arkansas Democrat*; United WEHCO Inc., which is the common carrier microwave corporation that transmits television signals and is partially owned (19 percent) by United Video Company; WEHCO Advertising Inc., which sells advertising on WEHCO cable stations; WEHCO Equipment Corporation, which owns and operates WEHCO equipment and rolling stock; and WEHCO Commercial Printing Inc., which is a printing operation that supports WEHCO activities. WEHCO Media Inc. also owns 25 percent of the *Jacksonville Daily Progress* in Jacksonville, Texas.

KCMC Inc., which was originally Palmer's Texarkana radio—and later television—company, has become the holding company for the electronic side of the Camden News Publishing Company. KCMC Inc. owns Memphis Broadcasting Inc. and Memphis Television Company, which has applied for licenses in the Memphis area. Additionally, it owns television station KTAL-TV and KTAL-FM in Texarkana, Texas, and Shreveport, Louisiana, and KCMC radio, also located in Texarkana. Music Business Inc. is a music service company that provides background music for stores and offices. A vital part of KCMC Inc. is WEHCO Video Inc. This corporation owns franchise cable company operations in Camden, Arkansas (Cam-Tel Co.); Vicksburg Video Inc., in Vicksburg, Mississippi; Resort Cable Television, in Hot Springs, Arkansas; Hope Community TV in Hope, Arkansas; Prescott Video Inc., in Prescott, Arkansas; Longview Cable TV Company, in Longview, Texas; Kilgore Cable TV Company and Kilgore Video Inc., in Kilgore, Texas; Pine Bluff Cable TV, in Pine Bluff, Arkansas; East Arkansas Video Inc., in Forrest City, Arkansas; White County Video Inc., in Searcy, Arkansas; Tahlequah Cable TV Company, in Tahlequah, Oklahoma; Morrilton Video Inc., in Morrilton, Arkansas; Dardanelle Cable TV Inc., in Dardanelle, Arkansas; and Augusta Video Inc., in Augusta, Arkansas. Palmer grandson David Palmer Mooney owns Gilmer Cable Television Company Inc. in Gilmer, Texas, independently of WEHCO Video Inc. Hope Community TV Inc. in Hope, Arkansas, was, in 1980, also owned by WEHCO Video Inc.

Two other operations under Camden News Publishing Company are Marigayle Realty Company, a privately owned Hussman family real estate company, and Camden Radio Inc., which owns and operates KAMD (AM) and KWEH (FM) in Camden, Arkansas.[50]

In 1980 Walter Hussman Jr., treasurer of WEHCO Video Inc., stated that the company held government securities of $4,307,978 and had a $5 million line of credit available from the Bank of New York. He also stated that WEHCO Video Inc. and its "affiliated companies invested over $8,756,000 in newspapers, radio, television and cable television operations."[51]

In June 1986, WEHCO Media Inc. enlarged its Board of Directors by adding four new members: Philip S. Anderson, a Little Rock attorney and member of a firm that represents the *Arkansas Gazette*; Allen D. Lassiter of Dallas, Texas; Paul R. Smith, general manager of the *Arkansas Democrat*, who had also worked on the staff of the *Camden News* and the *El Dorado News-Times*; and Marilyn Augur of Dallas, Texas. Mrs. Augur is the sister of Walter Hussman Jr. and the granddaughter of Clyde Eber Palmer. Walter Hussman Jr. said that "these outside directors will add strength to our company's commitment to serve the best interests of our readers, subscribers, viewers, listeners and advertisers."[52]

WEHCO Media Inc. and Camden News Publishing Company continue to be largely owned and operated by the Hussman family and are as complex as any of Clyde Palmer's various companies and corporations. The organization has diversity and is well financed. The organizations of the various corporations support each of the others in a way that appears to be fiscally prudent and would have met, no doubt, with Clyde Palmer's complete approval. It has grown, however, far beyond the organizational structure that Palmer left at his death in 1957.

Conclusion

Nowhere in the corporate structure of the Camden News Publishing Company or WEHCO Media Inc. is the Palmer name mentioned. However, in the section on newspaper groups in the 1984 edition of *Editor & Publisher Yearbook*, a listing of the "Palmer Newspapers" appears. The listing gives, as

Palmer newspapers, the *Camden News*, the *El Dorado News-Times*, the *Hope Star*, the *Hot Springs Sentinel-Record*, the *Arkansas Democrat*, the *Magnolia Banner News*, the *Texarkana Gazette*, and the *Jacksonville* (Texas) *Daily Gazette*. Walter Hussman Sr. is listed as publisher of the Palmer newspapers.[53] Historically, more than just time separates Clyde Palmer's old *Texarkana Courier*, which he acquired in 1909 and the multimedia world of WEHCO Media Inc. Modern communication companies are far more complex, far more regulated, and require much more complex management systems than existed in 1909.

Clyde Eber Palmer was a pioneer in publishing technology, and the impact of the Palmer Circuit remains today in the WEHCO Media microwave transmission operations. Palmer's activity in Arkansas politics was important, and he was involved in several of the major issues of his time. Additionally, his political influence was significant, both publicly and behind the scenes. Almost every Arkansas newsman and woman who knew him called him a "great newspaperman," perhaps the highest compliment they could give him. He influenced so many of the newsmen and newswomen, so many of the editors and publishers that followed him, that his impact reached far beyond his own newspapers. In his own family, Palmer's influence has reached into the third generation and is still having an impact. The impression that he made on friends, employees, and enemies was strong and vivid. Sam Papert Jr., president of the Papert Company, one of the nation's leading newspaper advertising companies, located in Dallas, Texas, grew up in Clyde Palmer's Texarkana newspaper plant. Papert remembers Palmer fondly:

> He always had a twinkle in his eye and a smile on his face, whether he was mad or happy or sad, he always had kind of an all-knowing smile on his face! I never saw him mad. I'm sure he got mad, but I never saw him mad ... he might have been mad and just controlled it. I remember he always took a 15 or 20 minute nap after lunch and he had a piece of apple pie at lunch every day of his life. But he credited his longevity to his nap which he took every day. He could sit in a room with 15 or 20 other people and they would be yelling or screaming or talking and he'd just close his eyes and nap for 15 or 20 minutes. He could *just do it*![54]

Clyde Eber Palmer was a unique individual, who understood fully the nature of the publishing business and understood the communities in which he published his newspapers. On the twenty-fifth anniversary of his tenure as publisher of the *Hot Springs Sentinel-Record*, the comic artist Chic Young drew a special panel of the "Blondie" strip with Blondie and Dagwood congratulating Palmer on his publishing success. The strip was run by all the Palmer newspapers.[55] As John Q. Mahaffey said so often, "Clyde Palmer, he was something!"

Fordyce publisher emeritus W. R. Whitehead has written of Palmer:

In my opinion Clyde E. Palmer was the most outstanding and most successful newspaper publisher to have lived during the 150 year history of Arkansas. He was not just a publisher in title—he was an all around newspaper man, he knew it all. He knew the value of local news coverage, he understood circulation, was very strong on advertising promotions with the saying "you must make a profit if you are going to provide good news coverage, good production facilities, etc." In addition to the foregoing C. E. Palmer was business genius.[56]

This is high praise from one of the state's veteran newsmen and publishers. It does not speak to the methods of Clyde Palmer, but it does speak to the success of Palmer and his newspapers. There is no doubt that Clyde Eber Palmer was the premier Arkansas publisher during the first half of the twentieth century, one of the state's leading businessmen, and one of the most interesting of the state's citizens.

I N 2020, THE FATE of local newspapers was clearly in distress, as documented by Penny Abernathy, the UNC Hussman School of Journalism and Media's Knight Chair in Journalism and Digital Media Economics, in her groundbreaking US news-deserts research.

However, the family-owned media company begun in Texarkana, Arkansas, in the early 1900s by Clyde Eber (C. E.) Palmer, whose legacy is chronicled in this book, was continuing into its fourth generation.

These pictures introduce us to the career of newspaper entrepreneur C. E. Palmer. But they also convey his legacy of a resilient media company that has weathered the vagaries of newspaper competition, technological disruptions, significant advertising declines, and financial challenges facing the entire industry.

We are proud to be called the UNC Hussman School of Journalism and Media and to reflect the Hussman family's values and commitment to local journalism and democracy. Another chapter of this newspaper family will need to be written, but these pictures give a glimpse of what C. E. Palmer built as a newspaperman and as the patriarch of a family committed to keeping communities informed and our democracy robust.

A line drawing of C. E. Palmer, Walter Hussman Jr.'s grandfather,
who started the family's media company in the early 1900s with the purchase
of the *Texarkana Courier* in Arkansas. This book tells his story and the
beginning of a newspaper family legacy.

Publisher C. E. Palmer, age thirty-five, in the Texarkana office of the
Four States Press, October 24, 1912. According to his family, in 1909, Palmer took
a train from Fort Worth to Florida with his new bride. They got off the train
in Texarkana to spend the night, and while they were there, they decided
they liked the town and chose to stay. Palmer paid $900 for one of
several newspapers in Texarkana at the time, the *Texarkana
Courier*, which he renamed the *Four States Press*.

The Linotype machine was invented by the German American Ottmar Mergenthaler in the 1880s. Just as movable type had done centuries before, the Linotype revolutionized setting type by allowing someone at a keyboard to create lines of type instead of just individual letters. The Linotype had competition but became the most popular, and C. E. Palmer standardized using the Linotype machine at all of his newspapers in the 1940s.

Prior to 1913, news was transmitted around the U.S. by telegraph using Morse code operators. Teletype replaced the telegraph with type printed on pages that could then be taken to a Linotype operator to set type. Next came teletype machines with a keyboard that allow the operator to punch paper tape. The tape would then go to a Teletypesetter, pictured above. The keyboard sits atop the Linotype keyboard, and the paper tape sends a signal to depress the keys to set the type.

C. E. Palmer came up with the idea of taking news delivered to one of his Arkansas newspapers via perforated tape—and transmitting it by telephone lines to reperforator machines at his other newspapers in Arkansas. In 1940, he pioneered this type of circuit to allow one perforated tape with news to be used in multiple locations without re-keyboarding. It helped address the labor shortage during World War II. By the 1950s, the national wire services had adopted his method. Pictured above is the transmitting distributor that was used to send the perforated tape from one newspaper to the others.

Portrait of C. E. Palmer.

C. E. Palmer with his closest associates, his son-in-law and
business manager Walter Hussman to his left, and J.Q. Mahaffey,
his editor of the *Texarkana Gazette*, to his right.

C. E. Palmer pickets the picketers during a strike by the International Typographical Union at the *Texarkana Gazette*.

Portrait of C.E. Palmer.

A picture of Betty P. Hussman, C. E. Palmer's daughter and
Walter Hussman Jr.'s mother. She met Walter Hussman Sr. at the University of
Missouri's journalism school and with him nurtured a lasting family legacy
of Arkansas journalism.

Walter Hussman Sr. built a media company from the foundation C. E. Palmer
began in Arkansas. This undated picture shows a man at the top of his profession
when newspaper publishers were local leaders.

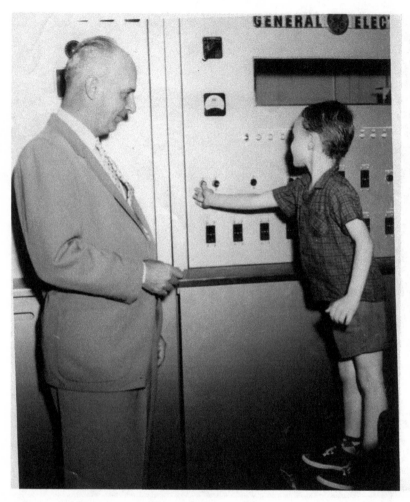

In 1952, Walter Hussman Sr. watches his son Walter Hussman Jr., age five, push the button to turn on the first television station in the Texarkana-Shreveport, Louisiana, market, KCMC-TV. In 1960, the station's call letters were changed to KTAL-TV after the station erected the second largest tower in the South, changed its affiliation from CBS to NBC, added studios in Shreveport, and became the first station in the market to broadcast in color. The Hussman family sold the TV station in 2000 to focus on newspapers and cable television.

Walter Hussman Jr. pictured at ten years old when he served as a page
in the Arkansas Senate.

Walter Hussman Jr. announces the purchase of the *Arkansas Democrat* on March 4, 1974. Marcus George, a previous owner of the newspaper, is pictured in the background. At the time, the afternoon *Arkansas Democrat* had slightly more than half the circulation of the morning rival, the *Arkansas Gazette*.

Walter Hussman Jr. announces the *Arkansas Democrat* will begin a
morning edition in January 1979. Later that year, the *Democrat* dropped
afternoon editions. In the following years, many other afternoon
newspapers switched to morning publication.

Donald W. Reynolds, left, and Walter Hussman Sr., right, at the University of Arkansas at Little Rock in the 1980s. The two men were roommates and college fraternity brothers at the University of Missouri. Both studied at the school of journalism there and were copublishers of *Yank* magazine in Paris during World War II.

Walter E. Hussman Jr. to head WEHCO

Walter E. Hussman Jr., publisher of the *Arkansas Democrat*, has been named president and chief executive officer of WEHCO Media Inc. and its subsidiaries. He succeeds his father, Walter Hussman, who has been elected WEHCO board chairman.

WEHCO Media Inc. owns and operates Little Rock Newspapers Inc., which publishes the *Arkansas Democrat*. WEHCO Media also owns companies which publish the *Texarkana Gazette, Hot Springs Sentinel Record, El Dorado News-Times, Camden News* and *Magnolia Banner News*. It also owns and operates 12 cable television companies with 56,000 subscribers in 15 cities in four states.

Other properties include two AM-FM radio stations and KTAL-TV, the NBC network affiliate for Texarkana and Shreveport, La.

Hussman Jr., 34, is a graduate of the Lawrenceville School, the University of North Carolina with a bachelor of arts in journalism and Columbia University where he received a master of business administration.

Walter E. Hussman Jr.

Walter Hussman

Since 1970, he has served as secretary-treasurer for WEHCO Media and affiliates, and since 1973, has been vice president and general manager of the company.

In 1974, he became president and publisher of the *Arkansas Democrat*, and in 1978, he became executive vice president of WEHCO Media Inc.

See WEHCO, Page 2F

A 1981 newspaper article announcing that Walter Hussman Jr., at age thirty-four, would become president and CEO of WEHCO Media Inc., while his father, Walter Hussman Sr., age 74, remained chairman.

Walter Hussman Jr. before doing an interview with President Ronald Reagan
in Little Rock, Arkansas, during Reagan's re-election campaign in 1984.

Walter Hussman Jr.'s three-year-old son Palmer is pictured in 1986 pressing the button to start the *Arkansas Democrat-Gazette*'s new 8-Unit double width offset lithography Goss Press, which allowed the newspaper to print color with greater clarity in all sections. Also pictured are Paul Smith, general manager, Hussman's wife Robena "Ben" Hussman, an unidentified banker who helped finance the press, and Larry Graham, circulation director. The *Gazette* would later install a similar offset lithography press.

This picture of Walter Hussman Jr. ran with a story in *Business Week* about the newspaper competition in Little Rock, Arkansas. The intense newspaper competition in Little Rock was not just an Arkansas story but a national one.

Walter Hussman Jr. celebrates with *Arkansas Democrat* employees on March 26, 1986, after a jury in federal court unanimously found the company not guilty in an antitrust suit brought by the competing *Arkansas Gazette* in 1984— just one moment in the dramatic Little Rock newspaper war.

Walter Hussman Jr. pictured after Gannett's announcement of the purchase
of the *Arkansas Gazette* on October 31, 1986.

Walter Hussman Jr. announces the purchase of the *Arkansas Gazette*
and the resulting merger of the *Arkansas Democrat* and the *Arkansas Gazette*
on October 18, 1991.

Walter Hussman Jr. pictured in 1997 at the announcement of the purchase of the *Chattanooga Free Press*. Pictured far left is Roy McDonald, the newspaper's publisher. To the right of Hussman is his wife, Robena ("Ben"). This purchase solidified Hussman's decision to strengthen the company's newspaper holdings.

Pictured are Walter Hussman Jr., his son Palmer Hussman, and Paul Greenberg, Pulitzer Prize winner and editorial page editor of the *Arkansas Democrat-Gazette* who was the keynote speaker at the *Post and Courier*'s 200th anniversary celebration in Charleston, South Carolina, in 2002.

Walter Hussman Jr. in 2009, the day he received the Distinguished Alumni Award from UNC, pictured with another of the day's recipients, professional soccer player and two-time Olympic gold medalist Mia Hamm.

Walter Hussman Jr. pictured with Erskine Bowles, the former White House Chief of Staff who introduced Hussman at his induction into the North Carolina Media and Journalism Hall of Fame in 2014. Bowles was president of the University of North Carolina System from 2005 to 2010 and has been friends with Hussman since both were in college at UNC.

Walter Hussman Jr. pictured with his children, from left to right, Olivia Hussman Ramsey, Palmer Hussman, and Eliza Hussman Gaines.

A picture of Walter Hussman Sr. later in life as he watched his son
both strengthen and grow the company.

Walter Hussman Jr. was named 2019 Arkansan of the Year by Easterseals Arkansas. The Hussman family is pictured at the event. Two of the three children are now part of the newspaper business—Palmer Hussman, far left, and Eliza Hussman Gaines, fourth from left.

In 2019, the *Arkansas Democrat-Gazette* celebrated the 200th anniversary of the *Arkansas Gazette*. At the celebration, former President Bill Clinton gave the keynote address. Clinton is pictured here with Water Hussman Jr.

Walter Hussman Jr. standing in front of iPads ready to be deployed to *Arkansas Democrat-Gazette* readers. In 2018, as part of the newspaper's ongoing digital transformation, the newspaper began providing subscribers with iPads so they could read a digital replica of the newspaper online, an innovative idea bringing the digital era to the newspaper world. In 2020, the newspaper ceased print home delivery except on Sundays.

Walter Hussman Jr. pictured with one of the iPads provided to subscribers.
This innovation mirrors the innovation of his grandfather, C. E. Palmer, who
created the first newspaper Teletypesetter network, and his father Walter Hussman
Sr., who created the first newspaper microwave facsimile network.

Walter Hussman Jr. is pictured with his daughter Eliza Gaines on November 21, 2019, at the event Eliza organized to celebrate the 200th anniversary of the *Arkansas Gazette*. In 2020, Eliza became the managing editor of the *Arkansas Democrat-Gazette*, following her father as the leader of the newspaper and paralleling the move to leadership that Walter experienced with his father.

Walter Hussman Jr. stands with UNC Hussman School of Journalism and Media
Dean Susan King, left, and his wife, Robena "Ben" Hussman, right, at the 2019
ceremony in which the Hussman family bequeathed a $25 million gift to the
school. The trio stand in front of the Hussman Core Values displayed in the
lobby of the school since the gift.

Chapter 1

1. "Publisher C. E. Palmer Dies," *Hot Springs Sentinel-Record*, July 5, 1957.

2. "Publisher C. E. Palmer Dies"; Ray Reid, "Romance of American Journalism: Stories of Success Won by Leaders of the Press," *Editor & Publisher* (August 1930), reprinted in *The Arkansas Publisher* (September 1930): 7–8.

3. "Publisher C. E. Palmer Dies."

4. "Publisher C. E. Palmer Dies."

5. Letter received from Edna Howe, October 1982.

6. Reid, "Romance of American Journalism," 7.

7. "Publisher C. E. Palmer Dies."

8. Reid, "Romance of American Journalism," 7.

9. "Publisher C. E. Palmer Dies."

10. Reid, "Romance of American Journalism," 7; J. Q. Mahaffey, "C. E. Palmer Kept His Reporters and Himself Busy," *Texarkana Gazette* (Texas), February 14, 1982.

11. Personal interview with David Palmer Mooney, October 2, 1986, Hot Springs, Arkansas.

12. Reid, "Romance of American Journalism," 7.

13. Mahaffey, "C. E. Palmer Kept His Reporters and Himself Busy."

14. "Publisher C. E. Palmer Dies."

15. Reid, "Romance of American Journalism," 7.

16. Personal interview with John Q. Mahaffey, December 4, 1984, Texarkana, Texas.

17. Personal interview with Betty Palmer Hussman, December 6, 1984, Little Rock, Arkansas.

18. Letter received from Gale Hussman Arnold, November 12, 1982.

19. Mahaffey, interview.

20. Robert W. Meriwether, A Chronicle of Arkansas Newspapers Published since 1922 and of the Arkansas Press Association, 1930–1972 (Little Rock: Arkansas Press Association, 1974), 75.

21. Fred W. Allsopp, *History of the Arkansas Press Association for a Hundred Years or More* (Little Rock: Parke-Harper Publishing Co., 1922), 253.

22. Palmer seemed to love to tell stories about his "beginnings" in the newspaper business, and the stories varied as he grew older and became less exact in real details but larger in scope.

23. All available historical accounts have been examined and attempts made to find the most correct dates for events.

24. "Publisher C. E. Palmer Dies." This story contains incorrect information, probably due to the haste with which it was written.

25. Clio Harper, *History of the Arkansas Press Association* (Little Rock: Parke-Harper Publishing Company, 1930), 69. Allsopp and Meriwether also confirm the date. See Allsopp, *History of the Arkansas Press Association*, 252; and Meriwether, *A Chronicle of Arkansas Newspapers*, 75.

26. Mahaffey, "C. E. Palmer Kept His Reporters and Himself Busy."

27. Harper, History of the Arkansas Press Association, 69.

28. "Clyde Eber Palmer," editorial, *Arkansas Gazette*, July 6, 1957.

29. Meriwether, *A Chronicle of Arkansas Newspapers*, iii.

30. Meriwether, *A Chronicle of Arkansas Newspapers*, 75.

31. Mahaffey, interview.

32. Meriwether, *A Chronicle of Arkansas Newspapers*, 75.

33. Letter received from Gale Hussman Arnold, November 12, 1982; "Funeral Sunday for C. E. Palmer," *Arkansas Gazette*, July 6, 1957.

34. Betty Palmer Hussman, interview.

35. Allsopp, History of the Arkansas Press Association, 614–15.

36. Mooney, interview.

37. Mooney, interview.

38. "Palmer-Mooney Vows," *Arkansas Gazette*, September 1937

39. Letter received from David Palmer Mooney, September 9, 1986.

40. Mooney, interview.

41. "Norphlet Paper Leased," *The Arkansas Publisher* (February 1933): 7.

42. Reid, "Romance of American Journalism," 8.

43. "Wellington Palmer Dead," *The Arkansas Publisher* (April 1934): 5.

44. Letter received from David Palmer Mooney, September 9, 1986.

45. Betty Palmer Hussman, interview.

46. Bessie Newsom Butler Allard, *Who is Who in Arkansas*, Vol. 1 (Little Rock: Allard House, 1959), 137.

47. "The Palmer Story," *The Texas Press Messenger*, n.d. Copy from the Arkansas Press Association.

48. Foy Lisenby, "Arkansas 1900–1930," in *Historical Report of the Secretary of State*, ed. Janice Wegener (Little Rock: Arkansas State Printing Office, 1978), 141.

49. Lisenby, "Arkansas 1900–1930," 143.

50. "Arkansas at 150: Celebrating Our Sesquicentennial," *Arkansas Times*, June 1986, 66.

51. Mahaffey, interview.

52. "Clyde E. Palmer Honored on 30th Anniversary as Publisher," *The Arkansas Publisher* (June 1939): 7.

53. Reid, "Romance of American Journalism," 8.

54. Reid, "Romance of American Journalism," 8.

55. Personal interview with Sam Papert Jr., September 17, 1986, Dallas, Texas.

56. Papert, interview.

57. Reid, "Romance of American Journalism," 7.

58. "Arkansas Dailies Group Hear Address by President Papert," *The Arkansas Publisher*(February 1931): 5.

59. Meriwether, *A Chronicle of Arkansas Newspapers*, 10.

60. Meriwether, *A Chronicle of Arkansas Newspapers*, 10, 75.

61. Meriwether, A Chronicle of Arkansas Newspapers, 75.

62. Allsopp, *History of the Arkansas Press Association*, 615.

63. Meriwether, *A Chronicle of Arkansas Newspapers*, 75.

64. Betty Palmer Hussman, interview.

65. Mahaffey, interview.

66. Betty Palmer Hussman, interview.

67. Betty Palmer Hussman, interview.

68. Mahaffey, interview.

69. Edwin Emery and Michael Emery, *The Press and America* (Englewood Cliffs, NJ: Prentice-Hall Inc., 1978), 431.

70. Meriwether, *A Chronicle of Arkansas Newspapers*, 109, 110.

71. Personal interview with Ray Kimball, March 25, 1983, DeQueen, Arkansas.

72. Mahaffey, interview.

73. Kimball, interview.

74. Betty Palmer Hussman, interview.

75. Meriwether, *A Chronicle of Arkansas Newspapers*, 10.

76. " El Dorado News-Times Purchased," *The Arkansas Publisher* (January 1928): 6.

77. Meriwether, *A Chronicle of Arkansas Newspapers*, 117–18.

78. Meriwether, A Chronicle of Arkansas Newspapers, 117–18.

79. Meriwether, *A Chronicle of Arkansas Newspapers*, 118, 120.

80. "Golden Fifty Service Award Program," The Arkansas Press Association, Little Rock, February 20, 1981.

81. "Golden Fifty Service Award Program," The Arkansas Press Association, Little Rock, February 20, 1981.

82. "Arkansas at 150," 78, 135.

83. Lisenby, "Arkansas 1900–1930," 152.

84. Boyce Drummond, "Arkansas: 1940–1954," in *Historical Report of the Secretary of State*, ed. Janice Wegener (Little Rock: State Printing Office, 1978), 180.

85. Betty Palmer Hussman, interview.

86. Mahaffey, interview.

87. Letter received from E. C. "Ernie" Deane, July 31, 1986.

88. "Jonesboro Paper Sold," *The Arkansas Publisher* (April 1930): 6.

89. Meriwether, *A Chronicle of Arkansas Newspapers*, 30.

90. "Arkansas Dailies Group Hear Address by President Papert."

91. "Busy Selling Arkansas to Advertising Space Buyers," *The Arkansas Publisher* (April 1931): 17.

92. "The Truth about Arkansas," *The Arkansas Publisher* (February 1931): 5.

93. "Arkansas Dailies to Promote State," *The Arkansas Publisher* (December 1931): 7.

94. "Busy Selling Arkansas to Advertising Space Buyers."

95. "Arkansas Dailies Group Hear Address by President Papert."

96. "Camden Paper Incorporated," *The Arkansas Publisher* (April 1929): 14.

97. "Camden Morning Times Sold," *The Arkansas Publisher* (February 1930): 12.

98. Meriwether, *A Chronicle of Arkansas Newspapers*, 86, 87.

99. "Palmer Buys Hot Springs Paper," *The Arkansas Publisher* (September 1929): 7.

100. Meriwether, *A Chronicle of Arkansas Newspapers*, 45.

101. Meriwether, *A Chronicle of Arkansas Newspapers*, 45.

102. Meriwether, *A Chronicle of Arkansas Newspapers*, 45.

103. "Spa Paper Has New Press," *The Arkansas Publisher* (February 1930): 7.

104. Meriwether, *A Chronicle of Arkansas Newspapers*, 49–50.

105. Kimball, interview.

106. Mahaffey, interview.

107. Mahaffey, "C. E. Palmer Kept His Reporters and Himself Busy."

108. Betty Palmer Hussman, interview.

109. Meriwether, *A Chronicle of Arkansas Newspapers*, 76.

110. "Stevick Injured," *The Arkansas Publisher* (December 1928): 12.

111. Kimball, interview.

112. Mahaffey, interview.

113. Betty Palmer Hussman, interview.

114. Meriwether, *A Chronicle of Arkansas Newspapers*, 76.

115. "Conway Dies," *The Arkansas Publisher* (June 1933): 6.

116. Letter received from Louis Graves, August 27, 1986.

117. Emery and Emery, *The Press and America*, 436.

118. Meriwether, *A Chronicle of Arkansas Newspapers*, 76. Count by actual tabulation from book.

119. Emery and Emery, *The Press and America*, 399.

120. Meriwether, *A Chronicle of Arkansas Newspapers*, 135.

121. George N. Gordon, *The Communications Revolution* (New York: Hastings House, 1979), 180–81.

Chapter 2

1. Ray Reid, "Romance of American Journalism: Stories of Success Won by Leaders of the Press," *Editor & Publisher* (August 1930), reprinted in *The Arkansas Publisher* (September 1930): 7.

2. "Texarkana Papers Promote State," *The Arkansas Publisher* (February 1934): 9.

3. "The Truth about Arkansas," *The Arkansas Publisher* (February 1934): 5. See additional notes in chapter 1.

4. Personal interview with John Q. Mahaffey, December 4, 1984, Texarkana, Texas.

5. Mahaffey, interview.

6. Personal interview with Edna Howe, October 30, 1982.

7. Letter received from Roy Bosson, June 9, 1986.

8. Letter received from George Brewer, June 16, 1986. Heilbron was a co-investor in El Dorado Newspapers Inc.

9. Letter received from John Q. Mahaffey, June 28, 1986.

10. Reid, "Romance of American Journalism," 8.

11. "Publisher's Daughter Wed," *The Arkansas Publisher* (February 1932): 8.

12. Letter received from Roy Bosson, June 19, 1986.

13. Personal interview with Betty Palmer Hussman, December 6, 1984, Little Rock, Arkansas.

14. Letter received from John Q. Mahaffey, June 9, 1986.

15. Bessie Newsom Butler Allard, *Who is Who in Arkansas*, Vol. 1 (Little Rock: Allard House, 1959), 137.

16. "Conway Dies," *The Arkansas Publisher* (June 1933): 6.

17. "Hussman, McGehee Named by Jaycees," *The Arkansas Publisher* (May 1940): 14.

18. "Hussman into Army," *The Arkansas Publisher* (July 1942): 12. Additional information from personal interview with John Wells, October 23, 1986.

19. "Capt. Hussman Goes to Army 'Yank,'" *The Arkansas Publisher* (December 1943): 1.

20. Wells, interview.

21. "Hussman Back on Job at Texarkana," *The Arkansas Publisher* (January 1945): 13.

22. "Two New Radio Stations Get FCC Nod; Others Pending," *The Arkansas Publisher* (December 1945): 13.

23. Mahaffey, interview.

24. Mahaffey, interview.

25. Letter received from George Brewer, June 8, 1986.

26. Letter received from George Brewer, June 16, 1986.

27. "Walter Hussman New President of TDNA," *The Arkansas Publisher* (July 1946): 8.

28. "Arkansas Newspaper Rates and Other Information," *The Arkansas Publisher* (May 1947): 31.

29. "Camden News Issues Mammoth Edition," *The Arkansas Publisher* (June 1948): 2.

30. Kimball, interview.

31. Mahaffey, interview.

32. Mahaffey, interview.

33. The Associated Press, *Reports and Discussions of the Continuing Study Committees of the Associated Press Managing Editors Association at Chicago, November 10–12, 1948* (New York: The Associated Press, 1949), 126.

34. The Associated Press, *Reports and Discussions of the Continuing Study Committees of the Associated Press Managing Editors Association at Fort Worth, November 2–5, 1949* (New York: The Associated Press, 1949), 33, 63, 150.

35. The Associated Press, *The APME Red Book* (New York: The Associated Press, 1951), 169.

36. The Associated Press, *The APME Red Book* (New York: The Associated Press, 1955), 23.

37. The Associated Press, *The APME Red Book* (1955), 159.

38. The Associated Press, *The APME Red Book* (1955), 147.

39. The Associated Press, *The APME Red Book* (1955), 211.

40. The Associated Press, *The APME Red Book* (1955), 217.

41. The Associated Press, *The APME Red Book* (1951), 239.

42. *Fifty and Feisty: APME 1933–1983* (St. Paul: The North Central Publishing Company, 1983), 27.

43. Robert W. Meriwether, *A Chronicle of Arkansas Newspapers Published since 1922 and of the Arkansas Press Association, 1930–1972* (Little Rock: Arkansas Press Association, 1974), 120.

44. Letter received from Ray Kimball, June 16, 1986.

45. Personal interview with Ray Kimball, March 25, 1983, DeQueen, Arkansas.

46. Meriwether, *A Chronicle of Arkansas Newspapers*, 113.

47. Meriwether, *A Chronicle of Arkansas Newspapers*, 113.

48. Meriwether, *A Chronicle of Arkansas Newspapers*, 15, 37, 52, 2, 26, 137.

49. Kimball, interview.

50. "Brown, Palmer, Kimball and Hussman Buy the *Stuttgart Daily Leader*," *The Arkansas Publisher* (March 1946): 8.

51. Kimball, interview.

52. Letter received from Ray Kimball, June 16, 1986.

53. Kimball, interview.

54. Kimball, interview.

55. Kimball, interview.

56. Meriwether, *A Chronicle of Arkansas Newspapers*, 3.

57. Letter received from Ernie Deane, July 31, 1986.

58. Kimball, interview.

59. Meriwether, *A Chronicle of Arkansas Newspapers*, 96.

60. Kimball, interview.

61. Letter received from J. William Fulbright, April 24, 1986.

62. Letter received from George Brewer, June 8, 1986.

63. Meriwether, *A Chronicle of Arkansas Newspapers*, 2.

64. Meriwether, *A Chronicle of Arkansas Newspapers*, 87.

65. Letter received from George Brewer, June 16, 1986.

66. Letter received from George Brewer, July 29, 1986. In an additional letter from Robert S. McCord, dated August 28, 1986, McCord says that he cannot provide any additional information.

67. Meriwether, *A Chronicle of Arkansas Newspapers*, 49, 27, 119.

68. Letter received from Sam Papert Jr., August 19, 1986.

69. Mahaffey, interview.

70. Letter received from Sam Papert Jr., August 19, 1986.

71. Letter received from Ray Kimball, June 16, 1986.

72. Letter received from Louis Graves, August 27, 1986.

73. Letter from Clyde Eber Palmer to Vern Sanford, January 10, 1955.

74. Letter from Clyde Eber Palmer to Vern Sanford, May 23, 1955.

75. Letter received from David Palmer Mooney, September 9, 1986. Mooney notes that the current owners of the Mt. Pleasant papers are named Palmer but are no relation to the Arkansas Palmer family.

76. "Arkansas Newspaper Rates and Other Information," *The Arkansas Publisher* (May 1947): 25–35.

77. Reid, "Romance of American Journalism," 9.

78. Mahaffey, interview.

79. "All Over Arkansas...," *The Arkansas Publisher* (March 1940): 3.

80. "Round the State: Newspapers and Newspaper Folk," *The Arkansas Publisher* (October 1948): 5.

81. "Palmer Honored by Texarkana Jaycees," *The Arkansas Publisher* (May 1940): 4.

82. Mahaffey, interview.

83. "Texarkana Sports Editor Awarded Distinguished Key," *The Arkansas Publisher* (February 1947): 5.

84. Mahaffey, interview.

85. "Arkansas–Texas Meet Agenda Set," *The Arkansas Publisher* (May 1928): 8.

86. Letter received from Lyndell Williams, August 4, 1986.

87. "Honored at TDPA Convention," *The Arkansas Publisher* (March 1956): 5.

88. "N.E.A. Members," *The Arkansas Publisher* (May 1930): 6.

89. "Named on Board," *The Arkansas Publisher* (June 1939): 10.

90. "Eight Arkansas Papers Represented at ANPA Meeting," *The Arkansas Publisher* (May 1952): 11.

91. "Clyde E. Palmer," editorial, *Arkansas Democrat*, July 7, 1957.

92. Howe, interview.

93. Kimball, interview.

94. *The Arkansas Publisher* is the official monthly publication of the Arkansas Press Association, distributed to all APA members.

95. "APA Agenda," *The Arkansas Publisher* (February 1932): 5.

96. "Palmer to Present World's Fair Talk," *The Arkansas Publisher* (June 1938): 1.

97. "Convention Speakers Say...," *The Arkansas Publisher* (June 1939): 11.

98. "Moses Given APA Life Membership, Governor Outlines Tax Program," *The Arkansas Publisher* (January 1957): 8.

99. Letter received from W. R. Whitehead, September 5, 1986.

100. "Press Association Convention June 20–21," *The Arkansas Publisher* (June 1941): 1.

101. Letter received from Louis Graves, August 27, 1986.

102. Mahaffey, interview.

103. "Publisher C. E. Palmer Dies," *Hot Springs Sentinel-Record*, July 5, 1957.

104. The Associated Press, *The APME Red Book* (New York: The Associated Press, 1949), 1.

105. J. Q. Mahaffey, "C. E. Palmer Kept His Reporters and Himself Busy," *Texarkana Gazette*, February 14, 1982.

106. The Associated Press, *The APME Red Book* (1949), 33.

107. The Associated Press, *The APME Red Book* (1949), 187.

108. The Associated Press, *The APME Red Book* (1949), 208, 190.

109. J. Q. Mahaffey, "Publisher Was a Great Newspaperman," *Arkansas Democrat*, February 26, 1982.

110. "AP Editors Meet," *The Arkansas Publisher* (June 1931): 15.

111. "Mahaffey Elected Head of A.P. Group," *The Arkansas Publisher* (July 1944): 13.

112. "State Associated Press Group Convenes in Hot Springs," *The Arkansas Publisher* (May 1948): 8.

113. Letter received by John Q. Mahaffey from Roy Bosson, January 27, 1986.

114. Letter received from Clement Brossier, September 4, 1986.

115. Letter received from Clement Brossier, September 4, 1986.

116. Allard, *Who is Who in Arkansas*, 189.

117. "Clyde E. Palmer Dead," *New York Times*, July 5, 1957.

118. "C. E. Palmer Establishes $100,000 Peace Foundation," *The Arkansas Publisher* (October 1945): 13.

119. "C. E. Palmer Establishes $100,000 Peace Foundation."

120. "C. E. Palmer Establishes $100,000 Peace Foundation."

121. "C. E. Palmer Establishes $100,000 Peace Foundation."

122. "Texas Journalist Wins Palmer 'Golden Rule' Award," *The Arkansas Publisher* (January 1947): 11.

123. "The Palmer Story," *The Arkansas Publisher*, reprinted from the *Texas Press Messenger*, from the Arkansas Press Association, n.d.

124. "The Palmer Story."

125. Betty Palmer Hussman, interview.

126. Betty Palmer Hussman, interview.

127. Letter received from Sam Papert Jr., August 19, 1986.

128. Kimball, interview.

129. Mahaffey, interview.

130. Letter received from John Q. Mahaffey, May 24, 1986.

131. Letter received from George Brewer, June 8, 1986.

132. Letter received from Louis Graves, August 27, 1986.

133. "Clyde E. Palmer," editorial, *Arkansas Democrat*, July 7, 1957.

134. "Clyde E. Palmer," editorial, *Pine Bluff Commercial*, July 7, 1957.

135. Mahaffey, interview .

136. Poindexter, 37, 47, 52.

137. Poindexter, 64.

138. Poindexter, 79.

139. Poindexter, 117.

140. Poindexter, 82.

141. Poindexter, 97, 101.

142. Poindexter, 268.

143. Poindexter, 268.

144. Letter received from John Q. Mahaffey, June 9, 1986.

145. Poindexter, 268.

146. Mahaffey, interview.

147. Poindexter, 118, 122.

148. Allard, *Who is Who in Arkansas*, 137.

149. Poindexter, 121.

150. "Roosevelt in Hot Springs," *The Arkansas Publisher* (January 1939): 7.

151. Poindexter, 122.

152. Poindexter, 123. Barton and his group would finally purchase several radio stations, including KARK, which later became KARK television.

153. Kimball, interview.

154. "C. E. Palmer Interested in Nine Arkansas Dailies," *The Arkansas Publisher* (March 1951): 9.

155. Betty Palmer Hussman, interview.

156. Mahaffey, interview.

157. Kimball, interview.

158. Letter received from Louis Graves, August 27, 1986.

159. Poindexter, 267, 268.

160. Betty Palmer Hussman, interview.

161. "Two New Radio Stations Get FCC Nod; Others Pending," *The Arkansas Publisher* (December 1945): 13.

162. Poindexter, 310. Meyers was often listed as being part of Palmer's radio enterprises and was involved with a number of Palmer/Hussman stations. Mahaffey recalls Meyers as being "one of the most bigoted men I have ever known . . . he hated Jews and Negros with a vengeance.. . . I often wondered why CEP kept him on." Letter received from John Q. Mahaffey, July 28, 1986.

163. "C. E. Palmer Interested in Nine Arkansas Dailies," 9.

164. Poindexter, 310.

165. Poindexter, 346, 305.

166. "Hussman Purchases Interest in Spa Radio Station," *The Arkansas Publisher* (November 1951): 5.

167. Ted Morgan, *FDR: A Biography* (New York: Simon and Schuster, 1985), 460.

168. Morgan, *FDR*, 461, 743.

169. Morgan, *FDR*, 460.

170. Letter received from David Palmer Mooney, September 9, 1986.

171. Personal interview with David Palmer Mooney, October 2, 1986, Hot Springs, Arkansas.

172. Allard, *Who is Who in Arkansas*, 138.

173. Letter received from George Brewer, July 29, 1986.

174. "C. E. Palmer," *The Arkansas Publisher* (July 1957): 3.

175. "Funeral Sunday for C. E. Palmer," *Arkansas Gazette*, July 6, 1957.

176. "C. E. Palmer," *The Arkansas Publisher*.

Chapter 3

1. Lawrence J. Bracken, "The Palmer Circuit: Hi-Tech in the '40s," *The Journal of Arkansas Journalism Studies*, 2 (Fall, 1984), 7–11.

2. Letter received from W. R. Whitehead, September 5, 1986.

3. Personal interview with Edna Howe, October 30, 1982

4. Boyce Drummond, "Arkansas 1940–1954," in *Historical Report of the Secretary of State*, ed. Janice Wegener (Little Rock: State Printing Office, 1978), p. 175.

5. Ibid.

6. "McGehee Times Suspends Due to Labor Shortage," *The Arkansas Publisher* (December 1943): 1.

7. "Women Run Shop of the Chicot Spectator," *The Arkansas Publisher* (July 1944): 13.

8. "Mrs. Aydelott Is New Editor of Monroe Co. Sun," *The Arkansas Publisher* (January 1945): 13.

9. "Abbreviated Paper," *The Arkansas Publisher* (July 1942): 12.

10. "Sell Sales Books," *The Arkansas Publisher* (November 1943): 4.

11. "Call Upon This Reserve Force," *The Arkansas Publisher* (November 1943): 4

12. "Government Entitled to Cooperation—Brown," *The Arkansas Publisher* (July 1942): 12.

13. Ibid.

14. Alex H. Washburn, "Five Arkansas Dailies Form First Teletype Circuit," *Editor & Publisher*, September 12, 1942, p. 34

15. George N. Gordon, *The Communications Revolution* (New York: Hastings House, 1979), p. 69.

16. El Dorado Papers Get New Machines," *The Arkansas Publisher* (June 1939): 217.

17. "New Machine Installed," *The Arkansas Publisher* (June 1939): 6.

18. Personal interview with Ray Kimball, March 25, 1983.

19. Edwin Emery and Michael Emery, *The Press and America* (Englewood Cliffs, NJ: Prentice-Hall, 1978), p. 300.

20. "AP Install Automatic Telegraph Printers," *The Arkansas Publisher* (January 1928): 4.

21. "The History of Telegraph Typesetting," *The Hope Star*, October 6, 1942, p. 1. This article, written by Alex Washburn, maybe not be the best source possible, but it does present a historical overview of the technology at the time.

22. Ibid.

23. Ibid.

24. Ibid.

25. Ibid.

26. Alex Washburn, "Five Arkansas Dailies Form First Teletypesetter Circuit," p. 34.

27. Ibid.

28. Ibid.

29. "Leased Wire Transmitting Type First Inaugurated by Group Arkansas Papers," *The Arkansas Publisher* (October 1942): 3.

30. Kimball, interview.

31. Ibid.

32. Letter received from Ray Kimball, June 16, 1986.

33. Letter received from Thomas A. Prentice, June 24, 1986.

34. Alex Washburn, "Five Arkansas Dailies Form First Teletypesetter Circuit," p. 34.

35. Kimball, interview.

36. Ibid.

37. Ibid.

38. Alex Washburn, "Five Arkansas Dailies Form First Teletypesetter Circuit," p. 34.

39. Ibid.

40. Alex Washburn, "Four Southwest Arkansas Dailies Set Up Automatic Circuit, First in Nation," *The Hope Star*, October 6, 1942, p. 6.

41. Ibid.

42. Kimball, interview.

43. Alex Washburn, "Five Arkansas Dailies," op cit.

44. Now that press service teletypes have been replaced by computer modems, much of the technology of the old teletypes is disappearing. Kimball described the "telephone pony" in an interview: "We were using a telephone pony at that time. That was where they [UP] would call maybe 30 minutes in the morning and 15 minutes in the afternoon and dictate news over the telephone to each of these newspapers from the Little Rock bureau. Of course, that was a rather inexpensive way of getting the news, but we didn't get very much. . . they had telegraph service on which they would send just a few words, say maybe 500, just a paragraph of two,

like some radio reports now, for the small daily newspapers. The telephone pony was the service we were getting at Magnolia, Camden, Hope and El Dorado and several other points in Arkansas at the time" (Kimball, interview).

45. Ibid.

46. Ibid.

47. Ibid.

48. Ibid.

49. Alex Washburn, photo caption, *The Hope Star*, October 6, 1942, p. 6.

50. Ibid.

51. Alex Washburn, "Four Southwest Arkansas Dailies," p. 6.

52. Ibid.

53. Ibid.

54. Ibid.

55. Ibid.

56. Ibid.

57. Ibid.

58. Ibid.

59. Kimball, interview.

60. Alex Washburn, "Five Arkansas Dailies," p. 34.

61. Ibid.

62. Ibid.

63. Alex Washburn, "Four Southwest Arkansas Dailies," p. 6.

64. Ibid.

65. Ibid.

66. Ibid.

67. Letter received from James H. Hale, August 6, 1986.

68. Alex Washburn, "Five Arkansas Dailies," p. 34.

69. Kimball, interview.

70. "Teletypesetter Circuit Now 10 Years Old," *The Arkansas Publisher* (July 1952): 9.

71. "Russelville C-D Joins Palmer Teletype Circuit," *The Arkansas Publisher* (November 1951): 6.

72. "Daily Citizen Gets Teletypesetter Transmission," *The Arkansas Publisher* (March 1947): 9.

73. "Fifth Anniversary of Southwest Arkansas Teletypesetter Circuit," *The Arkansas Publisher* (July 1947): 9.

74. "Hope Daily Star Installs Another Teletypesetter," *The Arkansas Publisher* (August 1946): 7.

75. "Teletypesetter Circuit Now 10 Years Old," *The Arkansas Publisher* (July 1952): 8.

76. Alex Washburn, "Four Southwest Arkansas Dailies," p. 6.

77. Ibid.

78. Ibid.

79. Kimball, interview.

80. Ibid.

81. Ibid.

82. Ibid.

83. "Ray Kimball Installs Teletypesetter in Clinton (Okla.) News," *The Arkansas Publisher* (July 1947): 10.

84. Kimball, interview.

85. "Inland Press Session Hears Kimball Speech," *The Arkansas Publisher* (March 1949): 9.

86. Kimball, interview.

87. Ibid.

88. Ibid.

89. "Union Pressmen Return to Work," *The Arkansas Publisher* (May 1941): 6.

90. "Comparing Force in Hot Springs Strike," *The Arkansas Publisher* (August 1941): 6.

91. Ibid.

92. "Compositor Strike in Texarkana Ended," *The Arkansas Publisher* (October 1941): 10

93. Donald Holley, "Arkansas in the Great Depression," *Historical Report of the Secretary of State*, ed. Janice Wegener (Little Rock: State Printing Office, 1978), p. 169.

94. Ibid., p. 168.

95. Ibid., p. 169.

96. Ibid., p. 149.

97. "Farm tenancy Commission Appointed," *Arkansas Gazette*, August 27, 1936, p. 1.

98. Ibid.

99. "Governors Advised of Tenancy Study," *Arkansas Gazette*, Augus 28, 1936, p. 5.

100. "Farm Tenancy Group Will Meet Today," *Arkansas Gazette*, September 21, 1936, p. 1.

101. "Commission Begins Study of Tenancy," *Arkansas Gazette*, September 22, 1936, p. 1.

102. Roosevelt Asks Plan to Solve Tenancy Issue," *Arkansas Gazette*, September 22, 1936, p. 1

103. Michael H. Mehlman, "The Resettlement Administration and the Problems of Tenant Farmers in Arkansas, 1935-1936" (PhD diss., New York University, October 1970), p. 235.

104. "Palmer Pleased with New Land Act," *The Arkansas Publisher* (April 1939): 3.

105. Ibid.

106. Mehlman, p. 232.

107. Holley, p. 170.

108. "Palmer Renamed," *The Arkansas Publisher* (December 1939): 3.

109. Personal interview with Ray Kimball, March 25, 1983, DeQueen, Arkansas.

110. "Printers Walk Out on Jobs at Palmer Papers," *The Arkansas Publisher* (July 1950): 8.

111. "Printers Walk Out on Jobs at Palmer Papers," 8.

112. "Texarkana ITU Paper Passes First Month's Publication," *The Arkansas Publisher* (August 1951): 3.

113. "Texarkana ITU Paper Passes First Month's Publication," 3.

114. "Texarkana ITU Paper Passes First Month's Publication," 3.

115. "Texarkana Tabloid Closes Doors April 23," *The Arkansas Publisher* (April 1954): 5.

116. "Printers Walk Out on Jobs at Palmer Papers," 8.

117. Letter received from Roy Bosson, June 19, 1986.

118. Letter received from James H. Hale, August 6, 1986.

119. Letter received from Roy Bosson, June 19, 1986.

120. Letter received from Roy Bosson, June 19, 1986.

121. Letter received from Roy Bosson, June 19, 1986.

122. Letter received from Roy Bosson, June 19, 1986.

123. Letter received from John Q. Mahaffey, June 9, 1986.

124. Letter received from John Q. Mahaffey, June 9, 1986.

125. Letter received from James H. Hale, August 6, 1986.

126. Personal interview with John Q. Mahaffey, December 4, 1984, Texarkana, Texas.

127. Mahaffey, interview.

128. Letter received from S. W. Papert Jr., August 19, 1986.

129. Letter received from James H. Hale, August 6, 1986.

130. Letter received from James H. Hale, August 6, 1986.

131. Letter received from Louis Graves, August 27, 1986.

132. Kimball, interview.

133. The Associated Press, *The APME Redbook* (New York: The Associated Press, 1951), 195.

134. Letter received from Edward H. Harte, June 6, 1986.

135. Letter received from Jenny Sakellariou, August 4, 1986.

136. Kimball, interview.

137. Kimball, interview.

138. Kimball, interview.

139. Edwin Emery and Michael Emery, *The Press and America* (Englewood Cliffs, NJ: Prentice-Hall Inc., 1978), 304.

140. Letter received from Louis Graves, August 27, 1986.

141. The Associated Press, *The APME Redbook* (1951), 127.

142. The Associated Press, *The APME Redbook* (1951), 127.

143. The Associated Press, *The APME Redbook* (1951), 196.

144. The Associated Press, *The APME Redbook* (1951), 198.

145. The Associated Press, *The APME Redbook* (1951), 199.

146. Letter received from Roy Bosson, June 19, 1986.

147. Letter received from Roy Bosson, June 19, 1986.

148. "AP to Convert to Teletypesetter Circuit," *The Arkansas Publisher* (August 1951): 3.

149. "Typesetter Circuit Now 10 Years Old," *The Arkansas Publisher* (July 1952): 8.

150. The Associated Press, *The APME Redbook* (New York: The Associated Press, 1955), 114.

151. The Associated Press, *The APME Redbook* (1955), 126.

152. The Associated Press, *The APME Redbook* (1955), 138.

153. The Associated Press, *The APME Redbook* (1955), 139.

154. The Associated Press, *The APME Redbook* (New York: The Associated Press, 1956), 12.

155. The Associated Press, *The APME Redbook* (1956), 126.

156. Letter received from Roy Bosson, June 9, 1986.

157. Personal interview with Mr. and Mrs. Walter Hussman, December 6, 1984.

158. "Clyde E. Palmer Dead," *New York Times*, July 5, 1957.

159. Kimball, interview.

160. Kimball, interview.

161. Kimball, interview.

162. Kimball, interview.

163. Alex Washburn, "Five Arkansas Dailies," 34.

164. "Funeral Services for C. E. Palmer at Texarkana Today," *Hot Springs Sentinel-Record*, July 6, 1957.

Chapter 4

1. Personal interview with John Q. Mahaffey, December 4, 1984; personal interview with Ray Kimball, March 25, 1983.

2. Personal interview with John Wells, October 23, 1986.

3. "Arkansas Newspapers Rates and Other Information," *The Arkansas Publisher* (May 1947): 23–35. The total for the *Arkansas Gazette* was 27 percent.

4. Fred W. Allsopp, *History of the Arkansas Press Association for a Hundred Years or More* (Little Rock: Parke-Harper Publishing Co., 1922), 614–15, 253.

5. Fred W. Allsopp, *The* Arkansas Gazette*: A History* (Little Rock: The *Arkansas Gazette*, 1980), 8. Palmer may well have agreed with populist Arkansas Governor Jeff Davis, who, speaking around the turn of the century, called the *Gazette* "an old red harlot" and said that he would rather "be caught with a dead buzzard under my arms or a dead polecat" than the *Arkansas Gazette* (quoted in this same work).

6. Allsopp, *History of the Arkansas Press Association*, 615.

7. Allsopp, *History of the Arkansas Press Association*, 253. The photograph of Palmer, who would have been about forty-five years old at the time of publication of Allsopp's book, shows a serious, young-looking man, wearing steel-rimmed glasses. His hair is short, parted just slightly off-center, and there is just the barest hint of a smile on his face. His eyes are intent, staring right at the camera lens.

8. Allsopp, *History of the Arkansas Press Association*, 251.

9. Clio Harper, *History of the Arkansas Press Association* (Little Rock: Parke-Harper Publishing Co., 1930), 69. Harper also included a photograph of Palmer in his listing. In this photograph Palmer is older (he would have been fifty-four in 1930) and more distinguished looking. Gone were the wire-rimmed glasses, replaced by a pair with larger, dark rims. His hair was short, and his noted half-smile was still present. He wore a plaid business suit and a bow tie for the sitting.

10. Robert W. Meriwether, *A Chronicle of Arkansas Newspapers Published since 1922 and of the Arkansas Press Association, 1930–1972* (Little Rock: Arkansas Press Association, 1974).

11. *The Arkansas Publisher* (September 1930): 1.

12. Ray Reid, "Romances of American Journalism: Stories of Success Won by Leaders of the Press," *The Arkansas Publisher* (September 1930): 7–9, reprinted from *Editor & Publisher* (August 1930).

13. "Joint Arkansas-Texas Meet Set," *The Arkansas Publisher* (January 1928): 5.

14. *The Arkansas Publisher* (July 1957): 1.

15. Letter from Roy Bosson to John Q. Mahaffey, January 27, 1986.

16. Letter received from George Brewer, June 8, 1986.

17. Letter received from John Q. Mahaffey, June 9, 1986.

18. Letter received from Roy Bosson, June 9, 1986.

19. Letter received from George Brewer, June 8, 1986.

20. Letter received from Roy Bosson, June 9, 1986.

21. Letter received from Louis Graves, August 27, 1986.

22. Letter received from George Brewer, June 8, 1986.

23. Kimball, interview.

24. Personal interview with Edna Howe, October 30, 1982.

25. Howe, interview. Howe also recalled: "He [Palmer] was the boss! Johnny Holder was the head of the advertising department and he would visit with Johnny about those kinds of things . . . in the editorial department Bob Dean took care of everything. Back in the back Frank Hampton was the manager of the mechanical department. The heads of the departments would meet with Mr. Palmer about personnel things."

26. Mahaffey, interview.

27. J. Q. Mahaffey, "80 No Cause for Worry: July Keep Double Shuffling On," *Texarkana Gazette*, January 19, 1986.

28. J. Q. Mahaffey, "C. E. Palmer Kept His Reporters and Himself Busy," *Texarkana Gazette*, February 14, 1982.

29. Mahaffey, "C. E. Palmer Kept His Reporters and Himself Busy."

30. Mahaffey, "C. E. Palmer Kept His Reporters and Himself Busy."

31. Letter received from John Q. Mahaffey, June 9, 1986.

32. Letter received from Roy Bosson to John Q. Mahaffey, January 27, 1986.

33. Letter from Roy Bosson to John Q. Mahaffey, January 27, 1986.

34. Letter received from George Brewer, June 8, 1986.

35. Mahaffey, interview.

36. Mahaffey, "80 No Cause for Worry."

37. Letter received from Louis Graves, August 27, 1986.

38. Letter received from George Brewer, June 8, 1986.

39. Letter received from George Brewer, June 16, 1986.

40. Mahaffey, interview.

41. Letter received from George Brewer, June 8, 1986.

42. Letter received from W. R. Whitehead, September 5, 1986.

43. Letter received from W. R. Whitehead, September 5, 1986.

44. Letter received from Louis Graves, August 27, 1986.

45. Mahaffey, "80 No Cause for Worry."

46. The Associated Press, *The APME Redbook* (New York: The Associated Press, 1955), 211.

47. Wells, interview.

48. Letter received from Louis Graves, June 27, 1986.

49. Letter received from George Brewer, June 8, 1986.

50. Mahaffey, interview.

51. Letter received from James H. Hale, August 6, 1986.

52. Letter received from George Brewer, June 8, 1986.

53. Howe, interview.

54. Letter received from Roy Bosson, June 9, 1986.

55. Mahaffey, interview.

56. "Hot Springs Leaders Pay Tribute to Palmer," *Hot Springs Sentinel-Record,* July 6, 1957.

57. Letter received from Sam Papert Jr., August 6, 1986.

58. Letter received from Roy Bosson, June 9, 1986. Roy Bosson, George Brewer, John Q. Mahaffey, and other former employees all used the term "Palmer Alumnus" to describe those who had previously worked for Palmer. It became a large group, and several of the members have suggested a "reunion."

59. Letter received from George Brewer, June 8, 1986. Brewer did not know Palmer when he left Texarkana for the El Dorado paper, but he knew of him. Brewer's father, who was in the department store business, knew Palmer and personally attended to Mrs. Palmer when she shopped in his store.

60. Letter received from George Brewer, June 8, 1986.

61. Letter received from George Brewer, June 8, 1986.

62. Letter from George Brewer to John Q. Mahaffey, January 27, 1986.

63. Letter from George Brewer to John Q. Mahaffey, January 27, 1986.

64. Letter from George Brewer to John Q. Mahaffey, January 27, 1986.

65. Letter received from George Brewer, June 8, 1986.

66. Letter from George Brewer to John Q. Mahaffey, January 27, 1986.

67. Letter from George Brewer to John Q. Mahaffey, January 27, 1986. Photographs that Brewer took of Palmer in Paris show him as an aging man, resplendent in his uniform, grinning happily, as he enjoyed the sights of the city.

68. Letter received from George Brewer, June 8, 1986.

69. Letter from George Brewer to John Q. Mahaffey, January 17, 1986.

70. Letter received from George Brewer, June 8, 1986.

71. Letter received from George Brewer, June 8, 1986.

72. "C. E. Palmer Returns from Overseas Trip," *The Arkansas Publisher* (1945): 4.

73. "The Family Circle," *The Arkansas Publisher* (January 1946): 4.

74. "Former Employee Sends C. E. Palmer War Souvenir," *The Arkansas Publisher* (January 1946): 2.

75. "The Family Circle," 4.

76. "The Family Circle," 4.

77. Howe, interview.

78. Mahaffey, interview.

79. Mahaffey, interview. Palmer frequently wore loud Hawaiian shirts. A photo in *The Arkansas Publisher* in July 1951 shows Palmer sitting in the lobby of the Arlington Hotel in Hot Springs with APA president C. A. Verbeck, *Memphis Press-Scimitar* editor Edward J. Meeman, and several other publishers, and he is wearing such a shirt. A number of his associates commented on his choice of shirts.

80. Letter received from Louis Graves, August 27, 1986.

81. Wells, interview.

82. "Palmer Takes Trip to Colombia, S.A.," *The Arkansas Publisher* (August 1953): 2.

83. "Publisher C. E. Palmer Dies," *Hot Springs Sentinel-Record*, July 5, 1957.

84. Howe, interview. Bob Dean was the long-time editor of Palmer's Hot Springs newspapers. He began his newspaper career as a sportswriter for the Hot Springs newspapers, then moved to Little Rock in 1933 and worked for the *Arkansas Democrat*. In the early 1940s, he returned to Hot Springs as night editor and then managing editor. In 1957 he became executive editor. He retired from the Palmer Group on January 1, 1969. Information of Bob Dean is from Louise Brown, "R. S. Brown," *The Record, Garland County Historical Society*, no. 18 (1980): 178–79.

85. "C. E. Palmer," editorial, *Hot Springs Sentinel-Record*, July 6, 1957.

86. Mahaffey, interview.

87. Clyde Eber Palmer, *Europe Today: A Collection of Overseas News Articles Reprinted from the* Hot Springs New Era *and* Sentinel-Record (Hot Springs, Arkansas: *Hot Springs Sentinel-Record*, 1952), i.

88. Palmer, *Europe Today*, 5.

89. Palmer, *Europe Today*, 7.

90. Palmer, *Europe Today*, 8, 9.

91. Palmer, *Europe Today*, 9.

92. Palmer, *Europe Today*, 10, 11.

93. Palmer, *Europe Today*, 11, 12, 13.

94. Palmer, *Europe Today*, 15, 16.

95. Palmer, *Europe Today*, 17.

96. Palmer, *Europe Today*, 17, 18.

97. Palmer, *Europe Today*, 19.

98. Palmer, *Europe Today*, 20.

99. Palmer, *Europe Today*, 21–22.

100. "Arkansas Newsman Tells of Recent European Visit," *The Arkansas Publisher* (December 1952): 8–10.

101. Mahaffey, interview.

102. Wells, interview.

103. "Publisher C. E. Palmer Dies," *Hot Springs Sentinel-Record*.

104. Janice Wegener, ed., *Historical Report of the Secretary of State, Arkansas 1978*, Vol. 1 (Little Rock: State Printing Office, 1978), 110.

105. Mahaffey, interview.

106. Wegener, *Historical Report of the Secretary of State*, 102.

107. Letter received from J. W. Fulbright, April 24, 1986.

108. Wegener, *Historical Report of the Secretary of State*, 100f.

109. "Funeral Services for C. E. Palmer at Texarkana Today," *Hot Springs Sentinel-Record*, July 6, 1957.

110. Kimball, interview.

111. Mahaffey, interview.

112. Letter from C. E. Palmer to Vern Stanford, September 30, 1954.

113. Mahaffey, interview.

114. Mahaffey, interview.

115. "President Will Have Best Time at Hot Springs," *Arkansas Gazette*, June 10, 1936.

116. "Roosevelt in Hot Springs," *The Arkansas Publisher* (January 1939): 7.

117. Wells, interview.

118. "May Continue Exhibit," *The Arkansas Publisher* (December 1939): 7.

119. "Palmer to Present World's Fair Talk," *The Arkansas Publisher* (June 1938): 1.

120. "All Over Arkansas," *The Arkansas Publisher* (March 1940): 3.

121. "C. E. Palmer in New York, Capital," *The Arkansas Publisher* (November 1938): 9.

122. "C. E. Palmer on Fair Committee," *The Arkansas Publisher* (May 1939): 3.

123. Donald Holley, "Arkansas in the Great Depression," in *Historical Report of the Secretary of State*, Vol. 3, ed. Janice Wegener (Little Rock: State Printing Office, 1978), 173.

124. "Clyde E. Palmer Honored on 30th Anniversary as Publisher," *The Arkansas Publisher* (June 1939): 7.

125. "Clyde E. Palmer Honored on 30th Anniversary as Publisher," 7.

126. "C. E. Palmer Quits Commission Posts," *The Arkansas Publisher* (June 1940): 2.

127. Wells, interview.

128. "All Over Arkansas," *The Arkansas Publisher* (January 1941): 2.

129. "Clyde E. Palmer Award Goes to Governor Adkins," *The Arkansas Publisher* (June 1941): 6.

130. "Convention Speakers Say . . . ," *The Arkansas Publisher* (June 1939): 11.

131. "Charles Goslee Leaves Hot Springs Papers," *The Arkansas Publisher* (May 1941): 4.

132. "Palmer Suggests Spa for UN," *The Arkansas Publisher* (December 1946): 7.

133. Mahaffey, interview.

134. Palmer, *Europe Today*, 14, 19.

135. Marion Hays, "From the Political Diary of an Unpolitical Person," *The Arkansas Historical Quarterly*, no. 36 (Summer 1977): 184.

136. "C. E. Palmer Entertains Congressional Delegation," *The Arkansas Publisher* (May 1946): 8.

137. *The Arkansas Publisher* (April 1949): 2.

138. Mahaffey, interview.

139. Wells, interview.

140. Letter received from George Brewer, June 16, 1986.

141. Mahaffey, interview.

142. Holley, "Arkansas in the Great Depression," 181, 182–85.

143. Personal interview with Betty Palmer Hussman, December 6, 1984, Little Rock, Arkansas.

144. J. Q. Mahaffey, "C. E. Palmer Kept Himself and His Reporters Busy."

145. Howe, interview.

146. Mahaffey, interview.

147. Kimball, interview.

148. Letter received from John Q. Mahaffey, July 28, 1986.

149. Letter received from Roy Bosson, June 9, 1986.

150. Howe, interview.

151. Howe, interview.

152. Wells, interview.

153. Wells, interview.

154. J. Q. Mahaffey, "Tale of Two Cities," *Texarkana Gazette*, July 10, 1955.

155. Mahaffey, interview.

156. Wells, interview. Wells said that he had been denied a press seat and had asked Palmer for help. Palmer appointed him as a designated correspondent for the Palmer Group, thereby giving Wells a seat in the press section and access to documents, debates, and other legislative activities.

157. Wells, interview.

158. Letter received from W. R. Stephens, June 30, 1986.

159. Wells, interview.

160. Personal interview with David Palmer Mooney, October 2, 1986.

161. Mahaffey, interview.

162. J. Q. Mahaffey, "C. E. Palmer Kept His Reporters and Himself Busy."

163. Kimball, interview.

164. Meriwether, *A Chronicle of Arkansas Newspapers*, 140.

165. Letter received from George Brewer, June 8, 1986.

166. Letter received from George Brewer, June 8, 1986.

167. Wells, interview.

168. Letter received from W. R. Stephens, June 30, 1986.

169. Letter received from George Brewer, June 8, 1986.

170. Wells, interview.

171. Wells, interview.

172. Letter received from George Brewer, July 29, 1986.

173. Letter received from George Brewer, July 29, 1986.

174. Wells, interview.

175. "Moses Given APA Life Membership, Governor Outlines Tax Progress," *The Arkansas Publisher* (January 1957): 8.

176. Wells, interview.

177. Mahaffey, interview.

178. "Publisher C. E. Palmer Dies," *Hot Spring Sentinel-Record*.

179. "C. E. Palmer, Newspaper Owner Dies," *Arkansas Gazette*, July 5, 1957.

180. "Clyde Eber Palmer," editorial, *Arkansas Gazette*, July 6, 1957.

181. "Clyde E. Palmer," editorial, *Pine Bluff Commercial*, July 5, 1957.

182. "Editorial Tributes to C. E. Palmer," *Hot Springs Sentinel-Record*, July 7, 1957.

183. "Clyde E. Palmer," editorial, *Arkansas Democrat*, July 7, 1957.

184. "Clyde E. Palmer Dead," *New York Times*, July 5, 1957; "Thirty – C. E. Palmer," *Editor & Publisher* (July 1957), copy in possession of Edna Howe.

185. Letter received from George Brewer, June 8, 1986.

186. Letter received from Roy Bosson, June 9, 1986.

187. Howe, interview.

188. Letter received from Louis Graves, August 27, 1986.

189. Wells, interview.

190. "Funeral Service for C. E. Palmer at Texarkana Today," *Hot Springs Sentinel-Record*, July 6, 1957.

191. *The Arkansas Publisher* (August 1956): 9, photo.

192. *The Arkansas Publisher* (July 1957): 1.

193. Bob Dean, "C. E. Palmer – An Editorial," *Hot Springs Sentinel-Record*, July 6, 1957.

194. Kimball, interview. Kimball said that Palmer bought the peach orchard, just outside of DeQueen, and was interested in it for a while.

195. J. Q. Mahaffey, "80 No Cause for Worry." Mahaffey said that Palmer loved to attend any circus. A few months before he died, Palmer went to a small circus in Texarkana and pronounced it the "Best damned circus I ever saw!"

Chapter 5

1. "17 Veteran Employees of SR-NE Boast a Total of 296 Years of Experience," *Hot Springs Sentinel-Record*, September 26, 1954. Mrs. Mooney joined the staff of the Hot Springs newspapers on December 18, 1929.

2. Letter from Roy Bosson to John Q. Mahaffey, January 27, 1986.

3. Letter received from Louis Graves, August 27, 1986.

4. Letter received from George Brewer, June 8, 1986.

5. Letter received from James H. Hale, August 6, 1986.

6. Ernie Deane, "The Arkansas Traveler," *Arkansas Gazette*, July 12, 1957.

7. J. Q. Mahaffey, "Tales of Two Cities," *Texarkana Gazette*, July 7, 1957.

8. Letter received from Clement P. Bossier, September 4, 1986.

9. Bob Dean, "C. E. Palmer – An Editorial," *Hot Springs Sentinel-Record*, July 6, 1957.

10. Dean, "C. E. Palmer – An Editorial." Dean quoted from a previous editorial that he had written.

11. Ray Reid, "Romance of American Journalism: Stories of Success Won by Leaders of the Press," *Editor & Publisher* (August 1930), reprinted in *The Arkansas Publisher* (September 1930): 7.

12. Reid, "Romance of American Journalism," 7.

13. Reid, "Romance of American Journalism," 7.

14. "Honorary Degree Conferred on Palmer," *The Arkansas Publisher* (June 1941): 4.

15. "Palmer Honored by Texarkana Jaycees," *The Arkansas Publisher* (May 1940): 4.

16. "Press Association Convention June 20–21," *The Arkansas Publisher* (June 1941): 1.

17. In Palmer's case, this meant, at least in Texarkana, Hot Springs, El Dorado, and Magnolia, a morning and an afternoon paper, both of which he owned.

18. Edwin Emery and Michael Emery, *The Press and America* (Englewood Cliffs: Prentice-Hall, Inc., 1978), 440.

19. George N. Gordon, *The Communications Revolution* (New York: Hastings House, 1977), 250.

20. John C. Merrill and Ralph L. Lowenstein, *Media, Messages, and Men* (New York: Longman, Inc., 1979), 174.

21. Ben Bagdikian, "Newspaper Mergers—The Final Phase," *Columbia Journalism Review* (March–April 1977): 18.

22. Ben Bagdikian, "The Media Monopolies," in *Mass Media Issues: Analysis and Debate*, George Rodman, ed. (Chicago: Science Research Associates, 1981), 4.

23. Bagdikian, "The Media Monopolies," 5, 7.

24. Peter M. Sandman, David M. Rubin, and David B. Sachsman, *Media: An Introductory Analysis of American Mass Communications* (Englewood Cliffs: Prentice-Hall, Inc., 1982), 123.

25. Ralph R. Thrift Jr., "How Chain Ownership Affects Editorial Vigor of Newspapers," *Journalism Quarterly* (Summer 1977): 130.

26. Frank Luther Mott, "News Controls," in *Mass Media and Communication*, Charles S. Steinberg, ed. (New York: Hastings House, 1971), 583.

27. "*McGehee Times* Suspends Due to Labor Shortage," *The Arkansas Publisher* (December 1943): 1; "Abbreviated Paper" [the *Carroll County Courier*], *The Arkansas Publisher* (July 1942): 1. Robert W. Meriwether, in *A Chronicle of Arkansas Newspapers Published since 1922 and of the Arkansas Press Association, 1930–1972* (Little Rock: Arkansas Press Association, 1974), lists numerous newspapers that failed, were sold, or combined with others during the period, including the *DeWitt Record* (1941); the *Gillett Record* (1936); the *Wilmott Weekly* (1933); the *Delta News* (1939); the *Colter Record* (1937); the *Bull Shoals Gazette* (1946); the *Baxter County Citizen* (1938); the *Decatur Herald* (1939); the *Siloam Springs Daily Register* (1934); the *Hill Billy News* (1940); the *Okolona Messenger* (1937); etc.

28. John Wells indicated that the Tenancy Commission eventually was involved in "leaking" information about future state land use that allowed some individuals to make large amounts of money on land purchases and resale, but this was after Palmer's tenure. Personal interview with John Wells, October 23, 1986.

29. Personal interview with David Palmer Mooney, October 2, 1986, Hot Springs, Arkansas.

30. There are no records of the details of the estate, except in private family records.

31. Alfred Steinberg, *Sam Johnson's Boy* (New York: The Macmillan Company, 1968), 650–52. Steinberg says that "two executives of Midwest Video Company of Little Rock, Arkansas" were at the LBJ ranch in late 1963 to work out a deal between the vice president and the Austin mayor. This was, of course, after Palmer's death, but Walter Hussman may have still been involved at this time. The FCC initially turned down Vice President Johnson's request for a Midwest Video/Capital Cable license, but, after the Kennedy assassination, re-voted and granted President Johnson a license, according to Steinberg.

32. Mooney, interview.

33. Mooney, interview.

34. "Hussman Formulates Plans for Newspaper Expansion," *Editor & Publisher* (August 31, 1974): 27.

35. Wells, interview; Mahaffey, interview. The fact that there were estate problems seems to have been common knowledge.

36. Personal interview with Mr. and Mrs. Walter E. Hussman, December 1984, Little Rock, Arkansas.

37. "Hussman Formulates Plans for Newspaper Expansion," 27.

38. "Hussman Formulates Plans for Newspaper Expansion," 27.

39. Letter from Richard S. Arnold to Charles W. Skelton, April 25, 1968.

40. Letter from Richard S. Arnold to Charles W. Skelton, April 25, 1968.

41. "Hussman Formulates Plans for Newspaper Expansion," 27.

42. "Hussman Formulates Plans for Newspaper Expansion," 27.

43. "Hussman Formulates Plans for Newspaper Expansion," 27.

44. The basis of the suit was the use of WEHCO Media profits from other holdings to support the operation of the *Arkansas Democrat*.

45. "Federal Jury Absolves *Democrat* of *Gazette* Antitrust Allegations," *Arkansas Democrat*, March 27, 1986; "Innocent," *Editor & Publisher* (April 5, 1986): 13.

46. John Brummett, "Sale of *Gazette* Not a Happy Thing, But It's Also Encouraging, Exciting," *Arkansas Gazette*, October 31, 1986, and other articles.

47. "Hussman Formulates Plans for Newspaper Expansion," 27.

48. "Arkansas Democrat $11,000,000 Expansion Underway," *Editor & Publisher* (April 26, 1986): 31 (advertisement). Ironically the *Arkansas Democrat* purchased the 229,000 square foot Terminal Warehouse Building for the expansion. This building housed publisher John Wells General Publishing Company, and the *Arkansas Democrat* and Walter Hussman Jr. forced Wells, Palmer's old friend, out of the building in late 1986.

49. Corporate ownership documents, obtained from the Office of the Secretary of State, Little Rock, Arkansas.

50. Material on the various Camden News Publishing Company holdings comes from a variety of sources, including information brought forward in the *Arkansas Democrat* vs. *Arkansas Gazette* case, the *Broadcasting Cable Yearbook* (1981 edition), personal interviews, correspondence, and other sources.

51. Letter from Walter Hussman Jr. to Board of Directors, City of Little Rock, February 5, 1980.

52. "WEHCO Media, Inc. Names Board Members," *Arkansas Democrat*, June 15, 1986.

53. *Editor & Publisher Yearbook – 1984* (New York City: Editor and Publisher Co. Inc., 1984), I-440.

54. Personal interview with Sam Papert Jr., September 17, 1986, Dallas, Texas.

55. Chic Young, "Blondie," *Hot Springs Sentinel-Record*, September 26, 1954.

56. Letter received from W. R. Whitehead, September 5, 1986.